New Postcolonial British Genres

Shifting the Boundaries

Sarah Ilott

Senior Lecturer in English Studies, Teesside University, UK

palgrave
macmillan

First published 2015 by
PALGRAVE MACMILLAN

Palgrave Macmillan in the UK is an imprint of Macmillan Publishers Limited, registered in England, company number 785998, of Houndmills, Basingstoke, Hampshire RG21 6XS.

Palgrave Macmillan in the US is a division of St Martin's Press LLC, 175 Fifth Avenue, New York, NY 10010.

Palgrave Macmillan is the global academic imprint of the above companies and has companies and representatives throughout the world.

Palgrave® and Macmillan® are registered trademarks in the United States, the United Kingdom, Europe and other countries.

ISBN 978–1–137–50521–7

This book is printed on paper suitable for recycling and made from fully managed and sustained forest sources. Logging, pulping and manufacturing processes are expected to conform to the environmental regulations of the country of origin.

A catalogue record for this book is available from the British Library.

A catalog record for this book is available from the Library of Congress.

Typeset by MPS Limited, Chennai, India.

For John, with love

Contents

Acknowledgments

There are many people whose influence, guidance and support I would like to acknowledge here, and I am particularly grateful to those who have read or advised upon drafts of this work: Chloe Buckley, Rachel Carroll, Stephen Curtis, Dara Downey, Kamilla Elliott, David Firth, Aroosa Kanwal, Lindsey Moore, Lynne Pearce, David Punter, Catherine Spooner and Andrew Tate.

I am also grateful to all the people with whom I have had the pleasure of working at Lancaster University, the University of Birmingham and, most recently, Teesside University, where I have received a warm welcome from new colleagues. Particular thanks go to the contemporary gothic reading group run by Catherine Spooner at Lancaster University, where I was able to test and develop many of the ideas for Chapter 2. I am especially indebted to Chloe Buckley, who has given me feedback on various drafts of chapters, and with whom I have worked through ideas on Helen Oyeyemi in anticipation of our next project together.

I am incredibly grateful for the support given by the team of staff in the Department of English Literature and Creative Writing at Lancaster University in the early stages of my career. In particular, Lynne Pearce could always be relied upon for both practical support and wisdom, as well as giving me the opportunity to work as a researcher for the AHRC-funded 'Moving Manchester' project. I also owe the deepest and most heartfelt thanks to my doctoral supervisor, Lindsey Moore, for her support and enthusiasm since my undergraduate days. Always patient and encouraging through my own periods of doubt she remains for me – in her political commitment, articulacy and wisdom – an inspiration.

The team at Palgrave Macmillan have been brilliant and I am particularly grateful for the generous comments and useful feedback of the anonymous readers, whose advice has been extremely helpful.

Warm thanks go to Chantal Zabus, Editor-in-Chief of *Postcolonial Text*, and to Sharanya Jayawickrama, Associate Editor of *Postcolonial Text*, for kindly granting permission to reprint ' "We are the martyrs, you're just squashed tomatoes!" Laughing through the Fears in Postcolonial British Comedy: Chris Morris's *Four Lions* and Joe Cornish's *Attack the Block*' in modified form, in *Postcolonial Text*, 8:2 (2013).

Finally, I want to thank my family and friends for their continued support and belief in my ability to see this project through.

I could never have written this book without the love, support and laughter of John, who saw me through the painful pyjama days of the manuscript's final stages, and whose pride and faith in me was a daily motivation, so it is to him that I dedicate it.

Sarah Ilott

Introduction: Remapping Boundaries – Postcolonial Britain and Literary/Cinematic Genres

As the 2015 general election approached in the UK, defining what it meant to be British was once again a hotly contested topic and one that was increasingly defined by an inward-looking and xenophobic nationalism. Yet, as always, this was not a debate that operated only in political circles but one that was taken up in various cultural and artistic works. One individual who was particularly keen to associate her work with an ideal of Britishness was film director Gurinder Chadha, who turned her film, *Bend It Like Beckham* (2002), into a musical that started in London's West End in May 2015. Openly lauding the film as a 'state of the nation piece' in a Guardian interview, Chadha linked the happy coincidence of the musical's opening with the general election, saying 'there are enough people out there who will be using race as a divisive mechanism during the election process, which traditionally and histori-cally always happens, as we know'.[1] Despite retaining its 2001 setting, it was marketed as a 'joyous new British musical about where we are now', suggesting a similarly hearty mix of myopia and utopianism that surrounded the release of the film.[2]

Given the rise in right-wing parties accruing popularity through anti-immigration policies and xenophobic sentiment that impacts not just upon future migration to Britain, but upon non-white British citizens and recent migrants too, I would agree with Chadha's sentiment that it's welcome to see a musical celebrating Britain's diversity with a feel-good plot-line centred on two girls from differing cultural backgrounds who work together to achieve their footballing ambitions. However, rather than celebrating the simple fact of diversity, it is important to consider who and what is included and excluded in this 'state of the nation' piece, by questioning how multiculturalism is managed and rep-resented. Commentary on the adaptation given by co-producer Sonia

1

Friedman describes it as 'a timeless tale of assimilation [...] an una-shamed celebration of what it is to be British, of diversity and difference and the richness and potential of all being on the same team, kicking the same ball and having the same goals!'[3] The language employed here, placing pride in assimilation and a certain level of uniformity comes close to Michael Gove's ominous revelation of the 'British values' to be taught in schools (June 2014) that supposedly unite us as a country, and causes me to pause and question how the terms 'Britishness' and 'diversity' are being mobilised and linked in Chadha's state of the nation.

To fully understand the way that Britishness is being deployed and negotiated in this musical and other similar cultural texts, it is necessary to understand the generic conventions of the medium in which it participates, which in this case is comedy. An awareness of genre conventions will enable audiences to read the hierarchies and stereotypes set up or undermined through the comedy. Linguistic conventions of the joke will signal patterns of inclusion and/or exclusion revealing who or what is the butt of the joke. The topic of joking exchanges and the focus of the comedy will demarcate what is constructed as taboo. Interpreting these generic conventions will establish how the topics of Britishness and diversity are being constructed. Interrogating the role that generic conventions play in constructions of Britishness is where this book, therefore, makes its intervention into postcolonial studies.

New Postcolonial British Genres identifies and explores four new genres that have evolved to accommodate and negotiate the changing face of postcolonial Britain since 1990. I focus on the way that notions of Britishness are challenged and rewritten in genre fiction that operates on the borders of mainstream literary fiction in terms of both market consumption and critical attention. My aim is to illustrate ways in which the new genres I identify simultaneously challenge and reinscribe both national and generic borders by opening up to postcolonial topics, authors and contexts. I consider British Muslim Bildungsromane, gothic tales of postcolonial England, the subcultural urban novel and multicultural British comedy as four new genres that interrogate both their generic forebears and traditions and the representations of Britishness that they are generically bound or designed to perpetuate. In the following sections I outline the key theoretical and critical paradigms pertinent to my subsequent analysis of literature and film. To finish, I introduce the subsequent chapters via readings of Salman Rushdie's *The Satanic Verses* (1988), a novel that serves as a precursor for the topics, debates, desires and fears engaged in the new genres, in terms of both the content and the furore surroundings its publication.

Narrating the nation

This book works on the premise that as a culturally diverse country, Britain needs something that transcends material, ethnic, economic and religious disparities to create a sense of shared national identity: it requires new modes of narration. The links between nation and narration have been thoroughly interrogated, most notably by Benedict Anderson, who considers nations as 'imagined political communit[ies]', and by Homi Bhabha, who claims that 'Nations, like narratives, lose their origins in the myths of time and only fully realize their horizons in the mind's eye.'[4] Bhabha expands on this, stating that: 'The people are not simply historical events or parts of a patriotic body politic. They are also a complex rhetorical strategy of social reference where the claim to be representative provokes a crisis within the process of signification and discursive address.'[5]

As such, peoples are fictional as well as factual entities, understood and understanding themselves variously through differing ideologies and frames of reference, rather than existing independently of forms of signification. There are implicit affinities between understandings of nation and storytelling; the nation is understood in terms of its constructed nature, its imaginative qualities and its mode of expression. It is important to note that narration is not the story but the way the story is told, and that there are important political and psychological implications to take into account when considering narration. Angela Carter highlights the political implications of narration, suggesting that 'narrative is an argument stated in fictional terms,'[6] which makes it apparent why the way that nations are imagined and mediated through fiction is important for an understanding of Britishness. The way that the national story is told leaves room for argument or political agenda, coercion or persuasion, whilst comprising power imbalances regarding who has the knowledge and who is able to narrate the stories. This is where the boundaries between nation and nationalism begin to blur, as the 'myth of nationhood, masked by ideology, perpetuates nationalism, in which specific identifiers are employed to create exclusive and homogenous conceptions of national traditions [...]. Constructions of the nation are thus potent sites of control and domination'.[7]

Narrative also has a psychological function in the mobilisation and actualisation of desire. Peter Brooks sums this up best when he states that we can 'conceive of the reading of plot as a form of desire [...]. Narratives both tell of desire [...] and arouse and make use of desire as dynamic of signification'.[8] For Brooks, desire is a structural agent utilised by authors to engage readers and draw them into the plot. He superimposes 'psychic functioning on textual functioning' to illustrate the 'movement *toward* totalization under the mandate of desire'.[9] This illustrates the importance of desire as a structuring tool in fictions of Britishness, as well as the potential of fictions (both novels and films) to re-imagine Britain and envision its future. As Mark Currie asserts, 'the archive is not a passive record, but an active producer of the present in anticipation of its recollection' and 'in life the future does not exist yet, but in narrative fiction it does,' illustrating fiction's potential for shaping our understanding of both the present and the future.[10] Although desire is often retrospective (*'concupiscence rétrospective*, desire oriented toward an irrecoverable past'), it often converges with a future-oriented desire (*'désir prospectif*, desire in and for the future'). The implications for national identity are apparent: by returning to Britain's colonial past and legacies as we see them addressed in postcolonial fictions, there is a simultaneous *'désir prospectif'* oriented toward shaping ideas of Britishness in the future.[11]

This book is timely in its analysis of 'Britishness' as the term seems to have become what Peter Morey and Amina Yaqin refer to as a 'floating signifier' – one that is swollen to include anything that interpreters might wish it to mean, which is especially unhelpful when used (as it frequently is) in contrast to Others that are narrowly defined to mean 'all that is threatening and foreign'.[12] Seen in an alternative, and more liberating light, this also means that fiction can be a powerful tool for de- and re-narrating ideas of Britishness. Accordingly, *New Postcolonial British Genres* locates the ways in which concepts of Britishness are negotiated in contemporary fiction and film that foreground the colonial legacies that have had such a crucial role in shaping current attitudes towards what Britain is identified in relation or opposition to.

Postcolonial genres

New Postcolonial British Genres marks a critical break with what has gone before through its exclusive focus on genre fiction and the unique contribution genre can make to the writing of a nation. Although individual genres have been theorised in relation to postcolonial criticism, there has not, until now, been a critical intervention that considers precisely what it is about genre *itself* that makes it useful for a postcolonial project and for writing about contemporary Britain. The chapters are structured around four different genres of literature and film (British Muslim Bildungsromane, gothic tales of postcolonial England, the subcultural urban novel and multicultural British comedy), as I examine how various genres are exploited to articulate differing negotiations of desire and fear that feed into constructions of Britishness and delineate what it includes and excludes.

Critiquing Benedict Anderson's work on imagined communities, film critic Rick Altman argues that 'Anderson concentrates on the moment when a nation was formed and stops there, failing to acknowledge the ongoing nature of the process he has described'.[13] Extending Anderson's project, Altman goes on to outline parallels between nation and narration that are highlighted specifically through reference to genre:

> Genres are not only formal arrangements of textual characteristics; they are also social devices that use semantics and syntax to assure simultaneous satisfaction on the part of multiple users with apparently contradictory purposes. That is, genres are regulatory schemes facilitating the integration of diverse factions into a single unified social fabric. As such, genres operate like nations and other complex communities. Perhaps they can even teach us about nations.[14]

The continuing tension between diverse factions and unification – identified by Altman as a property of genre – requires a mobile, evolving means of description. Similarly dynamic and embodying tensions between diversity and unity are national agendas, rendering the two systems comparable and mutually informative. This book takes up Altman's tentative suggestion that genres can perhaps teach us about nations and argues that both genres and nations have unstable boundaries that are, at least imaginatively, redrawn when the implications of postcolonial texts and contexts are taken into consideration.

I read shifting genre boundaries as a means of understanding shifting constructions of Britishness, as the genres expand or evolve to accommodate and provoke new sets of desires and fears that shape understandings of national identity. Furthermore, I assert that the unstable boundaries of genre can provide particularly fertile ground for authors that have traditionally been marginalised by virtue of their minority status. Altman's description of the link between generic boundaries and national communities highlights genre fiction's potential for a postcolonial project, in which those 'Satisfied with the current situation, users of generic and national terminology alike have a desire to slow the process of regentrification, while margin dwellers have every reason to speed it up.'[15] Notice the pun on gentrification, suggesting 'regenrification's' participation in divisive discourses of conservation and change.

I focus on 'margin dwellers' in both national and generic terms (examining Britishness and fictions respectively), arguing that the unstable boundaries of genre make useful sites for traditionally marginalised authors to make internal contradictions apparent and begin to negotiate both national and generic boundaries. Questions of categorisation are always political, as borders are redrawn and criteria of inclusion and exclusion are negotiated, so genre fiction and film provides a unique space for making apparent what Vron Ware has termed the contested 'politics of the border'.[16]

Genre is also intrinsically tied to specific historical periods, as has been argued by a number of critics who have tried to release genre criticism from what Fredric Jameson describes as 'semantic' approaches: those that 'aim to describe the essence or meaning of a given genre by way of the reconstruction of an imaginary entity [...] which is something like the generalized essential experience behind the individual texts'.[17] For Jameson, it is crucial that 'the "essence", "spirit", "world-view", in question is revealed to be an ideologeme, that is, a historically determinate conceptual or semic complex which can project itself variously in the form of a protonarrative, a private or collective narrative fantasy'.[18]

Many of the texts that I analyse work at the borders of generic frameworks and in so doing have the capacity to question the worldviews previously imagined by other participants of the genre. By situating works in the gothic genre, for example, postcolonial authors are able to exploit the aesthetics, style and conventions of gothic, whilst also questioning the 'essence' of imperial gothic in reference to structures of alterity. For the authors that I analyse, genre functions as an 'enabling device,' to borrow David Duff's term.[19] Texts are not bound to endless lists of conventions and rules but rewrite genres from within. It will become apparent that many of the postcolonial authors I have selected radically shift the parameters of the genres in which they participate.

This book also makes a critical intervention into the construction of genre and what the term itself constitutes. Moving away from a rather tired conceptualisation of genre, which in the footsteps of the likes of structuralist Vladimir Propp – who minutely identified the formal properties of the fairy tale – still tends to have an investment in rules and formulae, I alternatively theorise genre in relation to desire.[20] Articulating genres in relation to desire involves identifying the desires and fears that the genres are structured around and tracing how these desires are negotiated. The Bildungsroman, for example, negotiates conflicting worldviews in the expression of the desire for a coherent sense of identity, whilst gothic literature engages cultural fears, comedy engages with culturally repressed taboos and the subcultural urban novel is structured around the interpolation of consumerist and erotic desires. This is a less rigid and more enabling structure than has previously been granted to the study of genres, as it reflects human psychologies rather than mechanical rules. Accordingly, this book draws widely on psychoanalytic theorists, such as Sigmund Freud, Frantz Fanon and Ranjana Khanna, whilst maintaining attention to political and material realities and contexts.

Postcolonial Britain

Traditionally, postcolonial countries have been understood as those that were formerly colonis*ed*, rather than colonis*ing*. In their seminal work *The Empire Writes Back*, Ashcroft, Griffiths and Tiffin's introduction affirms that 'We use the term post-colonial [...] to cover all the culture affected by the imperial process from the moment of colonization to the present day.' They go on to list: 'the literatures of African countries, Australia, Bangladesh, Canada, Caribbean countries, India, Malaysia, Malta, New Zealand, Pakistan, Singapore, South Pacific Island countries, and Sri Lanka'.[21] A startling omission from this apparently exhaustive list is Britain, as a culture that has also been 'affected by the imperial process,' though this omission can probably be put down to the binarising structure that the critics work around, in which 'writing back' suggests a distance from the former colonial centre.

Throughout *New Postcolonial British Genres*, I stress the importance of understanding Britain as postcolonial, so as not to repress its shameful colonial history and to create an imaginative space for diasporic peoples whilst simultaneously taking into account Britain's ongoing neo-imperial involvements, particularly in the wake of the so-called 'war on terror'. I understand Britain as a postcolonial country because its peoples, legacies and national imaginings are shaped by its former colonial relationships. John McLeod explains the choice he similarly made when entitling his book *Postcolonial London: Rewriting the Metropolis*, acknowledging that 'the deployment of this term involves a degree of risk,' in terms of 'potentially deflect[ing] critical attention away from the economic, social and cultural circumstances in countries with a history of colonialism'; there is a 'danger of recentralizing the Western metropolis'.[22] He concludes that:

> When proceeding with a perception of London in terms of the post-colonial we must be careful to note that its postcoloniality is not at

all commensurate with sites of colonial settlement in once-colonized countries. But [...] it would also be inappropriate to consider London as solely the undifferentiated colonial 'centre' or immune from the consequences of Empire, its resistance and its decline.[23]

Like McLeod, I acknowledge that there are vital historical differences between Britain and the former colonies: emotional, physical and cultural traumas have been visited on the former British empire and have disrupted physical, psychological, economic and ideological landscapes accordingly. However, recognising Britain as a nation affected by its own history of colonialism ensures that the voices of peoples with a history of being colonised are included within the national narrative, and that migrants to Britain from the former colonies can be acknowledged as postcolonial peoples without being 'othered' through narratives that still rely upon historical binaries between colonial centre and margins.

To talk about 'postcolonial' (as opposed to black and/or Asian) British literature and film also avoids the essentialisms that have riddled previous literary categorisations and liberates ethnic minority authors from the sole 'burden of representation'. James Procter highlights ways in which black authors have historically suffered from a 'burden of representation,' or 'The problem of trying to say everything about black Britishness [...] in which the narration of black Britain feels a problematic pressure to delegate, or "speak for" the whole of that imagined community.'[24] However, by understanding Britain as postcolonial, the nation can be constructed around a shared history of colonial entanglement, and mediations of the nation must, therefore, include acknowledgment of its historical legacies and its present peoples. The political commitment to exposing and undermining the legacies of colonialism evident in contemporary inequities, stereotypes and discriminatory practices is one that can (and indeed should) be shouldered equally by white authors and directors. As such, acknowledging a history can create an imaginative space for diasporic peoples whilst equally beginning to make sense of Britain's ongoing neo-imperial involvements. Accordingly, sections of the final chapter engage films directed by white directors (Chris Morris, Joe Cornish and Damien O'Donnell) whose work I read as powerfully demonstrating the ways in which effort is required on the part of British society *en masse* so as not to further alienate or exclude people from migrant backgrounds according to prejudices stemming from Islamophobia, racism or class snobbery.

However, a problem immediately arises in employing Britishness as an inclusive term denoting a shared history in colonialism, as it subsumes devolving internal identities (English, Welsh, Scottish and Northern Irish). Furthermore, the colonial history is not equally shared. Although what is commonly understood as Britain's colonial history was mutually embarked upon, the imperial mission started from England, acquiring first Wales, and then Scotland and Northern Ireland, finally becoming the United Kingdom as known today following the 'Act of Union', which came into effect in 1801. In her autobiographical work, *Sugar and Slate*, Charlotte Williams, a Welsh-Guyanese author, parallels the English colonisation of the Welsh language and its resources to Britain's colonisation and, she goes so far as to claim, enslavement of the rest of the empire. Williams's discussion of quarry-workers and the quarry owner, Lord Penrhyn, employs imperial rhetoric, as she states that 'They were the black slaves to his white supremacy, the real Welsh to his Anglo-Welshness.'[25] Accordingly, Britishness itself is a loaded term and one that many may not (at least primarily) identify with. Although 'Britishness' might be a useful description for a multicultural nation inasmuch as it does not carry the same imperialist connotations as Englishness, it is problematic for eliding the differences between its constituent parts.[26] However, I would argue that Britain is still a politically viable term, if only because it encapsulates tensions between localisms, regionalisms and nationalisms effectively. Whilst talking about Britishness as both an ideal and a site of conflicting ideologies I therefore also pay heed to internal tensions and alternative strategies of identification.

New racism and Muslim identities

The book includes a preponderance of authors from Muslim backgrounds, which marks a critical shift from previous studies that have tended to focus on ethno-racial rather than religious signifiers of affiliation. I use the term 'Muslim' broadly, as suggested by Amin Malak, to include:

> the person who believes firmly in the faith of Islam; and/or, via an inclusivist extension, by the person who voluntarily and knowingly refers to herself, for whatever motives, as a 'Muslim' when given a selection of identitarian choices; and/or, by yet another generous extension, by the person who is rooted formatively, and emotionally in the culture and civilization of Islam.[27]

The reason for what might be seen as a disproportionate representation of Muslim authors and concerns lies in my intention to interrogate the inclusivity of 'Britishness,' which in blurring the lines between nation and nationalism has frequently expressed itself as an ideology that posits Muslim cultures and beliefs as its Other. By privileging those who are often on the receiving end of strategies of Othering, I am able to question the binaries created in national(ist) identifications. I share Kobena Mercer's opinion that rather than being overly concerned with representation, 'it always seems more important to know who or what you were writing against'.[28] In the case of contemporary narratives of Britishness, the most important thing to 'write against' is an increasing level of Islamophobia manifesting itself in policing, racist attacks, and selectively distorting media coverage.

My focus on (critiques of) Islamophobia mirrors and countermands the shift that James Procter identifies in racist discourse from 'imperial' racisms centred on '"biological" difference' towards 'new' racisms that operate on the basis of cultural differences.[29] The shift implied in 'new' racism has had profound political implications, engendering the necessity for a new parliamentary act to extend the protection from hate offences to religious as well as racial groups. Before the Racial and Religious Hatred Act was passed in 2006, Chris Allen argued that the shift in discrimination 'from race to religion' opened up what he calls a 'window of opportunity' for far-right groups like the British National Party that had previously been 'somewhat restricted by legislative protection', who found a group 'with a clear and definable yet unprotected marker: Muslim identity'.[30] He goes on to argue that this racist opportunism came to a head in 2001, as 'whilst the shift from race to religion clearly has its roots prior to 9/11, it was Ground Zero that provided the catalytic impetus to its quasi-justification'.[31]

The Satanic Verses and new postcolonial British genres

I include here an extended section on Salman Rushdie's *The Satanic Verses* (1988) as a crucible and historic precursor for many of the debates and genres detailed in the remainder of the book. I use readings of Rushdie's novel as a way of introducing the chapters that will follow, arguing that the novel and the surrounding furore acted as a historical tipping point in constructions of postcolonial Britain and particularly in British Muslim identities. *New Postcolonial British Genres* extends and updates approaches to the novel by reading it as a precursor to the new genres that have evolved in Britain in the wake of the Rushdie affair. Inclusion of *The Satanic Verses* in this book shifts the parameters of critique surrounding this text that have, to an extent, been defined by

polemic. Analysing Rushdie's novel here allows me to provide a historical context for many of the debates that extend into the genre fiction
of the last two-and-a-half decades that is the purview of the rest of *New
Postcolonial British Genres*. These include the contested relationship
between Britishness and Islam negotiated through the identity struggles
endemic of the Bildungsroman genre; deconstructions of monstrosity
and concepts of home in gothic tales; questions of exoticism, marketing and audience raised in the representation of minority cultures and
subcultures; and the ambivalent capacity of comedy to disrupt or to
preserve the status quo. This allows me to illustrate ways in which even
the most prestigious postcolonial literary fiction can be understood
as participating in genres before moving on to the new postcolonial
British genres that have arisen since 1990.

The Satanic Verses weaves together a number of plots spanning multiple histories and geographies through its two main characters, Gibreel
Farishta and Saladin Chamcha, who open the novel by falling from
an aeroplane hijacked by Sikh terrorists into the English Channel and
(improbably) surviving. Washed up on the shore, they encounter the
delusional Rosa Diamond, who clings to conflicting memories and
visions of the British empire. Alerted to the presence of an 'illegal'
immigrant, police arrive at the scene and arrest Saladin, who has grown
hooves and horns and begun to transform into a devilish creature that
literally enacts racist stereotypes. Gibreel, meanwhile, has developed a
halo and taken on an angelic likeness. Both men eventually make their
separate ways into Thatcher's London, their devilish/angelic metamor-
phoses progressing. Saladin has previously worked in England as a radio
actor, 'the Man of a Thousand Voices and a Voice' (60) and wishes to
make a hasty return to his career and English wife, Pamela Lovelace,
who unfortunately believes him dead following the plane crash and has
taken another lover, Saladin's friend 'Jumpy' Joshi. Gibreel, by contrast,
is an actor famed in India for his starring roles in 'theologicals' as a
variety of gods and supernatural beings. Having left India after a shattering loss of faith at the end of a long period of illness, he heads towards
London in search of Alleluia Cone, a mountaineer with whom he has
had a chance encounter in Bombay and fallen in love.

Set predominantly in the fictional London borough of 'Brickhall' in
the context of institutionalised racism, unjust policing and riot, the
novel draws upon and implicitly critiques the heavily-policed riots that
took place in the largely Asian areas of Brixton and Southall during the
early 1980s. It is this commentary upon postcolonial Britain that makes
the novel particularly pertinent to this study. However, the narrative

is not constrained to London alone, and when Gibreel's waking and dreaming lives begin to merge it is a vehicle for the novel's subplots to appear as a sequence of visions that the protagonist witnesses or participates in. The first of these visions is the most controversial and concerns the disputed story of the revelation of the 'satanic verses' that encourage Mahound (an appropriation of the Orientalist term for Muhammad, employed to 'turn insults into strengths' (93)) to allow the intercession of three goddesses as Allah's archangels, before his subsequent repudiation of the verses after realising that they had been fed to him by the devil. Gibreel's visions also develop subplots concerning the exile of a nameless Imam to London in a section that recalls Ayatollah Khomeini's exile in Paris, and the *hajj* led by prophetess Ayesha that sees the ambivalently successful parting of the Arabian Sea to allow pilgrims to pass through to Mecca. There are two questions that unite the various strands of the novel. The first is the question of how newness comes into the world, of what it is made and how it might survive. The second question, connected to the first, tests ideas for their ability or willingness to compromise. Each subplot tackles the conception and evolution of a new idea, from the early days of Islam, to the demands of the Sikh terrorists, to individual characters faced with life-changing events.

The novel is narrated by an 'omniscient' yet unreliable narrator who intervenes as a character and meddles with other characters at various points. Described in all-too-human terms as a man 'of medium height, fairly heavily built, with salt-and-pepper beard cropped close to the line of the jaw' and suffering from balding, dandruff and myopia (318), the trickster narrator bears a remarkable resemblance to Rushdie at the time of writing. This playful, irreverent, postmodern style is suited to predominant themes of the novel, including the questioning of grand narratives, identity crises that parallel the migration of people with the translation of selves and a magic-realist world in which fantasy and reality merge and intersect.

The legacy of *The Satanic Verses* is the result not just of the novel itself, but of the series of events and debates that followed its publication, commonly known as the 'Rushdie affair'. I refer to the events in this manner as the name has stuck, but as Paul Weller has noted in *A Mirror for our Times* (2009), 'many Muslims preferred to refer to "the Satanic Verses controversy" rather than "the Rushdie affair"' to signal opposition to the content of the book and subsequent reactions to their concerns, rather than focussing on the individual figure of the author.[32] I use inverted commas throughout in reference to the 'affair' to indicate that it is a contested term. However, the fatwa pronounced on Salman Rushdie for his blasphemous portrayal of Islam and the Prophet Muhammad, by Iran's Ayatollah Khomeini on 14 February 1989, served to ensure that the focus remained on the author himself, who was forced into hiding under the protection of the British government for almost a decade until the Iranian government undertook not to implement the fatwa in 1998.

The 'affair' has subsequently been defined largely in terms of opposition, although the terms of opposition have been fiercely contested, reflecting the high political stakes of the debate. Most commonly it has been understood as a cultural conflict 'represented in spatial terms and binary geopolitical polarities – Islamic fundamentalists vs. Western literary modernists',[33] painting the world in broad brushstrokes that obfuscate specificity and diversity of opinions and beliefs. The 'affair' has also been read as representing a collision between fundamentalism and the freedom of speech, a debate that has recently been rehearsed in relation to the assassination of *Charlie Hebdo* cartoonists for their representation of the Prophet Mohammad by Muslim terrorists in Paris (January 2015). The surrounding debate similarly refuses to see the irony or hypocrisy of declaring the sacrosanctity of free speech whilst refusing to acknowledge the sacred as constructed by religious believers. Gayatri Spivak deconstructs the premises on which the 'Rushdie affair' has frequently been conceptualised and in so doing forces us to re-evaluate the racist double standards that suggest 'freedom of expression' and 'other normative and private rational abstractions' (for which read religious affiliation) are mutually exclusive. This enables Spivak to 'recode the conflict as racism versus fundamentalism'.[34] I follow Spivak's assessment by considering the alienating effects of binaries that construct Muslim belief in opposition to 'western' values.

The 'Rushdie affair' has had a profound impact on British Muslims. Discontent over the novel was first publicly manifested in Bradford in northern England on 14 January 1989, a month before the fatwa, when a copy of the novel was publicly burnt for its blasphemous portrayal of the Prophet. This was a watershed moment as a crucible for British Muslim identity, as many united over this issue to protest the attack on their faith. Tariq Modood considers the socio-political specifics of the case of British Muslims, outlining reasons for offence and noting some particularities that more generalising accounts have ignored. Modood notes that British Muslim anger over *The Satanic Verses* was largely limited to South Asian Muslims who were provoked by the 'lampooning of the Prophet': 'This sensitivity has nothing to do with Qur'anic fundamentalism but with South Asian reverence of Muhammad (deemed by many Muslims, including fundamentalists, to be excessive) and cultural insecurity as experienced in England and even more profoundly in India.'[35] Modood interprets the politics behind the reactions (such as book-burnings in Bradford and the bombing of book stores) as a consequence of Britain's 'significant Asian working class [...] devotion to the Prophet [being] strongest among the rural peasantry from which Pakistani and Bangladeshi immigrants to Britain [...] originate'.[36] He uses these cultural specifics to argue for a more pluralistic legal approach in Britain, whereby 'Equality [...] may be best served by giving a minority group a legal protection that the majority does not want for itself.'[37] This response takes cultural and political frameworks seriously so as to outline the practical implications suggested by the novel's fallout. In sum, the 'affair' worked as a catalyst in the transition from racial to religious means of identifying in Britain, as the category of 'British Muslim' was increasingly identified with and employed by the media and politicians in place of 'British Asian'.

'I am always divided, always two or three or fifteen': hybrid identities and Muslim faith in *The Satanic Verses*[38]

In many ways, *The Satanic Verses* is a precursor to the British Muslim Bildungsromane considered in Chapter 1, insomuch as the novels considered there engage with and contest constructions of identity arising from both Rushdie's novel and the ensuing furore. *The Satanic Verses* has affinities with subsequent British Muslim Bildungsromane, as it negotiates identity crises arising from multiple sources of affiliation and grapples with questions of religious faith. However, that is where ostensible similarities end: where *The Satanic Verses* celebrates hybrid identities in what Rushdie has described as 'a love-song to our mongrel selves', authors have subsequently countered the desirability of hybrid identities; where *The Satanic Verses* ridicules 'the Pure' as a synonym for grand narratives, later novels have expressed the pain that accompanies the loss of meaning and authority; where '*The Satanic Verses* is for change-by-fusion, change-by-conjoining',[39] novels discussed in Chapter 1 foreground painful conversion narratives; where *The Satanic Verses* articulates problems with Islam, protagonists in subsequent novels turn to Islam as an unchanging source of identity and comfort; where Rushdie uses magic realism as a vehicle for the expression of religious belief, the British Muslim Bildungsromane considered in Chapter 1 are formally realist. It is useful, therefore, to consider the way that Rushdie engages with identity constructions and Muslim beliefs to understand the point of departure that subsequent novelists make, sometimes overtly with direct reference to *The Satanic Verses* or the 'Rushdie affair', sometimes covertly through choices in style and content that implicitly critique Rushdie's constructions.

Homi Bhabha frequently draws on Salman Rushdie's *The Satanic Verses* in his influential *The Location of Culture*, as exemplary of hybrid peoples and places, largely celebrating the author's fiction. He attempts to defend the novel from much of the opposition that was raised against it, stating:

> The conflict of cultures and community around *The Satanic Verses* has been mainly represented in spatial terms and binary geopolitical polarities – Islamic fundamentalists vs. Western literary modernists, the quarrel of the ancient (ascriptive) migrants and modern (ironic) metropolitans. This obscures the anxiety of the irresolvable, border-line culture of hybridity that articulates its problems of identification and its diasporic aesthetic in an uncanny, disjunctive temporality that is, at once, the *time* of cultural displacement, and the *space* of the 'untranslatable'.[40]

Accordingly, the theorist tries to draw the novel out of the ideological binary that it seemed to have fallen into over the preceding years, instead celebrating the 'culture of hybridity' that he argues is set up by the novel.

A 'culture of hybridity' emerges from the way in which identity is constructed in Rushdie's novel. One of the key questions posed within the novel is 'How does newness come into the world? How is it born? Of what fusions, translations, conjoinings is it made?' (8). As Rushdie himself answers in *Imaginary Homelands*: 'Mélange, hotchpotch, a bit of this and a bit of that is *how newness enters the world*. [...] *The Satanic Verses* is for change-by-fusion, change-by-conjoining. It is a love-song to our mongrel selves' (emphasis in original).[41] Rushdie's work is itself a reclamation of identity, as he rescues terms like 'hybrid,' 'impurity' and 'mongrel' from the negative connotations with which poets such as Jackie Kay had recently associated them.[42] But in so doing he simultaneously creates a new binary, where 'the absolutism of the Pure' is to be feared and combated.[43] *The Satanic Verses* boasts a plethora of characters that fall on either side of this binary, and the spokespersons for absolutism or uncompromising ideas are often demonised or ridiculed.

A prime advocate of the 'Pure' is a Sikh terrorist whose body, laden with bombs, 'provided her answer' as to 'what manner of cause' she and her accomplices are: 'Are we uncompromising, absolute, strong, or will we show ourselves to be timeservers, who compromise, trim and yield?' (81). The manner in which the head terrorist sees herself as embodying, or becoming her cause, signifies its purity and absolutism: 'What manner of cause *are we*?' (my emphasis) not 'What manner of cause is it/do we support?'. Saladin notices a visual unity between her body and the bombs, as he imagines the grenades to be 'like extra breasts nestling in her cleavage,' implying the absence of an extra-corporeal dimension to the all-encompassing idea that she has come to embody (81). Through Rushdie's terrorists (who gain a new resonance in the post-9/11 world), the author is able to question advocates of the absolute: all those who embody such uncompromising ideals that they are prepared to martyr themselves to the Grand Idea. The irony of this is that during the 'Rushdie affair', Rushdie suggested that there are some ideals that *should* be uncompromising and for which he was willing to risk his own life in defence, such as the freedom of speech and the right to blaspheme. It might be better, therefore, to reconceptualise the novel's binary not as purity versus hybridity, but as religion versus reason, terms that Rushdie suggests are mutually exclusive in his memoir, describing 'religion as the enemy of the intellect'.[44]

Rushdie levels his accusations higher than the faith of religious individuals by questioning the uncompromising nature of religious faith itself, as in order to be fully believed in, an idea must be absolute, something which in turn seems to make it a little pathetic in its inability to withstand questioning. When the 'Prophet Messenger Businessman' (118), the controversially-named Mahound, attempts to incorporate the three main goddesses of the Jahilians, (Al-)Lat, Uzza and Manat, into his verses, the Grandee's wife, Hind, points out the error of his compromise, eventually causing the Prophet to retract the previously uttered verses as satanic:

> I am your equal [...] I don't want you to become weak. You shouldn't have done what you did. [...] If you are for Allah, I am for Al-Lat. And she doesn't believe your God when he recognizes her. Her opposition to him is implacable, irrevocable, engulfing. The war between us cannot end in truce. And what a truce! Yours is a patronising, condescending lord. (121)

Herein lies the problem of religious faith according to the narrative: the absolute cannot compromise because doing so would make it weak and not worthy of belief. Yet if religious faith cannot question itself, it is unable to face the questions that the novel instructs must be asked of any idea in order to test its strength and value (335).

Rushdie justifies his choice of magic realism, a form of metafiction that deliberately blurs the boundaries between fantasy and reality, as 'essential' if one is to 'describe reality as it is experienced by religious people, for whom God is no symbol but an everyday fact'. For Rushdie, the 'rationalism' of the alternative form – realism – 'comes to seem like a judgement upon, an invalidation of, the religious faith of the characters being described'.[45] Rushdie's justification of his choice upholds the necessity of liberation from conventional modes of authorship to give voice to the religious content of the novel. However, his choice of a metafictional style of narration is not as innocent as he pretends. First and foremost it is immediately apparent that with the exception of the 'Parting of the Arabian Sea' section, the supernatural elements of the novel are almost entirely distinct from anything close to the Muslim religious belief that the author pretends to be stylistically engaging with and would be more appropriate to a gothic novel.[46] A closer interrogation into the way that metafictional style relates to religious content also reveals Rushdie's defence of his stylistic choice to be flawed.

The novel's metafictional approach to religious scripture is one reason for the many criticisms that have been launched against the novel, as the style conflicts with the common interpretation that the *Qur'an* is the direct word of God. Rushdie is forced to dethrone the book's divinely-ordained authority *to make available* the space necessary to challenge it. However, John Erickson exposes the dilemma that Rushdie is faced with in attempting to write on the subject of the satanic verses (also known as the *gharaniq*, or 'birds' verses in less Orientalist terms). 'As magisterial discourses,' Erickson argues, 'religious scriptures rely on a strictly defined "region of discourse" making them immune to outside discourses'. This effectively means that there is no way of challenging religious discourse; 'that is, the satanic verses may indeed survive but solely as an outside, unreliable, institutionalized variant, whose terms of opposition are set by the discourse of Islam'.[47] It is because of this distinction between modes of discourse that it remains an impossible task to critique the verses on their own terms. Metafiction denies absolute authority by exposing the processes of fiction, and as such, in metafictional writing the author/God is always already dead, or disempowered to the point of being worthy of such a status. These two different worldviews, evoked by (first) the Word as divine truth and (second) metafiction, start from mutually exclusive premises, meaning that it is impossible for them to launch significant critiques of each other.

Following on from the debates surrounding the content and publication of Rushdie's novel, Chapter 1 includes discussion of Hanif
Kureishi's *The Black Album* (1995), Leila Aboulela's *The Translator* (1999)
and *Minaret* (2005), and Robin Yassin-Kassab's *The Road from Damascus*
(2008) as British Muslim Bildungsromane. These novels engage questions of Muslim faith and identity in a British context, arising in part
from issues thrown up by – or during the messy aftermath of – *The
Satanic Verses*. Moving away from the celebration of hybridity enacted
within Rushdie's novel, I argue that this new genre of literature grapples with the discomforts of a hybrid identity, seeking instead stable
modes of affiliation and identification. I argue throughout that the
foregrounding of religious discourse in the novels is linked to a quest
for new narratives of Britishness that are open to alternative ways of
identifying.

'*Ellowen Deeowen*': unhomeliness, doubling and alienation in *The Satanic Verses*[48]

When describing *The Satanic Verses*, 'gothic' is perhaps not the first term
that would spring to mind. However, many of the manoeuvres made
in the 'gothic tales of postcolonial England' that I discuss in Chapter 2
have early precursors in Rushdie's novel. *The Satanic Verses* similarly
challenges the elision of alterity and monstrosity as constructed in
imperial gothic and appropriates familiar gothic tropes such as doubling and the uncanny to reflect the 'unhomely' experience of migration and the psychological and material traumas of alienation and
racism that cause ethnic minority characters to experience themselves
as Other.

Rushdie's novel explores the psychological damage incurred through
the lingering effects of a colonial ideology that constructs the English
self in opposition to the colonised Other through the fractured sense
of identity of its protagonists. This is particularly true of Rushdie's
Anglophile migrant, Saladin, who begins to see his English and Indian
selves as irreconcilable upon returning to India after a long period
abroad: 'he had begun to hear, in India's Babel, an ominous warning:
don't come back again. When you have stepped through the looking-
glass you step back at your peril. The mirror may cut you to shreds'
(58). Deploying the symbolically-laden motif of the mirror, the site of
misrecognition in Lacanian psychoanalysis, this scene demonstrates the
way in which Saladin believes that he has become irreversibly other to
himself through the act of migration. Even his name reflects an inability to have a translatable identity as he changes it from Salahuddin

Chamchawala to Saladin Chamcha, but is then subject to teasing as his adopted surname means 'spoon' in Hindi. This leads to Saladin being nicknamed as 'Spoono,' which is tellingly the slang for 'toady,' meaning a sycophant or hanger-on (54). The act of translation has made him a joke to his old Indian friends and his 'Indian self' is displaced by – rather than reconciled with – his English one.

This act of self-displacement is also reflected through Saladin's battle with his own shadow, which is depicted as an unacknowledged part of himself. He is warned, 'Watch out, Chamcha, look out for your shadow. That black fellow creeping up behind' (53). This indicates a split sense of identity, implying that his self and his shadow are not inextricably linked. Furthermore, the fact that it is his 'black' self that is stalking him also opens up a racial dimension, suggesting that he is victim to – and can never fully repress – his Indian self. The simple conflation of evil and blackness parodies racial stereotypes; a man's fear of his own skin colour seems absurd and thereby shakes the foundations on which racial prejudices are built, undermining imperial constructions of alterity.

As with the novels considered in Chapter 2, *The Satanic Verses* also draws on uncanny imagery to convey the spatial defamiliarisation that accompanies the experience of being unhomed through migration. Ian Baucom provides a compelling reading of the many immigrant families living above the Shandaar Café in the novel. Defining the scenario in legal terms, he describes a situation whereby migrants 'live in anticipation of a moment in which their legal identities will catch up with their bodies'. These 'wanderers' are termed 'the frustrated specters of the migrant uncanny. They are the empire's repressed, patiently waiting permission to return'.[49] These migrant families are forced to occupy liminal spaces, transgressing many borders and rendering themselves ghost-like as they subsist in the ultimate liminal space between presence and absence. Rushdie takes the conventional gothic trope of ghostliness and repurposes it to address contemporary socio-political circumstances that force people into a living death. A denied legal identity is writ large in migrants' ethereality.

However, *The Satanic Verses* also defamiliarises English spaces in ways that can be read as confronting the white majority with sensations of alienation and dislocation commonly experienced by migrant communities. The country is re-imagined from the centre, starting with its capital, which Saladin creeps up on like a child playing grandmother's footsteps. The phonetic spelling of the city – *Ellowen deeowen* – defamiliarises the name and has phonic similarities to

Halloween, creating an eerie and sinister sensation. 'In his secret heart, he crept silently up on London, letter by letter, just as his friends crept up to him. *Ellowen deeowen, London'*: the familiar is rendered distinctly unfamiliar (37).

Joyce Wexler's compelling argument that 'National identity needs some unifying principle that transcends empirical experience, some conviction that events are related to one another, some constant to establish a pattern among events', suggests that London needs to be more than a space, it needs to be a fiction.[50] This fictionalisation is enabled through the magic-realist framework of Rushdie's narrative that allows dreams and 'reality' to seep into each other. Like the blurring of actual and fictional cities enacted by referring to London as 'Airstrip One, Mahogonny, Alphaville [...] Babylondon' (459), the doubling of Gibreel's waking and dreaming lives performs a deconstruction of reality's hierarchical superiority to the extent that he cannot distinguish between the two, and fears that his waking life is in fact someone else's dream (83). Yet he eventually realises that 'The doctors had been wrong [...] to treat him for schizophrenia; the splitting was not in him but in the universe' (351). This translates psychological trauma onto a material level. Clearly a splitting world is more fearful than a single deranged mind, and Rushdie therefore creates a world where no one can feel safe, comfortable, or 'at home'. Yet this defamiliarisation of the once familiar serves a dual purpose, also allowing for the redemption of the once-uncanny: in a world where everything has become unfamiliar, in turn nothing is strange. This signifies how the gothic mode can be employed to enable a working through of trauma in a way that is taken up in some of the other novels considered in Chapter 2.

Chapter 2 considers gothic tales of postcolonial England that similarly serve to deconstruct colonial constructions of alterity, appropriate familiar gothic tropes to unfamiliar ends and give voice to the traumas that are both particular to specific moments in contemporary English society and generally evidence an uncomfortable and lingering relationship with the country's colonial past. This chapter includes discussion of Meera Syal's *Anita and Me* (1996), Nadeem Aslam's *Maps for Lost Lovers* (2004), Helen Oyeyemi's *The Icarus Girl* (2005) and *White is for Witching* (2009), and Hanif Kureishi's *Something to Tell You* (2008). I argue that this new genre of literature collapses distinctions between imperial gothic written from the former colonial centre and postcolonial gothic that 'writes back' from elsewhere to enable the vocalisation of experiences of racism, alienation and dislocation particular to contemporary England and born out of its colonial past.

'Ready to be anything they wanted to buy': performing ethnic identities in *The Satanic Verses*[51]

Chapter 3 considers the 'subcultural urban novel', a genre of fiction that reflects and refracts the erotic allure and economic opportunity promised by urban spaces as well as the flipside of these sexual and commercial desires in the form of gang culture, hypermasculinity and misogyny, greed and poverty. Novels considered in this chapter shift the conventional paradigm of postcolonial fiction, as rather than 'writing back'[52] to the (former) colonial centre, they are produced for the consumption of a community of insiders. However, this genre has affiliations with other novels about minority cultures in which the projected audience is largely white, middle-class and mainstream, such as *The Satanic Verses*.

In *The Satanic Verses*, both Gibreel and Saladin are actors, meaning that performance, audience and economic considerations are brought to bear on the way that the characters construct their identities. Saladin's character is most relevant to this study, as he negotiates his personal and professional persona largely in Britain. Here, he experiences the institutional racism of the British media: he is 'the big star whose face is the wrong colour for their colour TVs' (61), consigned to hide his brown face behind voices and masks. Yet for all that Saladin's 'choice' to play these invisible roles is derided, it is nevertheless an economic decision: he provides the required performance in order to retain a job in a precarious market. However, he loses this job when his 'universe' shrinks (a universe being 'the total potential market for a given product or service') (264). It becomes apparent at this point that his ethnic identity has become a commodity, something that can be traded in, bought, or in this case, made redundant.

The quotation given as the subtitle to this section describes how Saladin's professional and/or economic choices are mimicked in his personal life. Jumpy Joshi jealously watches on as 'Chamcha came up, reeking of patchouli, wearing a white kurta, everyone's goddamn cartoon of the mysteries of the East, and the girl left with him five minutes later' (174). In Joshi's opinion 'The bastard [...] had no shame, he was ready to be anything they wanted to buy, that read-your-palm bedspread-jacket Hare-Krishna dharma-bum' (174): the language explicitly denotes Saladin's performed identity as a commodity, something that women want to own. Although Saladin plays the role of the 'mimic men' in the sense of V. S. Naipaul's novel of the same name, these acts of mimicry (his disdain for subcontinental compatriots and manifest love of Britain) do not threaten white Britain, as socio-economic factors demarcate the range of identities from which Saladin can profit.[53] In his work on the *Postcolonial Exotic*, Graham Huggan describes Saladin's mimicry as 'a symptom of his subjection to a vast, metropolitan-based image-making industry [...] that continues to manipulate his multiple cultural self-fashionings for its own financial ends'.[54] However, Saladin is not portrayed solely as the victim of an exoticising and/or racist society, because he is ultimately complicit with the system that exploits him.

Saladin's seduction of women is an allegory for his seduction of the nation, which is shown to be his ultimate object of affection. His wife laments that 'Chamcha was not in love with her at all, but with that voice stinking of Yorkshire pudding and hearts of oak, that hearty, rubicund voice of ye olde dream-England which he so desperately wanted to inhabit' (180). Saladin's personal and national romantic advances are interdependent. During *The Satanic Verses*, in which erotic and political drives are paralleled, the perversion of what is shown to be an incredibly one-sided affair is exposed. Saladin occupies the position of the self-abasing lover: devoted, yet never deemed worthy of the affections of the beloved. Britain is portrayed as indifferent to the wooing of its immigrant peoples, yet is shown to be encouraging of a self-abasing attitude by buying into consumable ethnic identities when and where there is a market for them.

In Chapter 3, I discuss Hanif Kureishi's *The Buddha of Suburbia* (1990) and Zadie Smith's *White Teeth* (2000) as novels that similarly exoticise minority cultures for a mainstream audience whilst reflecting the erotic and economic allure of the metropolis. I then turn to subcultural urban novels, which make their departure from such works through a change in what I term 'imagined audience' from white majority to subcultural minority, as books are increasingly marketed to subcultural insiders. Examples of the subcultural urban novel are found in Karline Smith's *Moss Side Massive* (1994) and *Full Crew* (2002), Nirpal Singh Dhaliwal's *Tourism* (2006) and Gautam Malkani's *Londonstani* (2007). The novels discussed here, spanning two decades, illustrate a changing cultural and literary landscape with a shifting relationship between minority and mainstream, producer and consumer. This new genre re-imagines the configuration of interpersonal and intercultural relations in post-colonial Britain by foregrounding the sexual and consumerist desires through which these relations are frequently expressed.

'Pitting levity against gravity': irreverent comedy in *The Satanic Verses*[55]

An overview of the way that comedy is employed in *The Satanic Verses* highlights the crucial political and psychological functions of multicultural British comedy that are key to my readings of the films discussed in Chapter 4. The subtitle to this section, which ostensibly describes Gibreel's attempts at thwarting the force of gravity during his plummet towards the English Channel by 'spread-eagling himself' and 'adopting heraldic postures' (3), can also be read as a metaphor for the relationship between Rushdie's irreverent tone (his levity) and serious subject matter (including the 'grave' matters of the racist treatment of immigrants in Britain, the formative years of Islam, and terrorism).

Amidst debate surrounding the fatwa, Rushdie's novel was discussed so seriously that its status as a work of comedy has been somewhat over-looked, though as Tariq Modood has argued, the novel's irreverent style was the real cause of hurt for Muslims at the time. The novel 'was not objected to as an intellectual critique of their faith (libraries are full of those),' but the 'vulgar language, the explicit sexual imagery, the attribu-tion of lustful motives – without any evidence – to the holy Prophet, in short the reduction of their religion to a selfish and sexual appetite' was the real cause of offence. Modood concludes that the novel 'was no more a contribution to literary discourse than pissing upon the Bible is a theo-logical argument'.[56] Intention is hard to discern in the case of *The Satanic Verses*, not least because of the mixed responses given by Rushdie himself during the 'affair'.[57] However, the response to the novel's publication from minority groups forces me to question the utility of a 'postcolonial' novel that serves to retrench polarities and dredge up Orientalist stereotypes. The political functions of multicultural British comedies, to preserve or disrupt the status quo, are a key concern of Chapter 4, in which I consider the hierarchies, objects of satirical attack and relationships of inclusion and exclusion variously constructed in subsequent cinematic comedies.

Rushdie's primary comic style is satire, an aggressive mode of comedy that functions to attack and undermine a particular target. Whilst there are many objects of attack in the novel, including British institutions such as the police, the Queen and Margaret Thatcher (a wax effigy of whom is ceremoniously melted), the overall thrust of the novel serves as a prolonged and wholly irreverent character defamation of the Prophet Mohammad. Satirical attack on the Prophet is effected through the mimicry by the poet Baal and his harem of 'whores' of Mahound (the Orientalist name attributed to the Prophet Muhammad in the novel) and his wives. In the early days of 'Submission' (meaning Islam) in Jahilia (meaning ignorance), *The Satanic Verses* describes an increased appetite for brothels and a heightened interest in the Prophet's recently secluded wives. Filling this gap in the market, the whores of 'The Curtain' (a translation of *hijab*) each adopt one of the wives' identities.

This instance of mimicry operates on a number of levels: there is a queue to the brothel that rotates 'about its centrally positioned Fountain of Love much as pilgrims rotated for other reasons around the ancient Black Stone' (381); the whores marry the poet Baal, who thereby mimics Mahound/Mohammed; and the harem begins to mirror the 'political cliques at the Yathrib mosque' (382). As the residents of 'The Curtain' mimic the appearance and nexus of relationships between the prophet and his wives, the scenario also produces what Bhabha might term 'its slippage, its excess, its difference' by focussing on the sexual relationships of the characters, which sink as low as the necrophilic acts pretended on the whore impersonating Zainab-bint-Khuzaimah, the recently deceased wife of the prophet (382).[58] This ambiguity between the 'original' and the bawdy copy creates ambivalence that challenges the Prophet's authority. By means of 'that anti-mosque, that labyrinth of profanity' (383) the Prophet is rendered seedy by comparison and the veiling of Muslim women is portrayed as a cynical means of sexual enticement. Although the novel's comedy provides a resounding satire of postcolonial Britain, exposing, challenging and undermining racist and right-wing discourses, when it comes to Islam the object of satire is confused, meaning, as Lindsey Moore asserts, that the novel 'paradoxically [...] reinforce[s] the line it challenges'.[59]

As well as having a political function, Rushdie's novel also foregrounds the psychological function of comedy by challenging stereotypes that are the residual effects of a colonial mindset. This is effected through Saladin's transformation into a devilish goat-like creature, which takes place in tandem with his arrest for a crime that he has not committed and a degrading spell in a police van. Awaking in hospital and horrified at the bestial makeover that he sees reflected in those around him, he is told that the reason for the transformation is simply that 'They describe us [...]. That's all. They have the power of description, and we succumb to the pictures they construct' (168). This scene brings to the forefront an image of Britain's nightmare Other that illustrates both the comical absurdity of the stereotypes created and the damage done to those who are thus objectified.

Bhabha's work on stereotypes illuminates this scene, as he attests to the importance of 'fixity in the ideological construction of otherness'. Bhabha highlights the paradoxical nature of the stereotype, as it 'vacillates between what is always "in place", already known, and something that must be anxiously repeated'.[60] However, Saladin's transformation disrupts the fixity necessary for stereotypes to function effectively. Finding himself to have unfortunately acquired a goatish, devilish appearance, his body becomes the very picture of the grotesque and the following description shows a definite predilection for the workings of the 'lower stratum' that Mikhail Bakhtin identifies as the site of degradation and subsequent renewal:[61]

> His thighs had grown uncommonly wide and powerful, as well as hairy. Below the knee the hairiness came to a halt, and his legs narrowed into tough, bony, almost fleshless calves, terminating in a pair of shiny, cloven hooves, such as one might find on any billy-goat. Saladin was also taken aback by the sight of his phallus, greatly enlarged and embarrassingly erect, an organ that he had the greatest difficulty in acknowledging as his own. (157)

Saladin's body subsequently becomes what John Clement Ball describes in his assessment of Rushdie's 'pessoptimist' brand of satire as the 'defecating [...] body of the open apertures,' as he is horrified to find himself defecating uncontrollably in a police van.[62] Rather than the 'fixity' that the stereotype's power relies upon, Saladin's is a body in flux, altering and transforming constantly. This appropriates the stereotype as a site of struggle, incompleteness and potential transformation. As Saladin embodies a stereotype based on racist fears of animality and hypersexuality in the 'black' man's body, its changing and decidedly unfixed nature exposes the weak foundations on which the stereotype is built.[63]

An engagement with racist stereotypes is something that continues to be important for the films that I discuss in Chapter 4. However, changes in contemporaneous politics engender shifting causes for laughter and present new challenges for the negotiation of both state-endorsed ideologies and aspirations and shifting public attitudes, meaning that the genre is continuously evolving. Chapter 4 considers subsequent generations of comedy that have emerged to challenge or reflect new governmental policies and international affairs, including discussion of Gurinder Chadha's *Bhaji on the Beach* (1993) and *Bend It Like Beckham* (2002), Damien O'Donnell's *East is East* (1999), Chris Morris's *Four Lions* (2010) and Joe Cornish's *Attack the Block* (2011). Multicultural British comedy evolves rapidly in response to shifting attitudes towards multiculturalism, and this chapter covers two waves of comedy that have evolved since 1990. The first generation pursues a happy, multicultural idyll through the use of gentle and inclusive comedy. Although this type of comedy allows for the subtle undermining of stereotypes, I argue that its utopian tendency relies on the repression of social challenges that would threaten its potential harmony. A second generation of comedy employs laughter as an alternative response to fear, centring on the socially ostracised figures of the suicide bomber and the gangster that were repressed by the previous generation's idealism.

Final words

It is not within the scope of this book to comprehensively list and detail each work of fiction that might have affinities with the genres explored, nor are the genres engaged exhaustively. This does not mean, however, that works considered should be understood as representative, but instead as particular examples that engage with and/or expand the genres in unique ways. The intention of this work is to raise the profile of postcolonial genre studies by indicating ways in which British identity is approached, shaped and critiqued from the margins. In turn, I hope that this work will open up the field of postcolonial genre studies to academics researching other locations and histories.

This book is distinctive for the range of contemporary texts and films that are discussed, including both those that have a mainstream consumption but have seldom been read through the lens of genre (including works by Salman Rushdie, Hanif Kureishi and Zadie Smith) and those that have been marginalised by markets and academics alike (including works by Karline Smith, Nirpal Singh Dhaliwal and Gautam Malkani). The book works against models of Britishness that are overly-weighted on the metropolis through analysis of literature and film emanating from a range of locales. This has the benefit of tracing new patterns in contemporary British literature whilst crucially raising the profiles of authors and works that have been sidelined for reasons other than literary value.

1
British Muslim Bildungsromane

At the time of writing, members of parliament have recently felt justified in asking British Muslims to 'explain and demonstrate how faith in Islam can be part of British identity' in the wake of the *Charlie Hebdo* shootings (January 2015), in terms that imply their inherent opposition.[1] I argue, therefore, that it is more important than ever to consider the nuanced accounts of Muslim faith and identity provided in fiction and to evaluate critically the relationship between Britishness and Islam enacted therein. This relationship is foregrounded through the identity crises experienced by the protagonists of these Bildungsromane. The chapter title deliberately evokes the plural form of 'Bildungsroman' to indicate that the genre – as with the spectrum of 'belief attitudes'[2] displayed by authors and protagonists – cannot be considered as monolithic. The chapter examines Hanif Kureishi's *The Black Album* (1995), Leila Aboulela's *The Translator* (1999) and *Minaret* (2005) and Robin Yassin-Kassab's *The Road from Damascus* (2008).

Religious identity has been brought to the fore in western media following the 9/11 and 7/7 terrorist attacks, in ways that often seek (overtly or covertly) to distinguish between 'us' (secular, western, benign) and 'them' (Muslim, non-western, threatening). For Peter Morey and Amina Yaqin, what we see in the western media today 'is the distortion of particular features of Muslim life and custom, reducing the diversity of Muslims and their existence as individuals to a fixed object – a caricature in fact'.[3] They argue that this 'distortion' is brought about through 'framing structures' that 'rather than being descriptive and neutral [...] are defined by questions of belonging, "Otherness," and "threat"'.[4] This in itself highlights the importance of critically evaluating the representation of religious discourses in literature and the media. The critic Amin Malak goes one step further to highlight why the reintroduction of religion as a postcolonial topic is of paramount importance, arguing that the 'resistance to engage with religion as a key category pertinent to the debate about contemporary neo-colonial reality' effectively 'privilege[es] a secular, Euro-American stance that *seems* to shape the parameters of postcolonial discourses' (emphasis in original).[5] As he postulates, excluding religion from postcolonial studies is itself a preju-dice of a Euro-American project that should be remedied.

The birth of the Bildungsroman is often dated back to the publica-tion of Johann Wolfgang Goethe's *Wilhelm Meister's Apprenticeship* in 1795[6] and the form was popularised in Europe over the course of the following century, with a host of authors – including Jane Austen, Charlotte Brontë, Charles Dickens, Gustave Flaubert, Alessandro Manzoni, Stendhal, and Ivan Turgenev – adopting it to great effect. The Bildungsroman (from the German for a novel of education or transfor-mation) is a novel form predisposed towards discussions of identity in crisis, as youthful protagonists consider various ontologies that they will either accept or reject in their paths to maturity, self-awareness and autonomy. In his work on the significance of the Bildungsroman in European culture, Franco Moretti highlights a number of points that I read as indicating the particular suitability of the form for the purpose of representing and negotiating British Muslim identities. Primarily, Moretti terms it the '*most contradictory* of modern symbolic forms' in which 'we realize that in our world socialization itself consists first of all in the *interiorization of contradiction*' (emphasis in original). Accordingly, the form is fitting for negotiating perceived binaries, such as culturally constructed oppositions between Britishness and Islam, or between national and religious modes of affiliation. The Bildungsroman, for Moretti, enables not the resolution to the contradiction, but the ability to live with it.[7] This is particularly pertinent for the novels considered below, as rather than rejecting one identity in favour of another, pro-tagonists often eschew the construction of different modes of affiliation as mutually exclusive. Furthermore, the Bildungsroman has tradition-ally been concerned with the construction of normality '*from within* rather than from the stance of its exceptions'[8] (emphasis in original), which I suggest makes it particularly apt for the consideration of an identity group that, as Peter Morey and Amina Yaqin suggest, is often 'narrowed to mean all that is threatening and foreign'.[9] British Muslim Bildungsromane engage the quotidian construction of British Muslim identity from within, which serves in part to remedy the hyperbolised construction of the Muslim as nightmare Other, in the form of the ter-rorist or suicide bomber.

The subgenre that I identify here has parallels with what Mark Stein has termed the 'black British novel of transformation', in which the reworked Bildungsroman genre allows for the *'formation* of its protagonists' alongside the *'transformation* of British society and cultural institutions' (emphases in original).[10] Stein suggests that British society and culture is transformed through these novels as they enable the conception of a wider range of subject positions with which one might identify. British Muslim Bildungsromane similarly make available a broader range of subject positions that are crucial in challenging the representation of Islam as monolithic and in perpetual opposition to notions of Britishness. Yet while in Stein's remapping of the Bildungsroman genre the focus of affiliation and the site of transformation is resolutely national, I suggest that British Muslim Bildungsromane demonstrate that national affiliation is only one of many ways of identifying. Rather than transforming national identities through the transgression of space enabled through patterns of migration that Stein posits as 'eroding national borders',[11] religious affiliations coexist with and overlay national ones, as the Muslim *ummah* offers an alternative affiliative space and means of communal identification. In the texts I consider here, 'British' and 'Muslim' are not constructed as mutually exclusive, but rather represent two modes of affiliation that are negotiated and variously adopted by protagonists.

As well as being a genre well suited to the negotiation of identity, critic Feroza Jussawalla suggests that the postcolonial Bildungsroman also has an ideological function, as protagonists inevitably refuse a hybrid identity. Jussawalla denies the common equation of postcoloniality and postmodernity 'as a hybrid flux and merging, or the problematizing of cultures at various interstices,' arguing instead that 'postcoloniality constitutes a rejection of hybridity and a turn toward nationhood'. In support of this, she notes as a common trait that the 'postcolonial hero/ heroine/protagonist seems to refuse to inhabit a "border" liminal space and finds such a space uncomfortable'.[12] The Bildungsroman functions as a quest for identity, a means of finding an authoritative meaning in the protagonist's life, and as Stein and Jussawala have both recognised, it also serves to comment on society. But it is the additional concern for refusing hybrid identities as identified by Jussawalla that is the key conceptual turning point for all of the novels that I analyse in this chapter. Unlike the celebration of newness, hybridity and transformation exercised in Salman Rushdie's *The Satanic Verses*, the novels considered here have an affinity with the postcolonial Bildungsroman as defined by Jussawalla, insomuch as they similarly engage with the discomfort of a hybrid identity by seeking stable modes of affiliation and identification, or struggling with their absence.

Following the work of Esra Mirze Santesso in *Disorientation*, I argue that hybridity is a problematically celebrated term for the negotiation of affiliations and identities, particularly in the case of religious identities. Santesso highlights the inherently problematic manner in which hybridity is constructed in opposition to 'the pure or the traditional or the nationalist', effectively 'participating in the validation of binaries rather than circumventing the essentialist rhetoric associated with it'.[13] This tendency is outlined in my discussion of *The Satanic Verses* in the Introduction, in which 'the Pure' is the straw man against which flux, change, transformation and hybridity are pitted. Furthermore, in the process of opening up postcolonial criticism to the discussion of religious identities (often elided in the favour of national, ethnic or cultural ones) it is necessary to adopt an appropriate vocabulary, and hybridity is ill-suited to the topic. As Santesso rightly states, 'while hybridity can act as a productive site of self-fashioning in terms of race, nation and even sexuality, it ceases to function when it comes to organised faith. Simply put, given its monologic structure, religious identity resists any form of hybridisation'.[14] This chapter accordingly refers to the negotiation of affiliations in which the purported desirability of transformation is subordinated to desires for stability and the preservation of religious identities in an otherwise shifting world.

This (re)turn to religious identities countermands an emerging literary trend identified by Arthur Bradley and Andrew Tate in *The New Atheist Novel: Fiction, Philosophy and Polemic after 9/11*, in which the critics suggest that the absence of God is no longer experienced as a trauma:

> Whereas Matthew Arnold and the other giants of nineteenth century literary scepticism famously experienced the death of the Judaeo-Christian God as a terrifying, even bewildering, loss, Amis, McEwan, Pullman and Rushdie depict it as a natural, inevitable and entirely welcome phenomenon that is no more traumatic than disbelief in Zeus, Thor or Father Xmas.[15]

The authors considered in this chapter write *against* the trend that Bradley and Tate have identified among 'new atheists'. In their works, even if the idea of a God is not wholeheartedly embraced, the absence or 'God-Shaped Hole' is painfully experienced by the various protagonists, recapturing the sense of loss for the death of God and the desire to reformulate a basis for meaning.

British Muslim Bildungsromane explore networks of affiliations, representing the desire for a fixed mode of identifying by engaging with the trauma of its absence. The disorientation engendered by a collapse of meaning is explored via the trope of the absent father and through a return to realist modes of writing. Moving away from overly sanguine or optimistic accounts of hybrid identities, this chapter foregrounds readings of painful processes of transformation or conversion that bespeak the desire for a stable identity and belief system that will reinvest the world with meaning and the possibility of communal identification. The recentralisation of religion in the novels is marked via the use of metaphors of rebirth and conversion to understand processes of identification as well as the prioritisation of a religious identity that can transcend national borders. I argue throughout that the foregrounding of religious discourse in the novels is linked to a quest for new narratives of Britishness that are open to alternative ways of identifying.

'Mustafa's official version': fatherhood and authority[16]

Robin Yassin-Kassab's *The Road from Damascus* and Hanif Kureishi's *The Black Album* explore the loss of a sense of meaning and a desire for grand narratives to fill this void. In *The Road from Damascus*, the attraction of grand narratives is primarily enacted through the long and troubled soul-searching of British–Syrian protagonist, Sami Traifi, as he struggles to find a fitting identity. His spiritual journey takes him down a number of routes, as he dabbles with mind-altering drugs, contests his wife's decision to adopt the *hijab*, attempts an academic lifestyle and returns to his parents' homeland in Syria, all the while struggling with questions of belief and choices that affect both him and his loved ones.

The Black Album traces the story of Shahid as he moves from his parents' house in the suburbs into central London and begins college. As he tries to make friends in his new surroundings, he is caught between Riaz and his group of Muslim 'brothers' and his lecturer, Deedee Osgood, who lives and preaches a life of freedom, hedonism and pop-cultural mélange. The novel operates around a binary whereby these lifestyles are mutually exclusive and Shahid – caught in the middle (at times physically as well as figuratively) – must decide where he wants to locate his own sense of identity. The physical trauma that he feels as a result of these warring selves is expressed as the numbing sensation of being lost in 'a room of broken mirrors, with jagged reflections backing into eternity' (147).

Both Kureishi and Yassin-Kassab draw on the motif of the absent father to signify the end of a certain form of authority. For Sigmund Freud, dreams of killing the father mark a normal stage of (male) child-hood development.[17] But when the father-figure is (always) already dead – as is the case for Kureishi's and Yassin-Kassab's protagonists whose fathers died during their childhoods – there is a developmental gap and they are unable to seize the authority of the father, their fathers having been taken from them too early and against their will. Using Peter Brooks's formulation for aligning psychoanalytic and textual functioning, it is possible to understand how readers' desires might be manipulated into reflecting those of the protagonist. Brooks asserts that 'psychoanalysis promises and requires, that in addition to such usual narratological preoccupations as function, sequence, and paradigm, we engage the dynamic of memory and the history of desire as they work to reshape the recovery of meaning within time'.[18] By rendering the novels' patriarchs present in their absence, the authors ensure that their narratives structurally reflect the psychological absence in the characters' lives, creating desire in the reader for the 'recovery of mean-ing' as symbolised by the absent fathers. What is more, the fathers of the novels considered here are also symbolic of God, meaning that the moment of death simultaneously signifies the death of grand narratives and meaning.

Sami suffers a long period of estrangement from his mother, due largely to a (perhaps misplaced) idolisation of his father (Mustafa) who died during his childhood. As a hangover from this childhood admi-ration and subsequent loss, he frequently refers to 'Mustafa's official version' – the world according to the unquestioned authority of the boy's father (334). It is only later in the novel that his father is brought down to an earthly level through his mother's accusations, meaning that Sami is liberated from a one-dimensional view of the world and no longer has to live under his father's shadow. However, Sami's liberation from the idealised version of his father comes at a price and he feels the loss acutely: 'Of course his father wasn't up there. His father was far too small, like any of us. Sami felt fear and trembling. Felt the empti-ness of a burning heart' (348). The physical pain manipulating Sami's body demonstrates the significance of the loss and reveals the role that his father formerly occupied. The language employed also situates his father as God, 'up there,' meaning that the recognition that his father operates on the same level as himself entails a concurrent loss of the sense of any greater meaning. Such an easy, almost unquestioning con-flation of an absent father and a non-existent God is equally apparent in Kureishi's novel, where the protagonist Shahid intimates that 'All this reminded him of his childhood. He wanted to say: wait till Papa finds out. But Papa would never find out and there was, now – he was convinced of it – no one watching over them.'[19] The slippage between knowing that there is no (living, biological) father and making the inductive leap that there is no higher power whatsoever exemplifies the significant weight that fathers have in the novels, as embodiments of absolute authority.

A reading that equates childhood dependence on the authority of the father and religious belief is perhaps a rather reductive assessment of faith, yet it is one that is consistent with the way that religion is represented in the novels, at least at the outset. In a dismissive tone, Sami deems religion 'the long childhood of a people' early in the novel, allowing for the senility of 'ancient' believers but decrying religion as 'humiliation' among the 'healthy', 'sane' people of London (60). He implies that whilst religion might be pardoned as a benign affectation in the young, old and infirm, much like the inability to control one's bowel movements or to walk unsupported, it would be a shameful confession to make from a position of physical and mental stability. However, this patronising assessment is challenged by the end of the novel, at which point Sami conceives of himself as 'a bit more of a man now' with his 'trembling, contingent faith' (349, 348). The development of the narrative from immaturity and secularism to maturity and a carefully considered faith undermines the dominant narrative equating religion with mental infirmity set up at the beginning.

The Road from Damascus also countermands an easy dismissal of religious faith through an exploration of the appeal of grand narratives as Sami pursues different ways of reinvesting his life with meaning. In an article by Yassin-Kassab on the place of Islam in his own writing process, the author suggests that it 'is a fair generalization that grand narratives play a bigger role in the lives of British Muslims than in the lives of their non-Muslim compatriots' and proclaims himself a 'supporter of – if not a traditional believer in – the "grand narratives"'.[20] Unlike *The Satanic Verses*, in which believers in grand narratives are constructed as mad, requiring a hasty call to the 'straitjacket tailor,'[21] the inherent appeal of structures of meaning and belief are given space in Yassin-Kassab's novel, and it is the figure of Rushdie who is comically undermined. In this vein, C. E. Rashid reads the character of writer Rashid Iqbal in Yassin-Kassab's novel as 'an obvious caricature of Salman Rushdie' who 'positions himself as a novelist in opposition to Islamic dogma'.[22] Yassin-Kassab himself describes Rushdie's comment that '"Islam," in contrast to "the West," is not a narrative civilisation' as 'obvious nonsense' and uses writing as a means of exploring the complexities of Muslim belief in a climate in which they have been constructed as oppositional.[23]

The main stylistic difference between Rushdie's *The Satanic Verses* and those published in the 1990s and early twenty-first century that I discuss here is that whereas Rushdie chooses to express himself in metafictional terms, perennially questioning the status of authorship and the role of authority, these novelists return to realist modes of writing more commonly associated with the Bildungsroman form. The following discussion focuses on *The Black Album*, a novel that has an interesting intertextual relationship with *The Satanic Verses* as it engages a lot of the same arguments regarding the role of the author and theological debates but in a realist rather than a metafictional mode. Ironically, the absence of a metafictional writing style similar to Rushdie's is a reason that many of Kureishi's critics have been shocked or confused by his novel. For example, in an essay comparing Rushdie's novel with Kureishi's, Frederic M. Holmes suggests that 'The absence from *The Black Album* of such fictional self-scrutiny regarding the authority of its own representations is a curious blind spot in an otherwise postmodernist novel.'[24] However, I would argue that rather than an omission on Kureishi's part, the lack of 'fictional self-scrutiny' (or metafiction) actually intimates a desire for authority that is reflected in the protagonist's search for a structuring authority and source of identity in the novel. Here is where the tone of *The Black Album* differs from that of *The Satanic Verses*, as a shift is made from playfulness to an earnest search for identity and belonging.

Shahid struggles to find an identity by negotiating two ideologies offered in the novel: secular liberalism and Islam, or (to put it blandly as the blurb does) liberalism and fundamentalism. In the binary created and perpetuated by the novel, the former ideology is always destined to win out, as is suggested by the name of Shahid's postmodernist lecturer, Deedee Osgood, or, without much stretch of the imagination, D. Osgood: do is good. Deedee's 'dos' (encouraging him to partake in new experiences, be they gastronomic, hallucinogenic or sexual) rival his religious friends' 'do nots' (not partaking in sexual activities, not being friendly with white women and not taking mind-altering substances). Kureishi's protagonist superficially adopts the lifestyle of his lecturer, sharing with her a love of popular culture and a hedonist 'anything-goes' ideal, and he ultimately chooses to leave with her at the end of the novel. The 'horizon of expectations'[25] created by the Bildungsroman genre accordingly suggests that Shahid has come to an understanding of himself aligned with a postmodernity that is pitted against Islam.

However, the tone and style of the narrative go against the plot and instead provide a critique of postmodernism as a way of life that Shahid has apparently embraced. If *The Satanic Verses* challenges the authority of the absolute, *The Black Album* challenges the authority of postmodernism to provide a satisfactory explanation of things, in part through intertextual references to Rushdie's novel. Many of Shahid's personal dilemmas play out through the furore that arises following the publication and subsequent burning of a book that is disrespectful of Islam – Rushdie's novel is clearly implicated. As Maria Degabriele suggests: 'each novel [*The Black Album* and *The Satanic Verses*] discloses its source of inspiration (a previous text that has become canonical in its own genre) and then goes on to undo the conventions by which the previous text is recognised'.[26] Whereas Rushdie draws on the *Qur'an* in order to interrogate the way that scripture is read, Kureishi engages with *The Satanic Verses* in order to question the postmodernist hybridity that Rushdie both uses as a literary style and advocates as a way of life for his characters. To facilitate a challenge to the postmodern hybridity that Rushdie advocates, Kureishi's novel also engages with postmodern concerns, but it follows them through to their logical conclusions. He does this via Shahid's ontological questioning, ontology being the 'dominant of postmodernist fiction' according to Brian McHale's definition.[27]

Throughout *The Black Album*, Shahid demonstrates his desire to find a fitting identity for himself, acknowledging that 'he would have to study, read more and think, combining facts and arguments in ways that fitted the world as he saw it' (99). Yet despite the scholarly interest that he determines to act upon, the novel sees the protagonist embarking on different excursions and activities with his rival groups of friends, 'swung here and there by desire' and, I might add, by the intervening repression of desire (97). Despite the eschewal of authority embraced by his chosen mentor, Deedee, Shahid's *desire* for authority is nevertheless indicated in the willingness that he shows to submit to others, whether religiously, by taking orders from Riaz, or sexually, in the role-playing and cross-dressing that he enacts with Deedee. Holmes notes the parallel in the narrative between Shahid dressing up as a woman and Shahid 'dressing up' as a Muslim, when he accepts the gift of a *salwar kamiz* from Chad and tries it on for size, citing them as comparable 'ludic experiments with identity'.[28]

This understanding of identity, as something with little more permanence or substance than an outfit to be put on and taken off, comes to define Shahid's personal ideology. After a quest for identity that spans the novel, Shahid eventually decides: 'There was no fixed self; surely our several selves melted and mutated daily? There had to be innumerable ways of being in the world. He would spread himself out, in his work and in love, following his curiosity' (274). This quotation suggests the celebration of a hybrid, impermanent, postmodernist sense of self, yet when taken in parallel with a quotation cited earlier that similarly considers multiple ways of being, some of the phrases begin to jar. Whereas now the language is full of hope, suggesting a world of future opportunities and promise, the earlier passage examined the same sentiments from a more dystopian perspective, employing language of brokenness and war as he had the sensation of being lost 'in a room of broken mirrors, with jagged reflections backing into eternity' (147). Shahid still sees himself pulled in different directions; he still feels that his self is not whole, but melted, or jagged. However, this time he chooses to embrace a way of being that rejects authority, grand narratives and a stable notion of self. This would conclude the Bildungsroman format adequately if readers did not have such a recent memory of the upset that this ontology previously caused him.

Ultimately, for Shahid, authority and individual identity come from his own writing practice. This is interesting when taken alongside McHale's reminder that – like the Renaissance or Romanticism – 'postmodernism, the thing, does not exist' but is rather a 'literary-historical fiction [...] constructed either by contemporary readers and writers or retrospectively by literary historians'.[29] The problem in the narrative similarly arises from the conflation of postmodernism as a way of understanding or constructing art and literature, and the ideal of a postmodernism that can be lived out, 'out there' in the real world. Shahid is content when he is writing, creating and constructing a distinctive poetic identity fictionally, rather than 'out there'. Mimicking *The Satanic Verses* (which itself imitates the revelation of *Qur'anic* scripture), Shahid begins to meddle with Riaz's work that he has been entrusted to type out. Degabriele argues that Shahid's tampering with Riaz's work parodies the revelation of the 'satanic' verses in Rushdie's novel. 'The authority of Islam' – according to Degabriele – 'depends on the authority of "the book," the Qur'an, the sacred verses, and the Prophet'. Therefore, Shahid's 'tampering' can be understood as 'a transgression against the author as a god-like figure'.[30] Through the parallels that Degabriele identifies between this section and the comparable part of Rushdie's novel, it becomes apparent that Shahid uses this opportunity to assert his own authority. Becoming the author of his own life – 'He wanted to crawl back to his room, slam the door and sit down with a pen; that was how he would reclaim himself' (227) – Shahid effectively becomes a postmodern god, pretending and denying authority through his experiments with literature.

Yet this is a very limited vision that does not allow for any communal identification. The novel closes with Shahid and Deedee agreeing to stay together 'until it stops being fun,' a hedonist motto if ever there was one (276). The life that Shahid has spent trying to invest with meaning is now devoid or emptied of the same as he realises 'He didn't have to think about anything' (276). As Degabriele suggests, 'Throughout the novel Shahid looks for a sense of cultural belonging, to ultimately find that he belongs with pop culture where fragmentation, change, undecidability are the norm.'[31] But according to this logic, postmodernism becomes another grand narrative, with another set of norms, which must be fully believed in to confer identity upon its subjects. I therefore support Holmes's conclusion, that 'In the end, Shahid chooses Deedee over Riaz, but the ephemerality and indefiniteness of what she stands for as a postmodernist seems to undercut the value of his choice.'[32] Whilst Rushdie challenges the Absolute through his style of writing, Kureishi takes Rushdie's novel as his intertext and questions the (sad) implications of postmodernism as a source of identity, as the protagonist is left alone in the world with only the love of a woman many years his senior to rely on for stability.[33] In the fragmented, hedonistic and solipsistic postmodern lifestyle chosen by Shahid in the end, there is no hope of the communal identification that he has craved throughout the foregoing narrative.

The denouement to Shahid's narrative can be read as following what Moretti defines as the 'transformation principle' of the Bildungsroman. Suggesting that 'Maturity and youth are [...] inversely proportional', Moretti identifies two alternative strains of the Bildungsroman that differ according to whether youth is subordinated to maturity, or the reverse:

> Where the classification principle prevails [...] youth is subordinated to the idea of 'maturity': like the story it has meaning only *in so far as* it leads to a stable and 'final' identity. Where the transformation principle prevails and youthful dynamism is emphasized [...] youth cannot or does not want to give way to maturity: the young hero senses in fact in such a conclusion a sense of betrayal, which would *deprive* his youth of its meaning rather than enrich it. (Emphasis in original)[34]

Shahid's narrative prioritises continued transformation, yet this entails a sense of loss and pain that might be healed by a more stable identity. In the following section I discuss the ambivalent resolution to Sami's story in *The Road from Damascus*, which follows a similar pattern by prioritising the 'transformation principle'. Aboulela's novels alternatively prioritise the classification principle, by ending with the promise or rejection of marriage as moments in which maturity is reached and identity stabilised and fixed. Yet despite the conflicting resolutions of the novels considered here, the effect of these different strands of British Muslim Bildungsromane are comparable in the expression of desire for a stable sense of identity and a sense of loss or insecurity when this is not achieved.

'Who enters here is lost; who leaves is born again': painful conversion narratives[35]

The experience of conversion is often described through analogies to birth or rebirth, summoning images of new life and fresh beginnings. Renaldo J. Maduro and Joseph B. Wheelright explain the Jungian 'archetypal situation' of rebirth as

> The birth of the ego, or part of the ego, which renews the sense of self (feeling centred and whole). Ego-consciousness is reborn, experiences growth, is expanded; it emerges dynamically from a state of projective identification or fusion with a primordial state of unconsciousness (non-ego). This healthy process in later life repeats the earliest separation of the ego from identification and containment in the primary self. The ego feels threatened by death and experiences (perceives) rebirth.[36]

Rebirth is figured here in psychologically liberating terms, as flight from the threat of death and a return to a younger innocence. Similarly, Hindu, Jain and Buddhist beliefs advocate rebirth or reincarnation, whilst converted or practising Christians describe themselves as born again to indicate a spiritual (re-)awakening and share with Muslim doctrines a belief in the concept of an ultimate resurrection, using a physical process to symbolise a spiritual one. By contrast, the texts considered here strip the process of rebirth of its idealistic psychological and spiritual promise, instead associating it with pain and physical and emotional trauma. The section title, taken from *The Road to Damascus*, states that 'Who enters here is lost; who leaves is born again' (6).

In accordance with this dictum the novels I analyse here re-evaluate the concept of rebirth, foregrounding the aspect of death and painful effacement of an old self that is necessary for the (re)generation of a new self.

The maternal tropes figured in the following discussion provide a contrast to the previous section that revolved around predominantly patriarchal tropes of fatherhood, authorship and God. As Elleke Boehmer points out, 'nation [is] informed throughout by its gendered history, by the normative masculinities and femininities that have shaped its growth over time'.[37] Typically 'feminine' tropes can be found in the British Muslim Bildungsromane considered in this section, illustrating Boehmer's argument that in narratives of postcolonial nationhood women have traditionally embodied the role of mother, a position that 'invites connotations of origins – birth, hearth, home, roots, the umbilical cord – and rests upon the frequent, and some might say "natural", identification of the mother with the beloved earth, the national territory and the first-spoken language, the national tongue'.[38] This section covers similar critical terrain in its analysis of traditionally feminine tropes associated with motherhood. However, these tropes are deromanticised through my focus on their elision with narratives of trauma, guilt and pain in both its physical and spiritual manifestations. The following discussion centres on Yassin-Kassab's *The Road from Damascus* and Aboulela's *The Translator*.

Aboulela's *The Translator* tells the tale of Sammar, a young Sudanese widow who has moved to Britain with her husband and borne him a child, only for the former to be killed in a car accident. Having unsentimentally deposited her child with her mother-in-law back in Sudan, Sammar returns to Scotland to work as an Anglo-Arabic translator in Aberdeen University and subsequently finds herself falling for Rae, an academic working in Middle Eastern Studies. In the novel, birth is reduced to an adamantly physical process as elements of romance and sentiment are denied or forcibly repressed. For Sammar, the process of birth is always haunted by (another) death; a year after her first son is born, she miscarries and later recalls, 'She remembered Tarig [her husband] being calm, warm and sure of what to do. She remembered him on his hands and knees mopping the bathroom floor, her womb that had fallen apart.'[39] The image of the falling womb symbolically brings life and death into uncomfortable proximity, reminding the reader of the interdependence of the two states of being. This is further reflected when Sammar's husband dies and she displaces her feelings of anger and injustice onto her son: 'She was unable to mother the child. The part of her that did the mothering had disappeared. Froth, ugly froth. She had said to her son, "I wish it was you instead. I hate you. I hate you".' (7) The desire for her living son and dead husband to change places illustrates the less hopeful aspect of rebirth; her husband's rebirth would be dependent upon the sacrifice of her child, as one would replace the other. This problematises romanticised representations of birth and childhood; rather than 'trailing clouds of glory [...] from God' as does the infant subject of Wordsworth's poem, Sammar's children are described in more physically abject terms, engendering postnatal depression and guilt rather than symbolising hope.[40] Any links between birth and greater ideals (of God, in this instance) are cruelly severed. This brutal severing jars with the religious sentiments expressed by the main character throughout the rest of the novel – and I must clarify that Sammar is ultimately reconciled with her son – yet the focus on the painful process that Sammar endures first is given more space and depth of feeling in the novel than the later reconciliation.

Aboulela's narrative also offers a subversive critique of traditional ways of imagining the nation. Boehmer explains the marginalising effect that romanticising mother-figures has had on women: 'Often set in relation to the figure of her nationalist son', the woman's 'ample, childbear-ing, fully *representative* maternal form typically takes on the status of *metaphor*'. This, she states, has the detrimental effect of positioning the woman '*outside* the central script of national self-emergence', the 'cen-tral script' being reserved for her 'national sons' (emphasis in original).[41] Aboulela's protagonist serves as a corrective to the imbalance created by women so frequently being idealised in nationalist metaphors. The author employs tropes traditionally associated with feminine aspects of nationalism (birth, origins, the umbilical cord), but through a process of re-familiarisation with the physical and emotional traumas involved in birth, she reinserts Sammar as the central player in her narrative. This also enables her to examine processes of self-emergence, questioning whether national identification is the most useful starting point. I turn to Aboulela's move away from national identification further in the next section.

Rebirth is integral to the Bildungsroman genre as characters explicitly undergo processes of self-discovery that often involve the shedding of a former self. In Yassin-Kassab's novel, Sami's uncle is beaten up, forced into prison and tortured after being found out to be a Muslim Brother by the *mukhabarat*; as he is forced through the prison entrance he looks up and sees an ominous sign above the prison door: 'Who enters here is lost; who leaves is born again' (6). Whilst he is in the prison he is therefore addressed as 'Mr. Nobody' (7). This deliberate effacement of identity is a cruel example of what happens when anyone is 'born again,' a motif of pain and self-estrangement that Yassin-Kassab draws on throughout the novel, even when the change is self-motivated or ultimately brings happiness.

Sami himself goes through a prolonged process of conversion, which he fights violently until the end. When he finally converts, it is figured as a loss and a shattering of self rather than a glorious victory and the process of conversion that he undergoes before reaching a point of faith (and which the novel is largely concerned with) is figured in the language of trauma and self-destruction. In a haunting moment it is suggested that religion even takes the place of 'Sami', rendering him an automaton after his conversion: 'Pasts should die before you, but this past, this religion, cast itself as child rather than parent. It stood at the foot of his bed and watched him disappear' (169). Religion arrives as a child-like grim reaper, poised at Sami's deathbed and awaiting his demise in this uncanny image of rebirth that demands the death of the former sinning self in order to let the new life begin. Subsequently, Sami articulates his first prayer, but this moment is also accompanied by images of splitting, fragmentation and displacement. He 'Notices here that he's broken into two separate pieces: the piece that advises the other piece to relax. The two pieces in fact not two selves but two functions of the words. Speaker and speakee. The order to relax has made him briefly disappear' (330).

Although the process of Sami's conversion figures him as variously dead, fragmented and displaced, there is (tenuous) hope to be found at the novel's denouement where he has 'developed a trembling, contingent faith' (348). However, the narrative questions 'What is he, now?' and concludes 'Not much any more. Not Mustafa's son, nor Marwan's son-in-law. Not the child of corpse dust. Not an academic. Not a member of the eternal Arab nation' (348). His new faith-based identity is overshadowed by images of negation. Whilst the ending does instil a feeling of hope and newness and a sense of Sami's unburdening as he comes to a reconciliation with his wife and family, the imagery that surrounds the process illustrates the pain of conversion and of being 'reborn' to a new idea. Furthermore, the description of his new-found faith as trembling and contingent – suggesting that it is transitory, or dependent – questions whether or not he has ultimately found the 'new identity' that he had been seeking. Like *The Black Album*, discussed above, *The Road from Damascus* prioritises the transformation principle of the Bildungsroman.

The image of conversion is paralleled with translation in Aboulela's *The Translator*, as the act of 'converting' words into another language highlights the difficulties in moving from one identity to another and the loss that can be incurred through the metaphor of language. Sammar is said to '[work] hard pushing Arabic into English, English into Arabic' (152): the verb suggests a physical labour to the task (reminiscent of the act of labour itself). When she wants to write a letter to Rae she is compelled to write twice: 'She had an airmail letter pad with her, a ball-point pen, two envelopes. She was going to write two letters in two languages. They would say the same thing but not be a translation' (184). This illustrates the difficulty of the conversion of language, as it can prove a struggle, or an ideological challenge, to liberate words from their parent cultures.

Yet translation is not figured as a fruitless act. On the contrary, Waïl S. Hassan makes the connection between acts of translation and compromise; he suggests that translation 'has two components: linguistic transfer, which is the subject of frequent and open reflection by the characters, and the cultural mediation between disparate political discourses and ideological worldviews, which is often the more complicated part'. Hassan goes on to suggest that it is the negotiation of the 'relationship between translation and conversion that defines the novel's ideological project'.[42] Although translation – of words, cultures, bodies – is shown to be a difficult task, the results are fruitful, with marriage and conversion satisfying the generic conventions of the romantic and the religious strains of the novel. In an attempt to move beyond the pain of these (religious/nationalist) conversion narratives, it is the 'transnational' status of Aboulela's novels that I pick up on in the following section.

'I guess being a Muslim is my identity': prioritising religious affiliations[43]

It might be suggested that finding a single or primary point of identification is an unnecessary or even dangerous task. Amartya Sen argues in this vein that there should be multiple points of identification to avoid risking the violence of 'a fostered sense of identity with one group of people [that] can be made into a powerful weapon to brutalize another'.[44] For Sen, a 'proper understanding of the world of plural identities requires clarity of thinking about the recognition of our multiple commitments and affiliations [...]. Decolonization of the mind demands a firm departure from the temptation of solitary identities and priorities'.[45] Yet it is notable that whilst advocating plural identities, Sen nevertheless uses the loaded term 'decolonisation,' employing the discourse of colonialism and thereby suggesting that a 'unifocal' mind-set is another hangover from the colonial period. Aboulela's oeuvre, however, reworks the postcolonial Bildungsroman by dislocating itself from colonialism, or even migration, as a dominant discourse, thereby largely removing characters from narratives of national displacement. Instead, Aboulela centres her characters predominantly around religious (Muslim) affiliations. As Hassan succinctly puts it:

> The novelty of this brand of Anglophone fiction is that it moves away from the reactive position of 'writing back,' which has so far served as the primary paradigm of postcolonial fiction. [...] Aboulela is less concerned with reversing, rewriting or answering back to colonial discourse than with attempting an epistemological break with it.[46]

Aboulela instead recentres identity around Muslim faith, releasing her Bildungsromane from West/East, colonial/postcolonial, centre/margin binaries. She gives her characters a new stable and rooted mode of being whilst challenging Orientalist stereotypes (I expand on the latter point in the next section). In this vein, Anna Ball asserts that 'the faith-based rootings of Aboulela's characters prove generative, producing alternate cartographies that reinscribe and overwrite the official limits of national space, and relocate their inhabitants from the margins to the centre of community and belonging'.[47] As such, extra-national cartographies liberate Aboulela's characters from national 'limits'.

This may raise questions as to whether I am justified in discussing *The Translator* and *Minaret* in a book organised around the paradigm of postcolonialism, as this is not primarily the organising structure within which Aboulela situates her characters. I would argue, however, that this points to an omission in postcolonial theory, which is persistently ordered around national rather than religious structures, despite the crucial role that religion played during colonisation and continues to play in the construction and organisation of postcolonial nations. Indeed, the role of religion in the imagining of postcolonial national identities is of paramount importance in an era of 'new' racisms (see Introduction). Amidst increasing Islamophobia in Britain and abroad, especially in the wake of 9/11 and the 7/7 London bombings, obfuscating the role of religion in the construction of minority identities would seem perverse.

Colonial history is ostensibly relegated to the background of Aboulela's novels, as is made evident by the nod towards its 'crumbling' legacy near the end of *The Translator*:

> The hotel was built by the British in colonial times. It once glittered and ruled. Now it was a crumbling sleepy place, tolerant of rats and with showers that didn't work. But still the view was as before, something natural brimming over, the last stretch of the Blue Nile before it curved and met with the other river, changed colour and went north. (193–4)

This passage represents an ambivalent attitude towards 'colonial times'. Although the narrator's gaze is framed by the windows of the colonial hotel, implying a (world) view still partially constructed by a former colonial era, the natural order prevailing outside suggests a contrasting permanence that the colonial construction does not have. Although colonial interventions still have a major part to play in the history and politics of Sudan – a country that has been racked by civil war intermittently since the end of Anglo-Egyptian rule and that was divided recently (July 2011) along ostensibly religious lines to create a largely Arab Muslim North and a predominantly Christian and Animist South – nation-based and political postcolonial concerns are largely sidelined in Aboulela's work. What is prioritised is religion, which has increasingly come to define neo-colonial relations (one only has to think of the role that the West has played in the Israeli–Palestinian conflict). For postcolonial theory to remain relevant, it is important that it shifts its parameters in order to challenge neo-colonial interventions and ideologies alongside legacies of the 'crumbling' colonial era.

Aboulela's novel *Minaret* can be read as an example of the prioritisation of religion as a source of identity for her postcolonial, migrant characters. *Minaret* concerns itself with a Sudanese woman named Najwa, exiled as a teenager from her home in Khartoum on account of her father's corrupt dealings with an usurped government. Daughter of rich parents, her initial arrival in London is smooth, reminiscent of childhood holidays. Her class position produces a particular set of postcolonial possibilities that structure the crisis she undergoes, meaning that when the old regime is overthrown and her father arrested, it is financially viable for her family to uproot to Britain, where she finds a network of friends and relatives to help her. At this stage of the novel she can be considered one of those that Simon Gikandi terms 'postcolonial elites,' who 'are, by virtue of their class, position or education, the major beneficiaries of the project of decolonization'.[48] But after her father is executed, her brother is imprisoned and her mother dies, she finds herself increasingly isolated and uncertain of her status in London society, having been financially compelled to take a job as a maid with a local Muslim family. After many refusals to visit the mosque due to her association of Islam with the lower classes in Sudan, she realises that she has missed the Ramadan fast (an important cultural tradition for her, regardless of religious associations) and castigates herself, ultimately deciding to go along with an acquaintance, Wafaa. Unlike *The Translator*, *Minaret* ultimately eschews the closure of western 'romance' novels, because Najwa forsakes her love for her employer's son, Tamer, having been paid off by his mother, who believes Najwa to be too old for him. Nevertheless, the novel has a largely happy ending, with both Najwa and Tamer gaining spiritual fulfilment in the form of *hajj* for the former and a degree in Middle East Studies for the latter.

The question of how characters choose to identify is explicitly enacted in a conversation between the lovers, Najwa and Tamer:

'Do you feel you're Sudanese?' I ask him.

He shrugs. 'My mother is Egyptian. I've lived everywhere except Sudan: in Oman, Cairo, here. My education is Western and that makes me feel that I am Western. My English is stronger than my Arabic. So I guess, no, I don't feel very Sudanese though I would like to be. I guess being a Muslim is my identity. What about you?'

I talk slowly. 'I feel that I am Sudanese but things changed for me when I left Khartoum. Then even while living here in London, I've changed. And now, like you, I just think of myself as a Muslim.' (110)

National identity can evidently be impermanent, and appears arbitrary when applied to such cosmopolitan migrants. Furthermore, as illustrated by Najwa's last statement 'even while living here in London, I've changed,' identity is independent of resident status. This might appear self-evident, but it is worth consideration in light of the ways that identities are persistently constructed and labelled around place (of residency, ancestry, migration, for example). What the two characters in the novel find is that 'Muslim' is an identity that not only has the power to transcend national borders, but also signifies a communal set of beliefs, something that neither Sudan nor Britain is able to provide them with. The minaret of the title that Najwa uses to locate herself physically and spiritually is an emblem for the protagonist's transnational affiliation. When she asserts that 'We never get lost because we can see the minaret of the mosque and head home towards it', she situates the mosque as her physical and metaphorical anchor, an index of her faith and identity (208).

Against the backdrop of alienation and trauma that defines both Najwa's and Sammar's experiences of migration, Aboulela's novels offer religion as a source of comfort and solace. After the death of her husband, Sammar recalls 'Days in which the only thing she could rouse herself to do was pray the five prayers. They were her only challenge, the last touch with normality, without them she would have fallen, lost awareness of the shift of day into night' (16). Similarly, an act of worship is depicted as 'all the splinters inside her coming together' (72); through prayer she is able to reach a unified sense of selfhood again. Ball illustrates the significance of this reversal and the challenge that it can offer to postcolonial theorists:

> Aboulela's novels conjure diasporic landscapes formed not in the interstices, on the move or in the margins, but born out of the secure boundaries of faith-based community and identity, in which the establishment of roots – those constructs of essence, origin and belonging so often the site of deconstruction – are posited as central to the diasporic experience.[49]

Where postcolonial theory and practice is so often concerned with the *de*construction of binaries, Ball notes the *re*constructive bent of Aboulela's work, whereby identities are built and made whole through religious faith.

'A traitor [...] to the West': debating Orientalism[50]

Despite the reconstructive and paradigm-shifting nature of Aboulela's work, she has been criticised for the evasion of politics in her novels (discussed in the next section) and for her representations of the West. Hassan sees the author as homogenising and rejecting western practices, evidenced in her 'narrowly defined notion of personal freedom that she construes as Western and anti-religious'.[51] He describes her notion of freedom as a 'mixture of wholesale rejection of Western modernity, which means to her little more than secularism and Islamophobia, and nostalgia for an idealized Arab past paradoxically and unreflectively conceived of in Orientalist terms'.[52]

Aboulela does indeed voice a number of generalisations about the West through her characters, but her depiction of it is not as straightforward as Hassan has suggested. The subtitle of this section is taken from *The Translator*, where Yasmin explains Rae's situation to Sammar, saying that there are

> Those who would even accuse him of being a traitor
> just by telling the truth about another culture.
> A traitor to what?
> To the West. You know, the idea that West is best. (22)

This illustrates that for the professor, there are still prejudices that he is forced to negotiate, justifying his (at times) controversial work. Yet what it means to be western is never alternatively articulated, leaving a vacant space to be negotiated and considered. This might be problematic, falling into the trap that Morey and Yaqin have identified, by allowing terms such as '"American," "British," and "Western" [to] swell to operate as what semiotics would term "floating signifiers": words that have no single agreed-on definition and therefore can mean whatever their interpreters wish them to mean.' This is problematic because 'such distinctions are always highly ideological and never a natural outgrowth or inherent in the dictionary definitions of such words'.[53] Morey and Yaqin find the open use of these terms problematic *specifically* in comparison with terms like 'Islam' and 'Muslim,' which they see as being 'narrowed to mean all that is threatening and foreign'.[54] However, to close down the former set of words (American, British, western) at the same time as opening up the latter words (Islam, Muslim) would simply be to turn the hierarchy on its head. To my mind, what Aboulela's narratives bring to the forefront are individuals and personal choices that may be inflected by one affiliation or another but also illustrate individual desires.

Najwa's story entails a move towards the West, physically migrating from Sudan to Britain, but also a move away from the West as a loosely defined ideology or way of thinking. As a teenager in Khartoum she leads a rich and privileged lifestyle, attending a good college, frequenting discos and dreaming 'dreams shaped by pop songs and American films' (*Minaret*, 35). By contrast, when she moves to the geographical West, she simultaneously descends in class and begins her spiritual conversion to what has previously only been an aspect of her cultural background. Geoffrey Nash asserts that '[o]utwardly, Sammar and Najwa's choices (which are very similar) both involve refusal of the West and (on the surface) eschew a hybridity that would imply compromise with alien values'.[55] Whilst I agree that the characters 'eschew a hybridity,' the 'refusal of the West' is more complex. Rather than a wholesale rejection of the West, the novels engage in a debate with Orientalism, which has produced 'one of [the West's] deepest and most recurring images of the Other'.[56] Edward Said describes the 'relationship between Occident and Orient' as one 'of power, of domination, of varying degrees of a complex hegemony'.[57] The effect of this hierarchical doubling means that:

> Orientalism can also express the strength of the West and the Orient's weakness – as seen by the West. Such strength and such weakness are as intrinsic to Orientalism as they are to any view that divides the world into large general divisions, entities that coexist in a state of tension produced by what is believed to be radical difference.[58]

Aboulela's novels engage with East/West stereotyping without adopting an 'Occidentalist' attitude that, as Ian Buruma and Avishai Margalit argue, 'is like the worst aspects of its counterpart, Orientalism, which strips its human targets of their humanity'.[59]

Rather, by separating the geographical from the ideological Occident, Aboulela effectively questions a binary that has long been operative on an ideological level. When Nash accuses Aboulela's protagonists of a 'refusal of the West,' it tells us more about Nash's prejudice than Najwa's. Nash presumably uses the 'West' to signify the richer, more secular and more hedonistic lifestyle she led in Khartoum; he cannot be using the word to describe the geographic West, where Najwa is in the process of establishing a home and lifestyle. If critics were not so hasty to make the West signify all that is hedonistic and corrupt, then it would become apparent that Aboulela's work deftly challenges Orientalism by renegotiating stereotypes based on western affluence and 'third world' poverty. By divorcing ideologies and attitudes commonly associated with the West from the geographic West (and likewise for the East), Aboulela deconstructs the foundations on which Orientalist stereotypes are built. Similarly, *The Translator*'s Sammar only 'refuses' certain aspects of the West: ultimately she marries the Scottish Rae and plans to return to Scotland with him. It therefore has to be questioned whether what is at stake is really Aboulela's rejection of the West, or the straw-man visions of the West that critics such as Hassan construct, only to provide a platform from which to subsequently pull them apart.

In a more nuanced interpretation of understandings of the West in the novel, Ball points out that Sammar's narrative both incorporates and undermines the conventional western romance:

> She has just received Rae's proposal of marriage, and so is positioned as the heroine within the Western romance tradition; yet

this proposal also signals Rae's conversion, reversing the Orientalist tradition whereby the male subject is the bearer of knowledge and civilization, recasting Rae and Sammar within a diasporic Muslim feminist reversal of the romance tradition.[60]

Some critics have misread this ending as subordinating the Muslim framework of the novel to the western romance tradition: Tina Steiner, for instance, suggests that 'the romance plot drives towards a "happy ending" which sits at odds with Aboulela's politics since it suggests that Sammar needs Rae to convert, that Islam on its own is not enough to provide her with a sense of home'.[61] However, such a reading fails to understand the importance of marriage in Islam, a topic covered in numerous *Hadiths* and *Qur'anic* verses, such as the following: 'And one of his signs is that he created pairs for you from amongst yourselves, so that you might find peace in each other, and he puts love and mercy between you.'[62] The compatible aims of the romance genre and Muslim faith are also exemplified in Shelina Zahra Janmohamed's recent memoir *Love in a Headscarf: Muslim Woman Seeks the One* (2009), in which the author recounts the trials and tribulations she experienced in finding her husband in a form that incorporates generic conventions of the romance with an exploration of her Muslim faith.[63]

Apolitical Islam

Another criticism often levelled at Aboulela regards her protagonists' political apathy. Since the 'Rushdie affair,' 'British Muslim' has been understood as a highly politicised identity category, but for Aboulela's characters religion is a markedly personal affair, provoking questions of personal faith and responsibility rather than ones of political allegiance or polemic. Olivier Roy describes such identification as 'post-Islamist,' suggesting a return to spirituality as an alternative to the highly politicised 'Islamism': 'Post-Islamism does not go hand in hand with a decline of religion; rather it expresses the crisis of the relationship between religion and politics and between religion and the state.' This turn, Roy suggests, is also coupled with 'a reinforcement of "imagined identities", from religious communities to invented neo-ethnic, or even racial, denominations'.[64] Roy largely situates this religious, apolitical turn in the West, where predominantly Christian or secular governments mean that Islam has less political influence.

The question that concerns me, in terms of the post-Islamist turn that Roy identifies, is how these 'alternative' versions of Islam might

find expression in contemporary literature. Providing one framework
for understanding contemporary literature, Bradley and Tate argue
that 'the contemporary novel – both within and without the UK – may
more profitably be described as a kind of "post-atheist fiction"'. They
define this genre as 'an attempt to move beyond the Manichean clash
of religious and secular fundamentalisms epitomized by 9/11 and its
aftermath'.[65] The 'New Atheist Novel,' they argue, replaces a 'clash'
of ideologies with a belief in itself: 'it believes in the secular freedom
to tell stories, to imagine worlds and to say anything about anything
that it – alone – apparently embodies'.[66] But as they note, there are
British authors like 'Hanif Kureishi, Monica Ali and Zadie Smith' who
'are now offering more complex and variegated pictures of the multicultural, multi-faith world'.[67] Claire Chambers objects to the choice of
authors offered in support of this claim, arguing that 'Kureishi, Ali and
Smith – like McEwan, Amis and Rushdie – are preoccupied with the
sensational (and marketable) figure of the Muslim extremist and pay
little attention to religious people who have no truck with violence'.
Chambers continues, 'Nor do they engage in sufficient depth with
the genuine political grievances that drive extremism, or the way in
which Anglo-American foreign policy may itself be viewed as a form
of terrorism.'[68] The critic instead offers an alternative list of authors,
including Aboulela, who are 'producing more nuanced accounts of
religion [sic] doubt and multicultural politics'.[69] It is apparent, therefore, that Aboulela's novels are paradigm-shifting, moving away from
the 'Manichean clash' set out above, but in a different way to that
proposed by Bradley and Tate.

Aboulela strategically retreats from such politically charged debates
and ideologies, instead offering tales of personal faith within small
networks. In response to a question regarding the absence of Islamism
or extremist characters in her novels, Aboulela replies, 'I just wanted
to highlight the non-political part of the religion. I wasn't saying that
extremism doesn't exist, but showing other aspects of Islam and demonstrating that many Muslims aren't interested in politics, and not
interested in extremism.'[70] Whilst this deliberate rejection of political
elements is frustrating at times (*Minaret*'s plot extends to 2004 and is
based around a Muslim community, yet despite an increasing level of
Islamophobia experienced by her characters, the novel does not make
a single explicit reference to 9/11), it does have the benefit of forcing
the reader into a new understanding of identity. Roy notes that 'Muslim
religious sentiment is seeking, beyond or beneath politics, autonomous
spaces and means of expression, feeding contradictory and burgeoning

forms of religiosity, from a call for wider implementation of *sharia* to the revival of Sufism'.[71] Aboulela's work not only renegotiates nationalist affiliations, deprioritising them in favour of religious ones, it also opens up the space of religion, removing it from the highly publicised political sphere that Manichean binaries – such as liberalism versus extremism, or western democracy versus Islamism – are constructed around, and centring instead on religious individuals and small faith networks.

Aboulela's Najwa repeatedly rejects the political, or chooses to ignore or repress its significance, much to the frustration of her revolutionary boyfriend, Anwar. For Sadia Abbas, the novel's 'fantasy reconciliation between Islam and the West is achieved at the expense of the secular Sudanese, in this case working class, radical'.[72] The reconciliation between the portrayal of a female Muslim protagonist and imperialist desires, Abbas asserts, is similarly put down to portraying 'reasonably deft visions of Muslim women who desire their own subordination, thus making resistance to imperial dreams of female rescue simpler, more clean'.[73] Abbas's critique suggests that politics are sidestepped in Aboulela's novels in order to render the books more marketable to a western consuming audience. Although Aboulela does seem to duck out of explicit political questions, Abbas's critique verges on a deliberate misreading of the novel and a simplification of the plights of the various characters. In searching for the political polemic, it obfuscates the nuances of everyday struggle with faith and community that are presented in the novel. Abbas ignores the unfeeling and obnoxious character that Anwar is shown to be in order to mourn his political sidelining. She chooses to describe Aboulela's characters as 'desiring of subordination' rather than reading the nuances and power shifts that lead up to the happy romantic ending earned by Sammar and Rae, in which the former refuses to sacrifice her faith in order to attain an unbelieving husband.

However, while Abbas's readings of *The Translator* are somewhat blinkered, the conclusions that she arrives at merit consideration. Drawing comparisons with the furore surrounding *The Satanic Verses*, Abbas considers what kind of religious novel would be acceptable. She concludes:

> The attributes that allow the novels to be designated as Muslim and *halal* are thoroughly secular, by which I mean that they have little to say about divinity and bracket theological questions and the more troubling effects of religion on the world. In their chaste and narrow romantic focus, they make religion private. Secularism, it turns out, is constitutive of their *halal* goodness.[74]

The parallels between Abbas's description of the 'halal' goodness of Aboulela's literature and Roy's description of post-Islamism are immediately apparent, as both require Islam's removal from the political sphere. For this reason, Aboulela is *necessarily* limited in her version of the religious novel. But while Aboulela's work might not ask theological questions, the call for her to do so by critics like Abbas insists on a version of Islam with which Aboulela chooses not to engage. Abbas's questioning of what it would take to write a religious novel of the sort that she requires (politically questioning, theologically engaged) is far more convincing than her attempt to pigeonhole Aboulela as a failure at a type of novel that it appears she did not set out to write.

Aboulela's novels are paradigm-shifting without being political, by encouraging identification *with* characters frequently positioned as the Other of western discourse. I share Christina Phillips's opinion that *The Translator* is successful inasmuch as it makes a religious worldview palatable to a largely western audience: 'As narrative filter, Sammar's version of events – her Weltanschauung – is automatically presented as natural, while as protagonist she immediately commands the sympathy of the reader.' The implication of this is that 'the role of the reader is programmed – to be co-opted to the side of Sammar and forced to view the world as she does'. As Phillips suggests: 'Given that the novel is written in English, this will largely mean, in practice, the adoption of an Islamic perspective by a non-Muslim reader.'[75] As a counter to the methods of 'framing' that Morey and Yaqin observe in contemporary media, a change in outlook might be exactly the remedy required to combat increasing levels of Islamophobia evident in today's society. The amount of criticism and commentary that has already been published on Aboulela stands as testimony to her importance as a contemporary British author, whilst also indicating a new trend in British literature, as the faith-centred bent of her work points towards a new direction for the British Bildungsroman.

'The Muslims got in the way. They ruined the whiteness of the city, and the blackness too': religious identities and postcolonial criticism[76]

The quotation used in this subtitle comes from *The Road from Damascus* and considers the position of Muslims in relation to other identity groups, national and ethnic. For protagonist Sami Traifi, Muslims stand out, unchanging and isolated amidst the mimicry and 'mutual fascination' of other groups (60). I read this passage allegorically as representative of the wider exclusion of religion from constructions of identity more commonly organised around nationality and ethnicity in the British context. Ultimately, this calls for a new turn in postcolonial criticism and for new approaches to the British Bildungsroman. Contemporary authors – including Kureishi, Yassin-Kassab and Aboulela – critique the utopianism of hybrid constructions of identity espoused by the likes of Rushdie and Bhabha as a discomfiting position to occupy, and therefore turn elsewhere for direction. The terrifying absence of a structuring system or belief is expressed through absent fathers as symbols of a former age of grand narratives, certainty and trust, or at the very least, authority. In a more gruesome turn of events, narratives of traumatic (re)birth illustrate the pain of 'newness com[ing] into the world' (to borrow Rushdie's phrasing),[77] highlighting a situation in which frequent or dramatic change becomes painful at best, life-threatening at worst. Offering a change of perspective and priority, Aboulela roots her characters in their communities through shared religious faith, giving them an unchanging, transnational sense of identity that can be carried safely across borders. This effectively serves as a challenge to postcolonial critics to take religion seriously and to shift the parameters to include it, questioning postcolonial theories that still revolve solely around national or diasporic concerns. Challenging the Euro-American 'post-atheist' world identified by Bradley and Tate, it is necessary to make room for religion once more, as an important feature of both personal and national narratives and as a way of understanding how national affiliation is only one of many ways of identifying. Postcolonial writing in contemporary Britain is therefore at least in part a project of decentring ideas of nationhood as the only – or the primary – source of identification, instead opening up the 'imagined community' to multiple sources of affiliation that do not have to be mutually exclusive.

2
Gothic Tales of Postcolonial England

Contrary to prevalent constructions of postcolonial gothic that locate it elsewhere, in countries that were formerly colonis*ed* rather than colonis*ing*, this chapter alternatively considers postcolonial gothic that is concerned with the former colonial centre, engaging with revisitations of the colonial past in contemporary England through experiences of racism, dislocation and alienation. Postcolonial gothic literature foregrounds the haunting of the present day by the colonial past, confounding what James Procter and Angela Smith have described as the 'Eurocentric emphasis on a chronological break that implies colonialism is over'.[1] This chapter maps out a new subgenre, arguing that postcolonial gothic that is set in England and concerned with the haunting presence of an historic English identity has three crucial functions.

First, this new subgenre challenges its colonial forebears, which often equated alterity with monstrosity and voiced perceived threats regarding the foreign invasion of the self/nation. Second, it appropriates and repurposes familiar tropes of the gothic genre (such as the uncanny, the abject, haunting, terrifying silence and monstrosity) to reflect contemporary manifestations of fear and trauma associated with the 'unhomely' experience of migration and the psychological and material traumas of alienation and racism that cause ethnic minority characters to experience themselves as Other. Finally, following a trend in contemporary gothic as identified by Alexandra Warwick, a particular strand of gothic tales of postcolonial England manifest a 'desire for trauma'[2] by suggesting that the creation/commodification of a traumatised past can perversely act as a catalyst for communal identification in the absence of other unifying factors such as a shared language or heritage. This chapter discusses Meera Syal's *Anita and Me* (1996), Nadeem Aslam's *Maps for Lost Lovers* and Helen Oyeyemi's *The Icarus Girl* (2005) and *White is for Witching* (2009), also turning briefly to Hanif Kureishi's *Something to Tell You* (2008) in the final section. Outlined below are the connections that I am making between postcolonialism, gothic and English identity.

Postcolonial gothic

In his introduction to *The Oxford Book of Gothic Tales*, Chris Baldick asserts that 'a tale should combine a fearful sense of inheritance in time with a claustrophobic sense of enclosure in space, these two dimensions reinforcing one another to produce an impression of sickening descent into disintegration'.[3] Baldick's formula has gained currency in gothic criticism, but its potential application to a postcolonial agenda has not, to date, been explicitly handled. The parallels are, however, apparent. A 'fearful sense of inheritance in time' is shared by postcolonial literatures, in which closure on the colonial period is never fully accomplished. This means that history frequently intrudes upon the present in the form of colonial legacies of material, psychological and political traumas for which there have been insufficient reparations. Furthermore, in postcolonial Britain, former distinctions between colonial centre and colonised periphery are to some extent collapsed through the migration of peoples and products that could be seen to engender a 'claustrophobic enclosure in space' and is undoubtedly figured as such in the anti-immigration rhetoric adopted by Britain's main political parties.

Many critics have made links between gothic, postcolonialism and/or colonialism, citing common tropes to be found in the different bodies of literature.[4] In *Postcolonial Imaginings* (2000), David Punter conceptualises the functions of 'the literary' before illustrating postcolonial implications for the purpose of his study. What is significant is Punter's depiction of 'the literary' in exclusively gothic vocabulary, including 'the uncanny,' 'the haunting and haunted,' 'melancholy' and 'trauma' as defining characteristics.[5] By figuring the literary in this manner Punter suggests the innate gothicity of all texts, but also illustrates why these categories are especially pertinent to postcolonial fictions. The categories that Punter identifies are central to my own discussion of postcolonial gothic. Where this chapter makes its critical departure, however, is in the adaptation of postcolonial gothic to an English context.

Gothic England

Unlike other chapters in *New Postcolonial British Genres*, this one focuses predominantly on Englishness rather than Britishness. I address what is now perceived to be an antiquated and politically defunct national definition because it is, itself, the term that haunts constructions of Britishness. Although the imperial mission was politically a British one, cultural and linguistic colonialism was predominantly English in nature, resting upon internalised and transported ideas of 'Englishness' that often pre-dated the colonial period. This historical bind has hampered the generation of any new ideals to match present-day multicultural and multi-ethnic England. The Parekh Report, published in 2000, questioned the possibility of reimagining Britain 'in a multicultural way'[6] and (in Anne-Marie Fortier's words) decided that 'Because of its association with white supremacy, white privilege, imperialism, and its historical position at the centre of British political and cultural life, [it] rejects Englishness as an appropriate label for the re-imagined multi-ethnic nation.'[7] This suggests that ideas of Englishness are politically redundant in a multicultural, multi-ethnic society, and that the concept of Englishness itself is politically exiled to the past. I suggest that this, however, makes Englishness inherently gothic: if England locates (or is even politically *forced* to locate) its identity historically, it becomes the uncannily present absence, spatially here yet temporally removed. When figured like this, present space is irredeemably haunted by the nostalgic (and often perverted) memory of what it was, and what it denies or represses.

Furthermore, the desire to preserve or recapture a sense of quintessential 'Englishness' has an historical relationship with the gothic genre. As such, Robert Miles suggests that 'Englishness, the medieval and the Gothic are virtual synonyms' and that all are 'predicated on loss'. Miles conceptually draws the terms together under the umbrella of nostalgia, which he defines as 'a recognition of difference (the past as irretrievable) married to an insistence on sameness (the past, we hope, will tell us what we really *are*)'.[8] Nostalgia continues to play a significant part in the construction of national identity, as is apparent in the language that Paul Gilroy uses to explain the function of World War II for a 'melancholic' contemporary Britain as 'that particular mythic moment of national becoming and identity,' in which the country had a recognisable and suitably 'evil' enemy to unite against in the form of Nazi Germany.[9] Locating a sense of English national identity in a past that predates acts of decolonisation and the subsequent increase in migration from former colonies becomes increasingly problematic in contemporary multicultural Britain.

Additionally, I have strategically limited the texts considered here to English novels, as I would not want to subsume the distinct categories of Scottish, Irish or Welsh gothic under a British umbrella. Iain Banks' *The Wasp Factory* (1984), for example, is a Scottish gothic novel that critiques English imperialism. The novel would therefore sit uncomfortably under a label of 'British gothic' that would homogenise important local differences.[10]

Transgressed borders/abject bodies

Imperial gothic was frequently a vehicle for the expression of fears of foreign invasion of the self and/or nation. One only has to think of the threat posed by the Transylvanian Dracula in Bram Stoker's novel of the same name (1897), the 'mad' Creole Bertha Mason who provides an obstacle to Jane's marriage to Mr Rochester in Charlotte Brontë's *Jane Eyre* (1847), or even the more complex figure of Indian Dr Aziz, a figure of fear and mystery in the Anglo-Indian society of E. M. Forster's *A Passage to India* (1924). Novels such as H. Rider Haggard's *She* (1887) and Joseph Conrad's *Heart of Darkness* (1899) similarly documented anxieties regarding the decline and degeneration of the Englishman abroad in the colonies. Gothic tales of postcolonial England alternatively look at the experience of migration from a migrant's-eye perspective in which characters have to deal with the lived reality of racism and ensuing experiences of alienation and dislocation. In this section I discuss gothicised representations of migration in which physical, bodily abjection is frequently made to mirror – or to appear as a symptom of – the transgression of national borders, as national traumas of the colonial past and the neo-imperial present are played out on the body.

Meera Syal's *Anita and Me* documents the coming-of-age of Meena Kumar, a second generation immigrant and daughter of the only Punjabi family in the fictional Midlands village of Tollington. She is, to all intents and purposes a 'Tollington wench' and has never visited India, the place that her parents call 'home', but her skin marks her as Other to her peers at school and she becomes the victim of racist abuse. As a second-generation immigrant, she is doubly exiled: 'I knew I was a freak of some kind, too mouthy, clumsy and scabby to be a real Indian girl, too Indian to be a real Tollington wench'.[11] Having no first-hand knowledge of India (instead relying on overheard conversations behind closed doors, or patronising and archaic history lessons), Meena's sense of Indian identity is superficial and imposed by others who read her Indian-ness in her appearance. The control exerted over Meena simply by looking at her is significant; when she is audience to a racist speech ('This is our patch. Not some wogs' handout') she feels 'as if the whole crowd had turned into one huge eyeball which swivelled slowly between me and papa' (193). This monstrous synecdoche illustrates Meena's fear of the gaze, which is shown to outweigh any fear of physical aggression.

Meena's sense of alienation from the way that she looks is played out through the uncomfortable relationship that she has with her own skin. She views her skin as superficial and separate, claiming: 'I wanted to shed my body like a snake slithering out of its skin and emerge reborn, pink and unrecognisable' (146). Meena's story is a coming-of-age narrative (a gothic Bildungsroman), and in the steps she takes towards self-arrival she must distinguish what is and what is not intrinsic to herself. Unlike the Bildungsromane discussed in Chapter 1, in which characters' ontological choices are played out in the arena of ideology, Meena's battle for self-definition takes place on her own body. This gives rise to processes of abjection, which Kelly Hurley describes as occurring when 'the impulse towards self-differentiation overtakes the proto-subject'. However, because '"I" and "not-I" have not been (and as yet cannot be) counter-distinguished, this is also,' for Hurley, 'an agonising and convulsive moment of self-repudiation, self-expulsion [...]. One experiences oneself as the vile matter that must be cast off'.[12] There is little that could be considered more abject than the shedding of one's own skin, and portraying it as a snake's illustrates the feelings of alienation and betrayal that it provokes.

In *Powers of Horror: Essays on Abjection* (1982), Julia Kristeva famously defines abjection in terms of inassimilable threat, in which a psychological impulse to define the limits of the subject engenders feelings of visceral repulsion towards matter that disturbs boundaries of Self and Other, such as fingernails, corpses and shed hair.[13] Although many examples of abjection that Kristeva focuses on are bodily viscera, she asserts that it is 'not lack of cleanliness or health that causes abjection but what disturbs identity, system, order. What does not respect borders, positions, rules. The in-between, the ambiguous, the composite'.[14] Drawing on this broader description of abjection, it follows that Meena sees her skin as disturbing her identity. Operating in the boundary between inner and outer, her skin is something that she cannot assimilate into her sense of self and she therefore feels threatened by it.

Jess, the protagonist of Oyeyemi's *The Icarus Girl*, similarly identifies herself as Other, a sentiment that is variously represented through motifs of abjection and embodiment (the latter of which is discussed in the next section). Jess is an eight-year-old mixed-race girl, with a white British father and a black Nigerian mother. She struggles with her dual heritage, voicing her fears of being 'stretched' or 'hurt' if she submits to what she interprets as her mother's desire for her to 'be Nigerian or something'.[15] This identity crisis is made manifest when Jess visits Nigeria on a family holiday and meets Tilly, a child who follows her back to England upon her return. It becomes evident that no one but Jess can see Tilly, who is ambiguously an imaginary (and increasingly malevolent) friend created by Jess's disturbed psyche, an *abiku* (a Yoruba word that denotes a child who is reborn multiple times to the same family) and/or a manifestation of Jess's dead twin. As the narrative progresses, Jess must fight for the control and possession of her own body, which Tilly wants for herself. In an article on *The Icarus Girl* co-authored with Chloe Buckley, we argue that this sense of a surplus of identity is reflected both in 'physical abjection mapped onto bodies and places, and in the way writing functions as abject supplement' drawing on Kristeva and Jacques Derrida respectively.[16]

Like Meena, Jess also expresses a desire to shed her own skin when she believes that her body has been occupied by Tilly. Silently, she prays, 'please take my skin, take my feet and my hips, because she's been in them and spoilt them and made them not work' (205). It is significant that it is her skin that Jess wishes to cast off. Not only does the epidermis construct the boundary between inner and outer, but it is also the symbol of the contested realm of her national identity. According to binarising racial descriptions in Britain, in which 'black' is used to denote anyone who is not white, Jess is black. However, Jess cannot identify comfortably with her white British, black British or African friends, justifying the help that she requires from psychologist Dr McKenzie to Tilly with her dismay that she is 'not like Dulcie, or Tunde, or even Ebun. I'm just not –' (121). Focussing on negation or absence as the source of her identity ('I'm just not') conveys her desire to free herself from signifiers of identity that misrepresent her own self-conception. School bully, Colleen, crudely confirms a suspicion that Jess is ashamed to acknowledge and knows she cannot repeat to her mother: 'Maybe Jessamy has all these "attacks" because she can't make up her mind whether she's black or she's white!' (86). The binarising language employed here (black *or* white) suggests why it is that Jess struggles to find a fitting identity that negotiates both aspects of her ethnicity and heritage.

Nadeem Aslam's *Maps for Lost Lovers* similarly employs images of physical abjection to symbolise deeper psychological and social traumas linked to the experience of migration. The novel traces the interweaving lives of the families of adulterous Chanda and Jugnu following their murder, presumably (but not explicitly) at the hands of Jugnu's brothers. Set in an unidentified northern town, the novel follows a sequence of traumatic events in the lives of the two migrant families. Kaukab, Jugnu's sister-in-law, finds herself increasingly isolated in England, through alienation from the English language that her family have embraced. Her description of childbirth reworks what is commonly understood to be the primary site of abjection. She tells her daughter: 'They take the baby out of the mother but not all the way out: a bit of it is forever inside the mother, part of the mother, and she can hear and feel the child as it moves out there in the world.'[17] Rather than indicating repulsion and the desire to separate, this image evokes nostalgia for a time before the separation occurred. As if Kaukab's children need to signify their real separation, her womb (their first home) is described as 'slipping out of her vagina' (260). Lindsey Moore makes the connection between abjection and assimilation to English culture at this point, arguing that 'It is no accident, given the partial loss of her children to "Englishness," that Kaukab's womb is graphically falling out.'[18] Moore's reading highlights the novel's tendency to metaphorically displace psychological trauma onto bodily viscera. The novel's real transgressed borders are cultural and linguistic, but these are represented via Kaukab's body as she is unable/unwilling to assimilate to white English culture in the same way as her family. Kaukab yearns for a moment before separation, symbolising the considerable trauma that the experience of migration has inflicted upon her. Abjection is, after all, figured as a normal stage of social development.[19]

Aslam's novel moves abjection beyond personal identity crises in order to allegorise national traumas. The story of Jugnu's father, Chakor, frequently makes links between personal and political issues. Having lost his memory and subsequently forgotten his Hindu identity at the hands of an RAF bomb in Gujranwala, 1919, Chakor is subsequently brought up as a Muslim. This disturbs his family's religious identity for years to come. The description of Chakor's death over fifty years later returns readers to the national traumas that have spilled into his personal life:

> On the day in December that Chakor vomited dark-brown half-digested blood, grainy like sand – the aorta had ruptured and spilled

its contents into the stomach so that now his body was consuming itself – the Indian army moved into East Pakistan, and Pakistan surrendered after a two-week long war: East Pakistan was now Bangladesh – India had not only defeated Pakistan, it had helped cut it in two. (82)

The abject image of vomit and blood is coupled with the concurrent moment of national abjection, where identity is disturbed as borders are violated. Both traumas are the result of British imperialism, and of the rupturing of ineffectively constructed boundaries. Even the boundary between Chakor and his country is violated, as events render them mutually dependent when Chakor becomes a microcosm for the traumatised nation.

Judith Butler theorises the vulnerable interdependency of the public sphere and the private body, arguing that 'the skin and the flesh expose us to the gaze of others, but also to touch, and to violence, and bodies put us at risk of becoming the agency and instrument of all these as well'. For Butler, 'the very bodies for which we struggle are not quite ever only our own' due to their 'invariably public dimension'. She concludes: 'Constituted as a social phenomenon in the public sphere my body is and is not mine.'[20] Following Butler's argument, Chakor's body is not merely a microcosm for the nation, but always implicated by it, defined by it and a part of it, as scenes of national violence are played out on the stage of the individual body.

The blurring of individual and national bodies as subjects of violence is alternatively explored in Oyeyemi's *White is for Witching*,[21] in which nationalist and xenophobic fears of immigration are played out through the bodies and actions of both white Miri and black Ore. Oyeyemi's novel follows the lives of twins Miranda and Eliot Silver as they grieve the death of their mother. The majority of the novel is set in Dover, in an unwelcoming guesthouse (29 Barton Road) that takes on the racist and inhospitable character of the Silver family's female ancestors, who occupy and animate the house from beyond the grave. Yet Miranda, or Miri to her few friends, is the only character that is fully aware of this, as her father and brother continue with their lives unsuspecting. In the town, a series of murders takes place in the local refugee community and suspicion falls upon Miri, who is increasingly incapable of accounting for her whereabouts. Miri is later cleared of the crimes when her accusers fail to recognise her from a picture taken a year previously. Yet those close to her realise that Miri is undergoing a rapid change in appearance, perhaps driven by her eating disorder, or perhaps due to her increasing conviction that she is a host for what she refers to as the Goodlady. The figure of the Goodlady, nominally linked to her great grandmother, Anna Good, is also associated with the mythical soucouyant, as featured in stories told by Miri's black friend Ore, with whom she falls in love at Cambridge University. The novel reaches an inconclusive climax after Miri brings Ore back to the guesthouse that has a penchant for torturing and expelling foreign guests. After Ore flees, fearful for her life, Miri disappears, and readers are left with a choice of three possible outcomes: either she has committed suicide as a way of fighting the soucouyant, or she has been consumed by the racist house as a punishment for her transgressive love for Ore, or she has simply disappeared barefoot into the night.[22]

Whilst the novels discussed thus far have engaged with the experience of racism from the point of view of the victim using processes of abjection to indicate a sense of alienation that leads migrants to view their own bodies as Other, *White is for Witching* uses motifs of abjection to highlight the shoring up of a nationalist sense of self by white characters. By providing parallels between the policing and the violation of personal and national borders, the novel serves to highlight and contest constructions of British national identity rooted in distinctions against a foreign Other that is perceived as posing a threat to the integrity of the national body. Britain's tendency towards a xenophobic national politics is foregrounded through the Silver household, which becomes a microcosm for British border politics. This guest house has been passed down the maternal line from Anna Good, and it has become animated through her hatred. During World War Two, she had given the house the task of expelling foreign bodies following her husband's death at the hands of what she described as 'Blackies, Germans, killers, dirty ... dirty killers' (118). Mirroring Britain's duplicitous stances on immigration and asylum, the guesthouse imprisons and cruelly tortures foreign guests and employees, before expelling them, ensuring that they flee never to return. Further reference to British attitudes towards race and immigration are evident in racist attacks, BNP pamphleteering and a local refugee asylum that offers more in the way of terror than refuge to its occupants. Anna Good's words reverberate through the novel: 'We are on the inside, and we have to stay together, and we absolutely cannot have anyone else' (118).

The alienation experienced by the protagonists of these gothic tales of postcolonial England, in which subjects cast elements of themselves as Other, has an obvious historical connection with imperial discourse that (to borrow Ngũgĩ wa Thiong'o's phrasing) colonised the mind.[23]

This fractured sense of identity, experienced in postcolonial England, is comparable to that described by Patrick Colm Hogan in his analysis of colonised subjects' conflicting 'practical' and 'reflective' identities. He asserts that although 'One's reflective identity as defined by the colonizer is often brutally demeaning [...] the economic and political domination of the colonizers [...] impels one to accept the colonial categories, their implications and practical consequences.' The painful result of this colonial legacy of self-alienation manifests itself in 'very sharp and painful conflicts on one's self-understanding, aspiration, expectation, action, etc., leaving one almost entirely unable to take coherent action towards humanly fulfilling goals'.[24] This internal splitting and self-alienation is apparent in a number of the characters in the novels considered here.

Meena (in *Anita and Me*) experiences alienation that can be linked to a residual effect of colonisation, which informs the racist prejudices of those around her and even her own mindset. She frequently blurs boundaries between inner and outer and between fantasy and reality, confessing 'I was terrified that my body would betray my mind and all the anger and yearning and violent mood swings that plagued me would declare themselves in a rash of facial hives or a limb dropping off in a public space' (57). This quasi-Victorian understanding of physiognomy suggests an interdependence of inner and outer that Meena claims herself 'terrified' of, yet at other points she wishes for her inner and outer 'selves' to match up. In a state of discontent at seeing how the colour of her skin affects people's actions towards her, Meena writes to a magazine: 'Dear Cathy and Claire, I am brown, although I do not wear thick glasses. Will this stop me from getting a guy?' The reply, treating her skin as a 'problem' to be solved, encourages:

> You would be amazed what a little lightly-applied foundation can do! Always smile, a guy does not want to waste his time with a miserable face, whatever the shade! P.S. Michael Jackson seems to do alright, and he's got the *added problem* of uncontrollable hair! Most of all, BE YOURSELF! Love, C & C ... (145–6, my emphasis)

The advice to both 'be yourself' and to mask the skin with foundation is either vastly contradictory, or suggests that being yourself is *only* an inner affectation, making surface signifiers of identity completely irrelevant. This gives an indication as to why, in a so-called 'post'-colonial period, Meena still cannot help but imbibe the racist prejudices (residue of a colonial mindset) served up by those around her. As her practical and reflective identities do not match up, she constantly feels a sense of alienation and splitting.

A further way in which boundaries between self and Other are represented as being shored up or broken down in these novels is through motifs of deviant consumption and eating disorders, which are often the unhappy lot of Oyeyemi's female protagonists. Processes of abjection are often connected to feelings of disgust, a word that has its etymological roots in 'gustus', the Latin for *taste*. It is therefore fitting to consider ways in which psychological processes of abjection are mirrored in habits of consumption. I have previously detailed how 'hunger often functions as a metaphor for the transgression of borders and therefore the potential threat to personal identity' in *The Icarus Girl*, as is indexed through Jess's cibophobia and unwillingness to incorporate outside substances.[25] *White is for Witching* similarly deploys acts of consumption to index the contested 'politics of the border', both bodily and national, the latter of which Vron Ware describes as representing 'one of the most important issues of our epoch'.[26] In this novel, a fraught national politics is reflected in the protagonist's eating disorder, pica, which is 'an appetite for non-food items, things that don't nourish' that drives Miri to crave plastic and chalk (22). Given the novel's setting in Dover, I would suggest that it is no coincidence that Miri's condition leads her to consume a great deal of chalk, the landscape on which her town is built.

In both literature and culture, Dover has a long history of embodying Britain's contested national borders. The white cliffs are symbolically featured as a 'battlemented crown' in William Wordsworth's sonnet 'At Dover', as emblematic of 'Albion's earliest beauties' in Lord Byron's satirical *Don Juan,* and as representative of the hope associated with homecoming and the return of peace in Vera Lynn's nostalgic wartime anthem.[27] Yet in postcolonial England, the symbolic resonance of the 'white cliffs' takes on a new racialised dimension as an increasing anti-immigration rhetoric once again takes hold of British politics. In *White is for Witching*, the white cliffs that Miri consumes symbolise a privileging of whiteness. Miri's pica causes the national borders to be resurrected within her own body and because her consumption of chalk is also accompanied by a refusal of conventional food, this results in her gradual starvation. This can be read as a national allegory in the form of the refusal of the Other or the outsider. In this vein, Maud Ellmann contends in *The Hunger Artists* that 'starvation seems to represent the only means of saving subjectivity from the invasion of the other in the form of food'. Yet she points out the irony of this position, in that the self is undone 'in the very process of confirming its identity'.[28] When the national borders are translated onto Miri's emaciated body, the absurdity of denying the intrusion of the Other is revealed. Britain is no longer embodied in the thriving personification of Britannia that Anna Good played as a girl at school, but in her sickly, deluded, starving and self-absorbed granddaughter.

Miri's pica may be understood as a punishment inflicted upon her by her ancestors and the inhospitable guesthouse as a result of her taking a black lover, which is transgressive in the eyes of her female forebears. Indeed, one of the three possible endings (or beginnings) to the novel sees Miri trapped in the walls of the guesthouse eating plaster, because, as the house says, 'she has *wronged* me I will not allow her to live' (4, emphasis in original). Rather than rejecting the Other in an act of Kristevan abjection that would serve to delineate her sense of self, Miri's relationship with Ore is described almost entirely in terms of consumption, prioritising incorporation over distinction. They relate to each other over the sharing of picnics – which are the only times that Miri willingly eats normal food – and through sharing their own bodies as food. Miri describes Ore's body as a veritable feast:

> Ore's smell was raw and fungal as it tangled in the hair between her legs. It turned into a blandly sweet smell, like milk, at her navel, melted into spice in the creases of her elbows, then cocoa at her neck. Miranda had needed Ore open. Her head had spun with the desire to taste. She lay her head against Ore's chest and heard Ore's heart. The beat was ponderous. Like an oyster, living quietly in its serving-dish shell, this heart barely moved. (191)

Describing love in terms of hunger is so familiar as to sound cliché, but the language of consumption employed here indicates its own potentially transgressive nature. After pondering Ore's oyster-like heart, Miri confides that she 'could have taken it, she knew she could. Ore would hardly have felt it' (191). What starts out as a scene of erotic and gastronomic desire develops more sinister undertones as the language becomes selfish, greedy and even murderous. The novel implies that it is not, as the Silver women fear, the white majority who are at risk of being consumed.

Acts of consumption that blur the lines between bodily and national borders render Ore's body the stage on which a nationalist politics that is hostile to immigrants and their descendants plays out. Despite their mutual love, Ore's relationship with Miri is not represented as reciprocal, as they take on the roles of food and consumer. She complains of how 'draining it was to share a bed every night,' the pun on 'draining' implying something beyond sexual fatigue, as Miri is by now frequently linked to the vampirish soucouyant (185). Furthermore, despite having 'never eaten so much [... her] clothes ke[ep] getting looser' and she visibly diminishes, much to the consternation of her adoptive parents (185). Ore's ever-diminishing body performs the internalisation of racism, which climaxes when she dries herself after a shower at 29 Barton Road and begins to rub the blackness off her skin, watching it come off like 'black liquid, as dense as paint' (214). This humourless parody of antiquated racist rhetoric literalises the violence of racism, as the scene ends with Ore feeling ashamed and ugly, attempting to hide the towel that might give her away. I return to the language of consumption in relation to the deconstruction of a self/Other binary in the following section.

'I *am* the others': doubling and possession[29]

The previous section focussed on ways in which abjection was used to mirror the transgression or reinforcement of borders to delimit the boundaries between self and Other. Here, I turn to further ways in which such relationships are deconstructed, through tropes of doubling and embodiment that blur boundaries between self and Other, thereby mapping out alternative modes of identification and affiliation. By focalising narratives through ethnic minority characters and thereby complicating representations of those previously rendered Other, authors enable the deconstruction of a self/Other binary on which imperial gothic is frequently built. However, the fates of the characters considered here vary, as whilst some can move beyond a binarised sense of identity to achieve a unified sense of self, some are left in the limbo between identities that they fail to unite. First, I will discuss the detrimental psychological effects on ethnic minority characters who experience themselves as Other as expressed through mirror stages that represent a persistent state of misrecognition and alienation. I then go on to outline the damaging nature of relationships in which the Other is seen as the obverse of the self, as is the case with imperial gothic. Finally I outline ways in which self/Other relationships are undermined, particularly in Oyeyemi's novels, through motifs of possession that efface the simplicity of the doubled relationship.

Doubling frequently occurs through acts of misrecognition that cause characters to view themselves as Other. Jacques Lacan theorises the mirror stage (or 'Imaginary') as the stage in childhood development in which an infant sees themselves in the mirror for the first time and experiences both recognition of themselves as a discrete being and alienation as the independence of the image does not match with their sense of maternal dependency.[30] Bhabha brings this stage of childhood development into the postcolonial orbit by drawing parallels between the image witnessed in the mirror and the stereotype. For Bhabha, the image confronting the subject during the mirror stage is 'simultaneously alienating and hence confrontational,' attributes that he cites as the 'basis of the close relation between the two forms of identification complicit with the Imaginary – narcissism and aggressivity'.[31]

These two modes of identification (narcissism and aggressivity) are comparable to the stereotype, 'which, as a form of multiple and contradictory belief, gives knowledge of difference and simultaneously disavows or masks it. Like the mirror phase "the fullness" of the stereotype – its image *as* identity – is always threatened by "lack"'.[32] This parallel perhaps accounts for the multiple mirror stages undergone by characters on the receiving end of racist stereotyping, as the mirror symbolises an engagement with an unrecognisable identity that is aggressively imposed by others. In the following I examine the function of the mirror in these novels, as identity crises are played out later in life when characters persist in misrecognising the image of themselves that they are faced with, due to a sense of alienation reinforced through stereotyping and binarising accounts of self and Other.

In *The Icarus Girl*, Jess has two significant encounters with the mirror. The first occurs after she has been in trouble at school for cutting out pictures of twins from books upon finding out from Tilly that she had a twin who died in childbirth. When cutting the pictures out, Jess had taken particular interest in a picture that was not actually of twins, but of a 'girl with short blonde hair gazing into the mirror at herself. Two girls, two smiles, snub nose pressed to snub nose. It was like twins' (179). Having been reprimanded by parents and teachers, Jess retreats to the bathroom. The scene merits quoting at length:

> Still holding the mirrored blonde girl, she padded down the passage to the bathroom without switching on the light and peered into the mirror, watching herself intently, one hand pressed hard against the rim of the basin. She blinked several times, each time trying to catch her reflection out in the dim light. Then she pressed a finger against the cold glass, joining herself to her reflection, pointing, marking herself. It was something of an accusing gesture. (185)

I would argue that Jess approaches the mirror not to see herself as she is, but in the hopes of seeing someone else. This moment represents a desire emanating from a sense of lack, or a sentiment that she repeatedly cites of feeling incomplete. The revelation that she was born a twin offers a glimmer of hope to Jess, as this accounts for the sense of lack that she has experienced heretofore. Rather than the image threatening lack, Jess brings her own sense of lack to the mirror, desiring to see someone else that will complete her sense of identity. Not threatened by the image she sees, Jess instead threatens *it*, accusing it with a pointing finger. It is perhaps significant, therefore, that of all the pictures that she cuts out it is the figure of the solitary blonde girl to whom she is most drawn, a white girl who is complete without reference to anyone else, unlike Jess who must always negotiate conflicting senses of identity.

In a later instance, Jess approaches the same mirror expecting to see Tilly and is surprised just to see herself. Reversing a horror movie trope in which the mirror would reveal a monster, Jess sees only herself, 'her hazel eyes darting bemusedly around the mirror' (241). The moment of horror comes instead when Tilly starts speaking from the 'mirror-world she inhabited' through Jess's mouth, informing her that she wants to 'swap places' (242, 241). Diana Adesola Mafe reads this as a moment of Lacanian misrecognition, 'crucial to ego-formation and thus self-realization'.[33] She describes the moment as 'one of identification ("she was only looking at herself") and alienation ("I'm not swapping"), hence the misrecognition'. The stage is complete when the mirror shatters and 'Jess finally perceives herself as a separate being ("I"), albeit a fragmented being'.[34] Although Mafe's reading works up to a point, it ultimately depends upon an interpretation of the novel in which Jess achieves self-recognition and in which Tilly merely marks a stage in Jess's development. For me, the ending of the novel, to which I return later, does not mark the fulsome coming-of-age implied by Mafe's hopeful and celebratory reading of the possibilities of a happily hybrid identity and as such I read the shattering of the mirror as the final rending of the fabric separating Jess and Tilly's worlds, making the struggle that Jess has to prevent the colonisation of her own body even more precarious.

In these gothic tales of postcolonial England, the narcissistic mirror gaze is comparable to the gaze inflicted by others, as individuals' sense of identity is often conferred externally. Reasons for this are evident in Frantz Fanon's seminal *Black Skin, White Masks* (1952), a ground breaking work on the harmful psychological effects of colonial rhetoric on colonised subjects. Fanon discusses the difference between stereotypes of Jewishness and blackness, as whilst 'the Jew can be unknown in his Jewishness [...] I [Fanon] am overdetermined from without. [...] I am being dissected under white eyes, the only real eyes. I am *fixed*'.[35] This is a problem also encountered by Meena, in *Anita and Me*. Like Fanon, Meena is 'overdetermined from without,' but her second generation immigrant status and lack of knowledge of India leads her to identify as English, and all of the other English people she knows are white. Meena sees her inner identity as English, therefore white, so fails to recognise her image that – according to the 'image *as* identity' metonymy of stereotypes – should also be white. It takes her a while to learn that no matter how hard she tries to 'fit in,' those around her will construct her identity in terms of the colour of her skin. She has to learn this before she can overcome her 'fixed' sense of identity and reject the supposed superiority implied by the racist gaze often bestowed upon her by her friend Anita and others.

Due to her inclination to see the world through Anita's eyes, Meena is effectively displaced, as is suggested by the title of the novel: rather than using the nominative pronoun, 'I,' Syal employs the objective pronoun, 'Me,' meaning that Anita is the subject of the novel, and Meena (like the author, Meera) is displaced. This initial displacement sets the tone of the novel, as Meena has to struggle against Anita's overpowering and consuming sense of self:

> I followed Anita around like a shadow for the rest of the afternoon, keeping a respectful distance behind her [...]. I knew if I got too close to her during one of her wordless seething tempers, I would be sucked into it like a speck into a cyclone. Her fury was so powerful it was almost tangible, drew the energy and will from me until the world reversed like a negative and I found myself inside her head, looking out of her eyes and feeling an awful murderous hatred. (186)

Anita is a microcosm for the many white eyes through which Meena must view the world; due to her Indian heritage, Meena notices that she is unrepresented (unseen) in the media, whilst she is also unsee*ing*. Viewing the world through adopted eyes, she is blind to the injustices and cruelty inflicted upon her family.

Iterations of the mirror stage function to illustrate the effects of alienation when characters from ethnic minorities are made to experience themselves as Other, which is clearly a result of the binarising effects of an imperial logic. Tabish Khair describes two common representations of the Other in imperial gothic, first, as 'a Self waiting to be assimilated,' or second as 'the purely negative image of the European Self, the obverse of the Self'. Khair connects these differing representations under the rubric of being 'utterly knowable in its [...] unknowability'.[36] Such a representation of the knowability of the unknowable and binary structures based on the assumed superiority of the western Self is probably best articulated in Edward Said's influential work *Orientalism* (1978), in which the critic suggests that the Other is always already known and their image confirmed through scholarship based on assumptions about the moral and sexual laxity of 'Orientals'.[37]

Thus far I have considered the psychological damage that these binarising structures have upon those who have been discursively constructed as Other. Bhabha goes further by highlighting the problem with this binary for both coloniser and colonised, as it does not give 'access to the recognition of difference' within the fixed categories. 'It is that possibility of difference and circulation,' Bhabha argues, 'which would liberate the signifier of skin/culture from the fixations of racial typology, the analytics of blood, ideologies of racial and cultural dominance or degeneration'.[38] The gothic tales of postcolonial England that I analyse in this chapter often illustrate the damage inflicted by the dangerous self/Other relationship that arises when the Other is seen as the 'obverse of the self,' before deconstructing the binaries and thereby questioning their power.[39]

Syal's *Anita and Me* depicts the dangerous interdependency of such relationships in which the Other is understood as the obverse of the Self through the bond between Anita and her younger sister Tracey: 'Whilst Anita grew taller, browner and louder, Tracey became shrunken, hollow-eyed and silent, seeming less like a sibling and more like a fleeting shadow attached to Anita's snapping heels' (266). In this relationship the sisters are interdependent (relying on each other for their identities) as Anita's presence is predicated upon and confirmed by Tracey's increasing absence, but like two people on a see-saw they cannot thrive simultaneously, as Tracey becomes everything Anita is not, and vice versa. Indeed, later in the novel, Tracey is described as a ghost whilst Anita becomes more physical, violent and bullying.

Similarly, *Maps for Lost Lovers* presents simplified versions of self/ Other relationships that play themselves out in damaging stereotypes. A child is described by a white relative as being 'half Pakistani and half... er... er... er... human' (10), crudely implying that Pakistanis are other than human. But rather than moving beyond the parameters of such stereotypes, some of the Pakistani migrants in the novel deal with the effects of racism by merely reversing the hierarchy and creating a white bogeyman with which to threaten children (72). By simply reversing the binary opposition, the idea of racial hierarchy is upheld; clearly, to move beyond this, there needs to be a different mode of relating.

The damaging tendency to Other what people do not wish to identify with the self is also alluded to at the end of Syal's novel. Meena comes of age in the tradition of the Bildungsroman, finding that her body 'for the first time ever fitted me to perfection and was all mine' (326). She duly prepares to leave Tollington and writes Anita a letter, but the latter 'never replied, of course' (328). Beyond the ostensible reading that Anita could not summon the requisite energy to stay in touch, the chilling tone of the ending suggests that Anita's function is already over and that she perhaps never existed independently at all. It forces a retrospective reading of the novel, whereby Anita *is* Meena's double, and as I demonstrated previously, both cannot thrive together. In Freudian terms, the double is both 'assurance of immortality' and 'ghastly harbinger of death'.[40] A Freudian reading of this text would therefore imply that as Meena learns to see the world through her own eyes, the racist, self-alienating side of her personality represented by Anita effectively dies.

Earlier in the novel, Sam Lowbridge – Anita's boyfriend and the leader of a racist gang – claims that he is not referring to Meena when he publicly vents his racist prejudices. She retorts, 'I am the others, Sam. You did mean me' (314). I support Christine Vogt-William's argument that 'Meena sees through Sam's tempting offer to free her from the racist stereotypes [...] as if he were accepting her as an "honorary member" of white Tollington society'. In so doing, Vogt-William asserts, Meena is 'taking her stand as one of the others'.[41] The stubborn assertion that she is 'the others' does not, however, illustrate a complete rejection of her English identity. Rather, she refuses to accept any threats to her hyphenated (British-Asian) identity, or to sacrifice one part of her identity at the expense of another. Thus Anita does not represent Englishness in general, but one (white, racist) example of it, an example that Meena must reject as a threat to a unified sense of self.

While Meena overcomes the binarising racist structures that pose a threat to her unified sense of identity, Jess, in *The Icarus Girl*, does not reach such an uplifting conclusion. Patricia Bastida-Rodriguez brings together analysis of *Anita and Me* and *The Icarus Girl* under the rubric of 'evil friends', arguing that 'Choosing a harmful friend can [...] be interpreted as a rite of passage' for both protagonists, because 'it brings about a painful period in their lives which finally allows them to mature and enables them to establish more fulfilling relationships in the future, free from their previous feeling of unbelonging as bicultural individuals'.[42] Yet I would argue that whilst this reading holds true for Syal's novel in which Meena achieves a unified sense of self by overcoming fear and prejudice (her own and others'), it presents a questionable reading of Oyeyemi's novel. At *The Icarus Girl's* denouement, the battle for Jess's body is yet to be conclusively won and there is definitely no suggestion of more 'fulfilling' future relationships to come. When Jess is hospitalised after a car crash in Lagos and her spirit flies out, her body is subsequently occupied by Tilly, preventing Jess's spirit from returning. Jess is left to roam the Bush, a 'wilderness for the mind' (318). Though critics including Mafe and Bastida-Rodriguez have read optimism and hope into the image of Jess's final confrontation with Tilly that sees her waking 'up and up and up and up' (322), I would argue that it is described in confused and violent language (the collision of their spirits is described as 'hurting them both burningly', 322), which does not imply the fruitful amalgamation of Jess's conflicting identities. As I have argued with Buckley elsewhere, 'the floating and disembodied ending [...] conversely suggests that Jessy has submitted to everything that she fears and lost the battle for her own body'.[43] Where Meena's body is 'all mine', Jess is at best sharing hers unwillingly, if not displaced entirely.

The above readings indicate the damage incurred when binarising ideologies construct the Other as the 'obverse of the self'. Oyeyemi's *White is for Witching* provides a way out of oppositional self/Other relationships through motifs of embodiment and possession that indicate interconnectedness rather than opposition and question the entire construction of monstrosity that is at the root of such colonial structures. Monstrosity in the novel is ambivalently portrayed through the figure of the soucouyant, a creature of Caribbean folklore. Like many mythical and monstrous figures, it is hard to pin her down to one definition. Generally speaking, she is an old woman, normally a social outsider, who leaves her own skin at night and travels as a ball of fire to feast on the souls of the young, returning to her own body at dawn. In order to kill her, it is necessary to find her abandoned skin and treat it with salt and pepper, so that it burns and scratches her. This means that she cannot fully re-enter it in the morning and is instead forced to join her flame with that of the rising sun. She is described in the novel as 'the old woman whose only interaction with other people was consumption' (155) and although her predilection is for 'soul food' (147) she is portrayed in ways that connect her to vampirism and cannibalism. Miri is the living character most frequently portrayed as the host for the soucouyant, expressed through her cannibalistic desires and her fear that she has been possessed by her GrandAnna, the 'Goodlady'. I use the term 'host' here in the double sense implied by the French translation of the word, 'la hôte', meaning both guest and host, as it is unclear throughout whether Miri inhabits the Goodlady, or whether the Goodlady inhabits her. Miri openly reflects on the monstrosity of her own desires, absent-mindedly writing in her journal '*Ore is not food. I think I am a monster,*' thereby explicitly linking her desires to consume Ore to cannibalism (192, emphasis in original).

However, rather than confirming Miri's monstrosity in what would constitute a mere reversal of imperial gothic by casting the white character as irrevocably monstrous, *White is for Witching* instead challenges the construction of monstrosity as characters come to recognise the potential for agency and oral pleasure that the 'monsters' might represent. When Ore tells Miri the story of the soucouyant, the latter, incomprehensibly at first, sympathises with the soucouyant and reads her communion with the morning sun as a signal of her liberation. Ore has to remind her that the soucouyant is a monster, and that 'All monsters deserve to die' (166). But a consideration of the fears embodied in the soucouyant reveals the problematic ways in which she functions to demonise women who have freedom at night, non-conforming women who live on the outskirts of society away from their families, and old women. A sure way of spotting a soucouyant by day is her wrinkled skin, which is a marker of her having repeatedly donned and discarded it. Instead of labouring on the monstrosity of the monster, *White is for Witching* implicitly questions the social structures that 'monsters' are employed to uphold (such as imperial or patriarchal ideologies). Giselle Anatol argues that a feminist interpretation of the figure of the soucouyant, as recently undertaken by authors Edwidge Danticat and Jamaica Kincaid, 'can reclaim this folklorist figure as a paragon of female agency' and that the figure 'provides a model for sensuality and female sexuality that runs counter to the early colonial pressures on women to be chaste and sexually submissive, which later seeped into the moral codes of the postcolonial middle class'.[44] It is significant, in light of this, that Miri reads the soucouyant as a good figure, a woman trapped in ancient skin who recognises the potential for escape, flight and agency.

This ambivalent reaction to figures conventionally constructed as monstrous is repeated in Jess's relationship to Tilly in *The Icarus Girl*. Tilly, is an *abiku*, which according to Yoruba belief is an evil spirit that possesses children, causing them to die and to be reborn to the same mother several times over.[45] Yet Jess initially welcomes Tilly as a friend and role model. When asked 'Would you like to be like me? Like, be able to do the things I do, I mean?' Jess 'nodded so hard she felt as if her brains were bouncing about inside her head' (71). In Tilly, Jess recognises the opportunity for flight and an enviable ally against school bullies. As the novel progresses, Jess realises that Tilly is changing to mirror Jess's language and habits; she becomes 'a different Tilly from the one that she had first met in Nigeria' (155). This suggests that the 'monster' is not fixed but adapts to suit the requirements of the individual who appropriates them.[46]

In relation to this implicit questioning and undermining of monstrosity in Oyeyemi's work, I would argue further that the broken taboos commonly understood to define cannibalism are reversed in *White is for Witching*. Kristen Guest suggests that taboos surrounding cannibalism arise due to 'recognition of corporeal similarity,' which 'activates our horror of consuming others like ourselves' based on the assumption of a 'shared humanness of cannibals and their victims'.[47] However, *White is for Witching* foregrounds the harmful yet endemic construction of otherness, with a plot driven by xenophobic attacks, BNP pamphleting and an all-too-human hotel that tortures and expels indigestible 'foreign bodies'. I suggest, therefore, that the cannibalistic desires expressed by white Miranda towards black Ore outlined in the previous section are transgressive precisely *for* their suggestion of a shared humanity that the overtly racist Britain of the novel refuses to recognise, as racist discourse does not acknowledge the equal human right to resources, jobs or asylum.

Beyond implicitly challenging the construction of monstrosity, I would argue that *White is for Witching* goes so far as to celebrate certain forms of 'monstrosity' (and I use that term in inverted commas deliberately) by turning to Cixous' ideas of the feminine economy and 'good cannibalism'.[48] Cixous' idea of the 'feminine economy' attempts to deconstruct what she sees as the phallogocentric and binary values inherent in language. In *The Book of Promethea*, she reverses the fear and taboo of orality stemming from the 'scene of the apple' by linking the oral pleasure of sex to cannibalism, describing it as a 'good cannibalism' that, as Chris Foss suggests, is 'not ghastly or ghostly or grotesque, but rather generous and loving and fulfilling'.[49] Oyeyemi's frequent use of oral imagery can in this sense be read as the playful representation of lovemaking between two women. By reading Cixous's feminist work alongside Oyeyemi's novel, I would argue, therefore, that Oyeyemi is embarking upon a feminine gothic, not in the dualistic nature set up by Kate Ferguson Ellis, who contrasts feminine entrapment with masculine exile,[50] but through the deconstruction of monstrosity in which the sign of cannibalism can be interpreted as loving and generous. I return later to associated connections between female appetite and female voice engendered by reading Oyeyemi through Cixous.

In support of this unconventional reading of cannibalism, it is notable that Oyeyemi is a lifelong Catholic, so eating the body and drinking the blood takes on an alternative significance in which acts of human consumption might indicate communion rather than monstrosity. Indeed, Maggie Kilgour brings together communion and cannibalism in the title of a work dedicated to the spectrum of means of representing 'incorporation [...] a process concerned with embodiment and the bringing of bodies together'.[51] Read within a catholic tradition, therefore, one of the novel's possible endings – in which Miri is trapped within the walls of the inhospitable guesthouse – might be understood as a gesture of self-sacrificing love whereby Miri allows her own body to be consumed by the house in order to save Ore. Oyeyemi's novels provide ways out of oppositional self/Other relationships through the use of embodiment and possession to show interconnectedness and incorporation. However, they resist a 'happy hybridity' resolution such as Syal's in *Anita and Me*, as characters are left trapped in limbo spaces, such as the 'Bush' or the walls of a racist guesthouse. In so doing, Oyeyemi's novels resist a 'redemptive or cathartic ending',[52] which would imply that imperial legacies such as colonial discourse built on the assumed superiority of the western 'self' in opposition to the colonised 'Other' had been satisfactorily overcome. Oyeyemi's repeated reference to the persistence of racism and xenophobia in Britain today resists such an uplifting conclusion.

Unhomely spaces and the redemption of the uncanny

This section considers representations of home and space in the novels under consideration and articulates ways in which these gothic tales of postcolonial England have two key functions: first, English spaces are represented as unhomely and unwelcoming for migrant peoples, and second, uncanny spaces are sometimes (although not always) reclaimed and rendered unthreatening. To conceptualise the relationship between these two impulses it is necessary to turn to Freud's work on the uncanny before considering Bhabha's appropriation of the concept that highlights the particular experience of unhomeliness related to the experience of migration. In Freud's essay on 'The Uncanny' (1919), he explains the curiously paradoxical meaning of the German word *'heimlich'*. The word, he says, 'is not unambiguous, but belongs to two sets of ideas [...]: on the one hand it means that which is familiar and congenial, and on the other, that which is concealed and kept out of sight'.[53] Spaces are rendered particularly uncanny in novels centring on first generation migration, in which familiar spaces are migrated across continents and introduced into unfamiliar landscapes.

In Aslam's *Maps for Lost Lovers*, the concept of home is transported, and through its transportation becomes at once familiar and unfamiliar:

> As in Lahore, a road in this town is named after Goethe. There is a Park Street here as in Calcutta, a Malabar Hill as in Bombay, and a Naag Tolla Hill as in Dhaka. Because it was difficult to pronounce the English names, the men who arrived in this town in the 1950s had re-christened everything they saw before them. They had come from across the Subcontinent, lived together ten to a room, and the name that one of them happened to give to a street or landmark was taken up by the others, regardless of where they themselves were from – Indian, Pakistani, Bangladeshi, Sri Lankan. Only one name has been accepted by every group, remaining unchanged. It's the name of the town itself. Dasht-e-Tanhaii. (28–9)

According to Freud's analysis of the term, 'the unheimlich is what was once heimlich, home-like, familiar; the prefix "un" is the token of repression'.[54] Thus the English town that bears Pakistani, Indian and Bangladeshi names is unheimlich, containing for its immigrant communities elements of the once-homely that have now become unfamiliar. The original home (in India, Pakistan, Bangladesh) must be repressed so as to accommodate the new place that the migrants occupy, meaning that the new sites become uncanny *doppelgängers* of the old.

Bhabha translates Freud's *'unheimlich'* to the Anglicised 'unhomely' in order to represent a typical condition of migrancy, describing 'unhomeliness' as 'the condition of extra-territorial and cross-cultural initiations'. 'To be unhomed,' Bhabha argues, 'is not to be homeless, nor can the "unhomely" be easily accommodated in that easy division of social life into private and public spheres'.[55] The 'unhomely' nature of the English town in Aslam's novel is confirmed through its residents' insistence on referring to their countries of origin as home, in accordance with which Kaukab's house is figured as 'temporary lodgings in a country never thought of as home' (96). Indeed, this is a community defined by its loneliness, as the religious connotations of 'Wilderness of Solitude' and 'Desert of Loneliness' denoted by the name 'Dasht-e-Tanhaii' suggest a place of trial and suffering. The downbeat connotations of the name prevent it from being a rejuvenative and communal act of unofficial naming and instead signify resignation and sorrow, even punishment. The temporary and unfamiliar home in England becomes a repeated reminder of the initial experience of being unhomed.

The experience of being 'unhomed' manifests itself differently in narratives focussed on second generation immigrants, for whom England is the place known as home whilst racist rhetoric insists on their origins being elsewhere. This is expressed in *White is for Witching* through the assumptions that people make about Ore, who was adopted by a white couple at a young age from a 'legal immigrant' who 'suffered from quite serious postnatal depression' (148). Well-meaning or otherwise, people frequently make assumptions about Ore's affiliations outside the UK, whether it is her adoptive mother returning with books from the local library on African folklore, people at university asking her to join the 'Nigeria society', or Sade – the Nigerian housekeeper at 29 Barton Road – using the pronoun 'we' to distinguish herself and Ore from the white characters, a gesture that Ore resents (148, 149, 210). The 'unhomely' experience of non-white Britons when British identity is located in whiteness is allegorised in Oyeyemi's novel through the racist guesthouse. Inhabited and animated by the spirits of the matrilineal Silver line, the guesthouse is given the job of expelling those constructed as Other to the British self. This alterity is constructed along lines of both nationality and ethnicity. In the words of 29 Barton Road, who is one of the novel's narrators, white, French Luc (Miri and Eliot's father) 'knows he is not welcome (if he doesn't know this he is very stupid)' (118). However, while Luc's presence is tolerated by the house, 'those others' (presumably referring to the 'Blackies' summoned in Anna Good's venomous diatribe earlier in the paragraph) 'shouldn't be allowed in though, so eventually I [29 Barton Road] make them leave' (118). The guesthouse serves as a microcosm for British nationalism and like first generation immigrants, such as guesthouse workers Azwer and Ezma, 29 Barton Road also tortures and expels Ore in an act of metaphorical and literal unhoming that denies her equal claim to a British identity.

However, the way that these novels interact with the uncanny is not solely defined by the unhoming of migrants and their descendants. I argue that this subgenre of postcolonial gothic also rewrites English spaces in acts of reclamation for migrant peoples. In order to conceptualise the way that traditionally English spaces have been rendered uncanny in a colonial context, it is useful to turn to Ian Baucom's analysis of the transportation of 'locales of Englishness' during the colonial period. As 'the empire's court chambers, schoolhouses, and playing fields' were exported to the colonies, colonised subjects 'took partial possession of those places, transforming the narratives of English identity that these spaces promised to locate'. According to Baucom, this not only changed the spaces in the present, but 'made the English past available to a colonial act of reinvention, a disobedient labor of remembrance'.[56] Spatial transformation is employed as a metaphor for greater acts of subversion and reclamation in some of the novels considered in this chapter. In *Maps for Lost Lovers*, for example, the English town is slowly 'exoticised' through the transformation of nature. By the end of the novel, the town is home to fireflies, parakeets and wild peacocks, all typically native to the subcontinent rather than England. The migrant birds and insects acclimatising to their new English locales bridge the gap between what is conceived of as 'home' (the subcontinent) and 'abroad' (England) by familiarising the space and nature.

In a related impulse, things that start out as uncanny are redeemed and made unthreatening and familiar in Syal's novel. This is facilitated primarily through the motif of the gothic house overlooking the village, which engenders rumours and speculation that a child-killer stalks the place. The gothic house stands out as an antiquated symbol of fear in a novel embroiled in the far more immanent threat of racist violence, yet it provides much of the fuel for Meena's wild and terrible fantasies: 'There was someone in the grounds of the Big House and they were watching us. [...] A figure, huge and shaggy as a bear was standing just beyond the fence near the crossroads' (206). In a narrative containing much psychological trauma in the form of racism, bullying and alienation, this traditional – and more than a little ridiculous – gothic trope initially seems unnecessary as a further source of horror, yet it serves a particular purpose in the novel. At the climax, Meena finds that the house is owned by an Indian gentleman and his French wife, and she no longer feels threatened by the place. In the unfamiliar she has found someone familiar – an Indian man amidst the sea of white faces confronting her in the village – and she is able to shed her childish fears. As such the space is redeemed and made unthreatening.

In a parallel scenario, Meena speaks of the effect that her father's singing has on her:

> Papa's singing always unleashed these emotions which were unfamiliar and instinctive at the same time, in a language I could not recognise but felt I could speak in my sleep, in my dreams, evocative of a country I had never visited but which sounded like the only home

I had ever known. The songs made me realise that there was a corner of me that would be forever not England. (112)

Immersing herself in the Punjabi language is for Meena (initially) like entering an unknown world where all is strange and unfamiliar. Yet in the world summoned by the language, India seems less distant to her, enabling her to start reconciling herself to a country that has always been unknown. This passage simultaneously reverses the colonial impulse of Rupert Brooke's World War One poem 'The Soldier':

If I die think only this of me:
That there's some corner of a foreign field
That is forever England.[57]

The implication is that the colonising mission (as implied by Meena's mimicry of Brooke's rhetoric) has not fully claimed her for its own, as she begins to become a postcolonial subject rather than being defined by leftover colonial rhetoric.

However, as I have illustrated in previous sections, Oyeyemi's novels often do not allow for such a feel-good ending in which fear and the uncanny are overcome and rendered unthreatening. Whilst gothic motifs of the uncanny *can* be deployed to signify surmountable objects of trauma, alienation and unease, they can equally be used to reiterate a lingering colonial trauma that cannot be mended through good feeling and utopian literature. As explored in the previous chapter, the 'Third Space' of enunciation in which Bhabha suggests that cultural identity is negotiated is often an uncomfortable space for individuals to occupy. The optimistic resolution to Bhabha's work on this subject – that 'by exploring this Third Space, we may elude the politics of polarity and emerge as the others of our selves' – is revealed to have more sinister implications when considered alongside Oyeyemi's *The Icarus Girl* in which Jess becomes other to herself not through an amalgamation of selves but through alienation from her own body.[58]

The plot of *The Icarus Girl* spans three spaces: Nigeria, England, and the supernatural space of the 'bush'. The novel is also divided into three sections that roughly match these spaces in terms of the location of the main action. The final section is mainly devoted to the bush, which is accessed at this point of the narrative from Nigeria following the car crash that hospitalises Jess in Lagos. However, this spiritual wilderness of the mind is also accessed from England, as Tilly takes her on journeys beyond the realms of physical possibility from the comfort of her own home. It is fittingly the bush, this hybrid 'Third Space,' in which Jess's most crucial struggles for her own identity take place. Following the vein of criticism that celebrates the possibilities of a hybrid identity, Mafe describes the bush as a 'feminine and postcolonial space' and reads the ending as depicting Jess emerging 'from the "eerie bush" intact' and carrying 'all its supernatural possibilities with her in her new hybrid form'.[59] Yet as I have outlined previously, such a reading conveniently ignores the language of pain and impending disaster of the ending, in which 'the silent sister-girl' tells Jess that 'it wasn't the right way, not the right way at all' (322) to reclaim her physical body. Rather than unquestioningly celebrating the happy amalgamation of places and identities supposedly represented by the bush that Tilly brings Jess into, it is necessary to consider Tilly's own sentiments regarding belonging: 'Land chopped in little pieces, and – ideas! These ideas! Disgusting ... shame, shame, shame. It's all been lost. Ashes. Nothing, now, there is no one. You understand? [...] There is no homeland' (249). Reflecting the destruction of spaces, Tilly's language comes apart at the seams, including unsurpassable ellipses and fractured sentences. As Jess fails or refuses to understand, Tilly reiterates, 'There is no homeland – there is nowhere where there are people who will not *get* you' (250), and as readers will be aware, to be 'got' in the novel signifies not to be understood, but to be attacked – it is Tilly's mode of avenging those who have upset Jess.

Thus space is deployed to convey contrasting negotiations with belonging in these gothic tales of postcolonial England. While Syal and Aslam draw on motifs of the uncanny that are later redeemed to signify a process of cultural acclimatisation and belonging or an understanding of parents' distant previous lives, Oyeyemi refuses to provide a stable sense of identity through spaces that have been unalterably ruptured through colonisation ('land chopped into pieces'). Instead, characters become trapped in liminal spaces that allow not for an amalgamation but for a severing of identity.

Terrorising speech/terrifying silence

Colonisation had a role both in the act of silencing and in equating silence with Otherness. One of the great 'successes' of imperialism was that of rendering its victims voiceless, by refusing to engage with native languages. Thomas Macaulay's 'Minute on Indian Education' proposes forming 'a class [...] Indian in blood and colour, but English in taste, in morals, in intellect' simply by teaching Indians the English language.[60] This demonstrates that whilst the educated classes then have a voice (of sorts), the uneducated classes are effectively rendered voiceless, as they are unable to communicate in the language of the ruling class. When taken alongside the equation of silence with Otherness articulated in gothic fiction – in which 'The screams and sulky silences of Gothic fiction do not set out to "represent" the Other; they primarily register the irreducible presence of Otherness' – the real power exerted through silencing becomes apparent.[61]

Gothic tales frequently deal with the unspeakable or the terror too terrible to give voice, registering the greatest horrors through what is left unsaid. This occurs in Syal's novel, where horrific events hover on the periphery of the story, never fully expressed in words: 'I wished I had not seen what I was sure I had seen, the row of bruises around Tracey's thighs, as purple as the clover heads, two bizarre bracelets perfectly mimicking the imprint of ten cruel, angry fingers' (142). The horror of child abuse is hinted at but never fully articulated, and the physical signs trigger the imagination to supply the rest of the information, which becomes (if possible) even more fearful in its infinite possibility. Punter describes child abuse as 'the great unwritten narrative of the twentieth century', putting this down to an observation that 'the pressure of the secret, the pressure of the unspoken and unwritten, has become more evident'. He links this pressure to 'the postcolonial,' in which this '"open secret", is directly related to the dehumanisation attendant upon deprivation and, in the final analysis, on the relation between deprivation, slavery and colonialism'.[62] Punter's observation coincides with a reading of *Anita and Me*, in which I understand Tracey's story as mirroring the novel's other 'open secret': that colonialism is the unspoken root cause of the racism that Meena and her family receive.

So how can these gothic tales of postcolonial England deconstruct the bonds between silence, terror and alterity? I consider three responses that *Maps for Lost Lovers*, *White is for Witching* and *The Icarus Girl* offer to my question: first, they highlight the terror inherent in the *act* of silencing; second, they register the voices of characters that imperial gothic has traditionally Othered; finally, they gesture towards the potentially terrifying power of *speech* and the accompanying empowerment offered by silence, thereby destabilising the equation of terror with silence.

The violence inherent in the act of silencing is foregrounded as silence becomes a source of alienation and loneliness for characters populating Aslam's novel. The character most affected by the infliction of silence is Kaukab, who feels increasingly alienated from the country and her family due to her inability to speak English. This is specifically linked to her gender and class positions, which work together to keep her at home. Her husband's high status job means that she does not need to work herself, but rather than knocking on the doors of friends for company as she used to in Pakistan, she finds herself not knowing how to approach strangers and 'full of apprehension regarding the white race' (32). Her children have also moved out and begun their own lives in England and when they return home Kaukab describes them as having a 'new layer of stranger-ness on them' (146). As second generation migrants, brought up with England as their home, they seem increasingly alien to their mother. Kaukab's alienation is further highlighted through her observation that because onomatopoeic words are translated 'even things in England spoke a different language than the one they did back in Pakistan' (35). Alienation occurs at the site of language itself, as not only does it alienate her from the people around her, but from 'things' too.

In Maps for Lost Lovers, Jugnu's story similarly foregrounds the terror of silencing. Repeatedly associated with moths that have no mouths and are therefore 'born to die' (21), Jugnu effectively haunts the narrative every time moths are mentioned. Although the moths' lack of mouth primarily signifies an inability to eat that engenders their death, there is an uncanny resemblance between this 'mouthlessness' and acts of deliberate and often violent silencing that occur in the novel. The ultimate silencing effected by Jugnu's murder is paralleled to the creatures without mouths by which he was so fascinated during his lifetime.[63]

The interconnectedness of violence, silence and exile has parallels with Gayatri Spivak's work on subalternity and silence, in which she grapples with the issues of representation in both its discursive (*Darstellung*) and its political (*Vertretung*) senses to describe the 'epistemic violence' involved in representing those locked out of the systems of knowledge and power within which they are being represented.[64] Spivak draws attention to the impossibility of the subaltern speaking as follows: 'You make the subaltern the conscious subject of his – in the case of Subaltern Studies – own history. The subaltern disappears.'[65] Despite Spivak's advocacy of 'antisexist work among women of color or women in class oppression' and 'information retrieval in these silenced areas,' she warns that 'the assumption and construction of a consciousness or subject [...] will, in the long run, cohere with the work of imperialist subject-constitution, mingling epistemic violence with the advancement of learning and civilization. And the subaltern woman will be as mute as ever'.[66]

Aslam's novel engages with this dichotomy by giving a voice to characters such as Kaukab who 'cannot speak' (or, more precisely, do not have voices that can be heard within English discourse), yet simultaneously foregrounding her burden of silence and thereby depicting a constant and insistent denial of speech. For Moore, 'the use of shifting perspective and the interweaving of speech and silence suggest that subaltern experience may be transmittable only in contingent and aporetic fashion'.[67] This suggests that the very style of the novel reflects a concern with representing subaltern subjects and engages with Spivak's concern that 'It is the slippage from rendering visible the mechanism to rendering vocal the individual [...] that is consistently troublesome'.[68] The novel instead serves to illustrate acts of actual and effective (or political) silencing without fully ventriloquising the subjects.

A similar manoeuvre is effected in *White is for Witching*, in which the silence of the local refugee community is foregrounded. Although the context of the silence is specific to the plot of novel – Kosovan refugees are refusing to speak up in relation to a string of murders that has seen four of their number killed – parallels with the national media in which the actual voices of asylum seekers are rarely sought are undeniable. A local news report that Eliot reads in the *Dover Post* comments on the 'silence of the refugee community' (30), which leads to a discussion with his father, Luc. While Eliot offers a series of explanations to account for the silence that (in the words of his father) makes him 'sound like [he's] quoting from some sort of textbook' (31) or undertaking a 'sociological exercise', Luc tries to make his children appreciate the human factor and draws parallels with their own lives by talking about the situation in terms of a family. The novel foregrounds the silence of the refugees and rehearses the dangers of depersonalising mechanisms that risk turning people into case studies or statistics.

In a gesture that I read as a critique of insidious racist discourse, *White is for Witching* also foregrounds other voices not often heard in imperial literature: openly racist voices. Although countless anti-colonial thinkers and critics have highlighted ways in which literature has been used in the service of colonial ideologies to uphold structures of alterity and assumptions of western superiority, these ideologies are commonly cloaked in the language of Enlightenment reason and paternalism and served up as adventures and travellers' tales to make them more palatable to reading audiences.[69] Oyeyemi exposes the workings of imperial literature and ideologies by foregrounding the venom and cruelty of racist discourse before indicating how this becomes institutionalised and hidden. During a scene occurring as part of what readers are encouraged to interpret as a daydream (it takes place after Miri has closed her eyes), Miri descends into what appears to be a World War Two bomb shelter and meets her mother, grandmother and great grandmother, or GrandAnna. The representation of the two older women is grotesque: 'They stared at Miranda in numb agony. Padlocks were placed over their parted mouths, boring through the top lip and closing at the bottom. Miranda could see their tongues writhing' (127). The older generations of Silver women are portrayed as having been violently silenced, yet readers are already aware that it is the 'task' given to the house by Anna Good (now GrandAnna) that has animated it and caused it to expel foreign guests (118). Although overtly silenced, Anna Good's voice speaks loudest in the novel as she animates her environment and possesses her great granddaughter. It is in this manner that Oyeyemi foregrounds the insidious nature of racist ideology as it becomes institutionalised and cloaks itself in more appealing guises.

As well as foregrounding acts of silencing, *Maps for Lost Lovers* structures much of its violence around acts of gossip or destructive words. In so doing, the potentially terrorising nature of speech is employed to challenge the elision of silence with terror. One of the victims of slander in Aslam's novel is Suraya, who goes to a feuding family's house in order to request them to be compassionate towards her pregnant niece. Deeming that it would 'cast a mark on their honour' if they did not rape Suraya, a woman 'from the other side of the battle-line,' the men agree to tell people that they have taken advantage of her (158). Gossip dictates popular understanding of events to the extent that Suraya describes the mere aspersion of rape to be 'as bad as if they had raped her', because 'What mattered was not what you knew yourself to have actually happened, but what other people thought had happened' (158). Events deteriorate further as the stigma incurred by a rape that has not in fact happened leads her drunkard husband to divorce her, simply by 'uttering the deadly word [*talaaq*] in triplicate' (159). According to *Qur'anic* scripture, as rendered by the novel, Suraya has been divorced from her husband and must remarry another man before she can go back to him, even though he is remorseful and cannot remember having uttered the words in the sobriety of the morning.[70]

Patricia Meyer Spacks praises the liberating qualities of gossip, portraying it as a democratising discourse because it 'incorporates the possibility that people utterly lacking in public power may affect the views of figures who make things happen in the public sphere'.[71] Yet as I have indicated, gossip has a far more powerful (and destructive) effect in Aslam's novel than Meyer Spacks's libertarian view allows for. Private and public discourses are brought into much closer proximity as private relationships come under public scrutiny: 'The neighbourhood is a place of Byzantine intrigue and emotional espionage, where when two people stop to talk on the street their tongues are like the two halves of a scissor coming together, cutting reputations and good names to shreds' (176). Thus the novel expresses the dangers of both silence/ secrecy *and* speech, and the violent imagery surrounding it indicates both the power of language and the force of repression required to contain it.

Oyeyemi's *The Icarus Girl* similarly portrays the danger and duplicity of speech as Jess's possession by Tilly is manifested in the words that she speaks. After the scene outlined in the previous section during which Jess confronts Tilly in the mirror and the mirror shatters, her parents hold her accountable for the broken mirror, which Jess interprets as the grossest miscarriage of justice, blaming it on Tilly instead. It is ambiguous as to whether Jess is speaking on her own behalf or on Tilly's at this point, or whether it is even wise to make such a distinction, but Jess continues to shout hurtful words at her mother whilst recognising the damage that they inflict, whether out or in: 'Jess couldn't stop spitting out words, because they were words like blades to hurt, and if she swallowed them, she'd be scraped hollow. She didn't like saying these things, but she didn't know how to stop' (246). The image of spitting the words out speaks of violent abjection and an attempt to rid herself of things that she does not want to keep inside and negotiate, that are perhaps not even her own. In a related incident, Jess insults her best (living) friend, Shivs, on the phone: 'As if through rippling sheets of cloth, Jess heard herself sneering: "Don't phone me again with your stupid stories, white girl"' (230). Whether Jess's words are read as the psychological return of repressed violent emotions or as possession by Tilly, the dangerous potential of speech to hurt and to betray the intentions of the speaker is made apparent in this novel. Speech, in this sense, is colonised and made Other; it does not serve as a reliable assertion of identity.

Speech and silence are shown to be ambivalently empowering in *Maps for Lost Lovers*. Chakor, Jugnu's father, cuts out his own tongue in an act that ostensibly reads as horrific self-mutilation, silencing in its most violent guise. However, this act is simultaneously self-assertive: he 'had cut out his tongue before setting fire to himself lest the pain cause him to call out for help' (85). This decision enables him to cremate himself as a Hindu thereby preventing his family from giving him a Muslim burial. Chakor's desire to remove his own tongue suggests that it can be a mocking impediment and that speech itself can be treacherous. This violent image implies the ambivalent power of both speech *and* silence, and in so doing challenges both the violence of colonial silencing and the elision of terror and silence effected in imperial gothic.

I have already outlined how *White is for Witching* deploys images of consumption to convey metaphorically the processes of incorporation and abjection necessary to establish identity, but I now want to go further by following Tamar Heller and Patricia Moran's claim that 'appetite can function as a form of voice' to indicate both the potential violence of silencing and the ambivalent empowerment of silence.[72] Heller and Moran claim that 'In anorexia and other disordered eating [...] female authority and female appetite emerge as related issues' due to the dual association of the mouth with eating and speech.[73] Accordingly, eating disorders in literature can be read as indexes of protest, dissent or the reclamation of power and authority absent in speech. It is therefore possible to read Miri's pica in a number of ways: as possession, as transgressive desire or as punishment.

Pica is a disorder often associated with pregnant women due to mineral deficiencies that lead to cravings for alternative sources of nutrition, particularly iron. The fact that Miri suffers from pica might therefore suggest that she is carrying a parasite, that she is feeding something that has different nutritional needs to herself. Her reactions after eating non-nutritious substances also resemble demonic possessions. Her brother describes: 'there'd be cramps that twisted her body, pushed her off her seat and laid her on the floor, helplessly pedalling her legs' (23). The language used portrays Miri as the passive victim of the disorder. Pica might in this sense serve as an indication that Miri is hosting the soucouyant.

However, Miri's decisions to eat plastic and chalk are more often presented as an active choice on her part, and in interview Oyeyemi describes Miri as having 'an unnatural appetite. A girl who eats chalk but probably with a desire to eat something else'.[74] The non-nutritious foods can in this sense be interpreted as an index for transgressive desires. When Miri's mother offers to bring her any food she would like and asks her what she wants, Miranda shakes her head, initially claiming that 'She didn't know,' but revising this to suggest 'She knew, but she couldn't say it' (127). The only other thing that Miri expresses a desire to consume is her lover, Ore, as outlined previously.

The links between female appetite and voice are further theorised in Heller and Moran's reading of what Hélène Cixous refers to as the 'scene of the apple', on which I am basing the following discussion of symbolically-laden encounters with apples in *White is for Witching*. Heller and Moran summarise that 'In the Genesis narrative of the fall, sin and death enter the world when a woman eats'. They read Cixous'

'Extreme Fidelity', in which she claims that 'this Eve story [...] is the guiding myth of Western culture, a fable about the subjection of female "oral pleasure" to the regulation of patriarchal law'. Following Heller and Moran's summary, this is the moment at which the individual discovers both 'the body and the cultural prohibitions surrounding it'.[75] In their groundbreaking feminist criticism, *The Madwoman in the Attic*, Sandra M. Gilbert and Susan Gubar similarly use the apple to describe a 'paradigm of female conflict',[76] arguing that by 'rejecting the poisoned apples her culture offers her, the woman writer often becomes in some sense anorexic, resolutely closing her mouth on silence ... even while she complains of starvation'.[77] I therefore read 'scenes of the apple' in *White is for Witching* as signifying moments of crisis in which characters must negotiate tensions between desire and repression focussed on the mouth as the site of both voice and appetite.

In *White is for Witching*, both Miri and Ore are offered 'Eve's apples' at moments of crisis in the narrative. Ore finds a poisoned apple on her bed when she stays at the hostile guesthouse. It is half red and half white like the one offered to Snow White. The implication is that it is placed there by the animated house to scare her away, or even to poison her. Her desires are thereby constructed as dangerous, as to eat the apple or to pursue her relationship with Miri would lead to Ore's destruction. Moments before her suicide or departure (depending on the choice of endings), Miri is also offered a piece of apple pie that Eliot has made from a pile of winter apples that have inexplicably appeared in the kitchen. I would argue that the presence of the apple at these crucial moments of the narrative is symbolic of the characters' shared sexual knowledge and desire, and the self-abnegation, or silencing, required not to bring destruction upon each other. This reading is confirmed by one of the possible endings, as narrated by Ore, the only character who recognises that it has been necessary for Miri to allow her body to be consumed by the guesthouse in order to save her lover. Ore returns to another 'scene of the apple' to describe Miri's demise, describing Miri's throat as 'blocked with a slice of apple (to stop her speaking words that may betray her)' (1). The image of the apple is appropriated to symbolise female assertion and the active choice to let her consuming desires speak louder than her voice, through which her racist ancestors might speak.

Horrible histories/traumatic desires

In Aslam's and Syal's novels, there is an ongoing tension between inescapable traumatic pasts that return to haunt characters in the present, and the perverse desire to cash in on, claim, or create a traumatised past as a point of personal or communal identification. This dualistic impulse is captured in *Anita and Me*, as Meena learns that history is something to be taken seriously: 'I realised that the past was not a mere sentimental journey [...]. It was a murky bottomless pool full of monsters and the odd shining coin, with a deceptively still surface and a deadly undercurrent' (75). Delving into history is depicted as potentially lethal, but the image of the 'shining coin' also indicates its exchange value. My suggestion is that postcolonial gothic can create or commodify a traumatised past in order to engender new points of identification through shared experiences. By constructing this argument, I am synthesising the functions of postcolonial theory, trauma theory and gothic literature in unusual ways, so I shall explain my connections below.

In a discussion on 'the wound and the voice', Cathy Caruth describes the delay in processing trauma, as it is unassimilated and repressed in the first instance and only 'returns to haunt the survivor later on'.[78] Furthermore, she suggests that the wound created by trauma 'bears witness' and demands to be heard, which leads to connections with other people and other traumas: 'one's own trauma is tied up with the trauma of another, [...] which may lead, therefore, to the encounter with another, through the very possibility and surprise of listening to another's wound'.[79] I understand Caruth's description of the experience of trauma at a remove as illustrative of its potential significance to a postcolonial condition. Caruth argues that 'since the traumatic event is not experienced as it occurs, it is fully evident only in connection with another place, and in another time'.[80] It is possible, therefore, to read in the traumas of contemporary characters the echoes of the remnant traumas of colonialism at a historical and spatial remove in contemporary England, as individuals make connections through trauma to historical wounds not yet healed.

The relationship between trauma and literature is also a crucial one, calling into question the function that literature might play in trauma recovery. Susan Brison outlines the cathartic function of storytelling, arguing that as a 'speech act that defuses traumatic memory', it enables survivors to take control and 'remake a self'.[81] According to Brison's argument, storytelling enables activity after the debilitating passivity of trauma, and I want to extend this to suggest that the propensity of trauma for 'remaking a self' encourages its appropriation (or even fabrication) *in order* to remake a national 'self'. Yet the idea of storytelling and narrative catharsis as the *telos* of trauma recovery has been criticised by many postcolonial scholars as being a westernised and individualist way of dealing with the effects of trauma. Stef Craps and Gert Buelens question why 'the study of trauma has traditionally tended to focus on individual psychology', when colonial trauma is a 'collective experience' requiring 'material recovery'. They express a concern that the dominant study of trauma in the West tends to prioritise what they term 'immaterial' over material recovery.[82] Although I agree that to overlook material recovery in the case of colonial trauma is politically evasive, to devalue the suffering of individuals seems, to me, equally perverse. Therefore, in my analysis of these gothic tales of postcolonial England – which can admittedly do very little in the way of material reparation – I balance a consideration of individual psychologies with broader socio-political concerns regarding the national digestion and appropriation of trauma.

Gothic literature has a long history of narrating trauma, sharing a vocabulary of wounds, transgressions and haunting. Yet the relationship between trauma and gothic takes an unusual turn in a particular strand of contemporary literature. Alexandra Warwick describes the current 'prevalence of Gothic' as 'the effect of a kind of aftershock [...] of psychoanalysis'. She notes the current pervasiveness of the 'discourse of "therapy"' that is employed to represent 'individual and collective emotional experience'.[83] Contemporary gothic's indebtedness to the discourse of therapy as a framing device for the revelation of trauma is exemplified in Hanif Kureishi's novel *Something to Tell You* (2007), in which the main character is both analyst and analysand.

Gothic tropes of haunting, incestuous families and repressed desires litter Kureishi's novel, but its main concern is with how past trauma constitutes and creates the self. The body is once again the canvas on which psychological trauma is painted, as is illustrated when the protagonist, Jamal, describes leaving his first appointment with an analyst:

> When I was outside, standing on the street knowing I would return in a couple of days, waves of terror tore through me, my body disassembled, exploding. To prevent myself collapsing, I had to hold onto a lamp post. I began to defecate uncontrollably. Shit ran down my legs and into my shoes. I began to weep; then I vomited, vomiting the past. My shirt was covered in sick. My insides were on the outside, everyone could see me. [...] I came to love my analyst more than my father. He gave me more; he saved my life; he made and re-made me.[84]

This abject description mimics the process of analysis, crudely bringing the 'shit' to the surface for all to see. What is most shocking about this scene is the love Jamal expresses immediately after the retelling of such a humiliating moment, indicating a desire for the 'trauma' to be evident. His gratefulness at having been remade relies upon having previously been un-whole. A love for the manifestation of trauma coincides with the way that Warwick redefines contemporary gothic as 'the desire *for* trauma,' in which 'the experience of trauma, and not the healing of it, is that which will make us whole'.[85]

Bearing this is in mind, what is most interesting about Kureishi's novel is the subtle linking of personal and national trauma. Whilst the storyline superficially follows a personal narrative, it also operates on a political level, with contemporaneous political events providing the backdrop to the novel. The personal climax neatly coincides with the 7/7 London bombings: 'That day and night we were haunted by TV images of sooty injured figures with bloody faces, devastated in their blamelessness, being led through dark blasted tunnels under our pavements and roads whilst others screamed' (313). The subterranean image of the London Underground bombings acts as a kind of national psychopathology, a trauma that must be dealt with and not repressed. Furthermore, the idea that English citizens watching television on the day of the bombings are immediately haunted indicates that the haunting occurs simultaneously to the event, as if it has already been transferred to the nation's traumatised past.

The combination of individual and cultural trauma is integral to Kureishi's novel, as both traumas are handled in the same way: by narrating the trauma and reinstating linguistic order so as to move on. The *desire* for trauma is evident in the speed that it is recognised, named and dealt with. Yet the very speed with which this act of healing and transferral to the 'past' is meant to occur makes it seem ridiculous and brings to the forefront the impossibility of dealing with cultural trauma in such a manner.

Ranjana Khanna's theorisation of critical melancholia highlights the impossibility of fully narrating the past:

Melancholia as symptom and reading practice [...] offer[s] a way of gauging how critical agency functions constantly to undo injustices performed in the name of justice and novelty. The impossibility of completed digestion of the past, and its calm production of novelty, manifests itself in constant critique.[86]

This encourages a critical engagement with postcolonialism, as to assert that colonialism is fully 'post' – that its past traumas have been effectively dealt with and that we are able to move on – would be damaging and belittle its real impact. Warwick summarises the 'dominant rhetoric of contemporary experience' as the understanding that 'there are defining events in our individual, social and national lives that are insufficiently assimilated or experienced at the time of their occurrence, which we are then belatedly possessed by, unable to proceed until the fallout is dealt with'.[87] Khanna argues, however, that the 'fallout' cannot be fully 'dealt with' as Warwick's statement implies, but that this in itself can be put to a positive use, as 'critical agency emerges because a remainder always exists that cannot be assimilated into the normalizing constraints of the superego on the ego'. Rather than narrating the past in order to move on, the fact that trauma cannot be fully digested leads to a state of melancholia, or permanent mourning, where the loss cannot be overcome but must always be critically evaluated.[88]

The psychoanalytic backdrop of Kureishi's novel may raise questions over the way that trauma is handled on both individual and cultural levels, but its real achievement is in tapping into the *desire* for cultural trauma. In an article on cultural trauma, Kai Erikson asserts that 'trauma can create community' and that 'trauma shared can serve as a source of communality in the same way that common languages and common backgrounds can'.[89] I would argue, therefore, that trauma can be a tool for unification *in the place of* common languages or common backgrounds: this could be the tool for writing postcolonial England. I am not suggesting that this is cause for celebration, that trauma as cultural glue is a fine thing. As Erikson states, 'The point to be made here is not that calamity serves to strengthen the bonds linking people together – it does not, most of the time – but that the shared experience becomes almost like a common culture, a source of kinship.'[90] The desire for similarly traumatic pasts (be it individual or communal) to engender a new sense of identity can also be traced through *Anita and Me* and *Maps for Lost Lovers*.

Before any of Meena's real troubles begin in *Anita and Me*, she repeatedly fantasises about horror, complaining, 'I wish I was a tortured soul' (20). Yet the kind of horror that she desires illustrates a large element of displacement, making the horror safe and at a distance, as she plans a night of fun that involves 'playing a screaming blonde heroine being pursued by nameless wailing monsters' (109). Syal locates Meena's fantasising and often deceitful manner in a decided absence of an accessible history, as her protagonist excuses herself at the start by saying, 'I'm not really a liar, I just learned very early on that those of us deprived of history sometimes need to turn to mythology to feel complete, to belong' (10). Her sense of disinheritance from history is marked by listening to her parents' conversations behind closed doors, as she imagines India to be 'a country that seemed full to bursting with drama, excitement, history in the making, and for the first time [she] desperately wanted to visit India and claim some of this magic as [hers]' (211). This indicates a desire for both individual and national definition that she thinks that she can achieve by 'claiming' an authentic and sufficiently 'troubled' history.

In Aslam's novel, ghosts are employed as a recurrent motif, pointing to a similar desire to claim trauma. Roger Luckhurst defines ghosts as 'the signals of atrocities, marking sites of untold violence, a traumatic past whose traces remain to attest to a lack of testimony'.[91] By seizing the ghost one can effectively lay claim to the 'untold violence' that it signifies, whilst their unfinished business represents a blank canvas, enabling the person that claims the ghost to map their own story upon it. *Maps for Lost Lovers* boasts two ghosts, one with a glowing stomach, and one with glowing hands. This pair of ghosts is variously named as Shamas and Suraya (by Shamas), a murdered Muslim girl and her Hindu lover (by the Hindu lover) and Jugnu and his girlfriend Chanda, the murdered couple around which the narrative revolves (again by Shamas). There are various explanations given for the luminous bodies, and the lack of consensus over the identity of the ghosts again illustrates a desire to be the 'haunted' (or even haunt*ing*) one, as it is notable that at least two of the people identified as ghosts are not even dead at the time that they are named as such.

However, it may be that characters in Aslam's novel dwell on past traumas as a way of avoiding the more pressing horrors of the present. Kaukab comforts herself with a connection to history, enjoying the work that links her to her female ancestors and preferring to be trapped in her house with ghosts than outside facing the world:

> There's nothing for her out there in Dasht-e-Tanhaii, to notice or be interested in. Everything is here in this house. Every beloved absence is present here. An oasis – albeit a haunted one – in the middle of the Desert of Loneliness. Out there, there was nothing but humiliation. (65)

This signifies a desire for communal belonging, but suggests that she can only find it in a romanticised past rather than the lonely and alienating present. Kaukab's daughter, Mah-Jabin, also defers to the past to take the sting from the present. After blaming an irritability towards her mother on thinking about her uncle's murder, 'She winces inwardly at what she has just said, feeling degraded, that already the death of the two loved people is being used in deceit because she does not wish to hurt this living person by her side' (102). Here trauma is used as an excuse, illustrating the danger and duplicity involved in unjustly appropriating a real trauma for one's own ends.

It is necessary to note, however, that Oyeyemi's novels resist the tidy resolution offered by the working through of trauma, real or imagined. As Victor Sage and Allan Lloyd Smith note in a statement that has a clear resonance with Oyeyemi's work, whilst 'early Gothic proposed a delightful excursion through the realms of imaginary horror, contemporary use of the gothic register strikes a darker and more disturbing note. It is the horror now that is real, and the resolution that is fanciful'.[92] In the context of Oyeyemi's fiction, the real horrors are contemporary racism and xenophobia, and attempts at healing the traumas of alienation, bifurcated identities and self-hatred are left incomplete and 'fanciful'. Conclusions draw readers away from the located and historicised sites of trauma into supernatural or impossible places, implying the impossibility of the complete healing of traumas that are ongoing.

This chapter has illustrated the key imperatives of a subgenre of literature that has evolved out of postcolonial gothic to suit an English context: to challenge the destructive binaries found in imperial gothic, to appropriate familiar gothic tropes for a new context in order to comment upon contemporary desires and fears, and sometimes to posit ways beyond the lingering effects of colonial trauma. The novels considered here explore traumas specific to experiences of migration, positioning colonialism as the original trauma that has prefigured generations of people suffering from displacement, alienation and racism. Appropriation of familiar tropes of doubling and monstrosity rewritten from the perspective of those who have been othered by imperial gothic highlights and deconstructs a tendency to displace onto the Other traits that cannot comfortably be assimilated to the Self. Silence – which has been both a tool of colonialism and a way of registering terror in the gothic – is deconstructed as characters negotiate the ambivalent empowerment enabled by both speech and silence. In accordance with the wider genre of postcolonial gothic, these tales continually make connections between the personal and the national body, as traumas overlap and mutually infect. English spaces are rendered uncanny as a step towards their reclamation for a postcolonial society or to foreground the persistence of the alienating effects of racist discourse. However, it is not possible (or even desirable) completely to homogenise the subgenre and a distinct division emerges between texts that seek to foreground the lingering effects of colonial trauma in narratives that end without a satisfying sense of resolution, let alone reconciliation, and those in which a perverse desire for trauma is appropriated as a means of generating a sense of collective heritage.

3
The Subcultural Urban Novel

Sex and shopping have long been associated with constructions of the urban space, as the modern city presents, or is presented as, a place of erotic allure and economic opportunity. The subcultural urban novel reflects and refracts the promise of these sexual and commercial desires by exposing their more unpleasant counterparts: gang culture driven by hypermasculinity and unsatiated materialistic desires, women that are interchangeable with material commodities in the eyes of their misogynist beholders, and the underlying poverty that is a logical out-working of the capitalist system. The subcultural urban novel shifts the conventional paradigm of postcolonial fiction, as rather than 'writing back'[1] to the (former) colonial centre, it is produced for the consumption of a community of insiders. As examples of this new genre of fiction, this chapter considers Karline Smith's *Moss Side Massive* (1994) and *Full Crew* (2002), Gautaum Malkani's *Londonstani* (2007) and Nirpal Singh Dhaliwal's *Tourism* (2006). Authors that I study here have, to date, received very little academic attention and I argue that this is because they often present a picture of multicultural Britain that is largely unpalatable to mainstream audiences.

Before moving onto the 'subcultural urban novel' proper, I will discuss the representation of minority cultures in Hanif Kureishi's *The Buddha of Suburbia* (1990) and Zadie Smith's *White Teeth* (2000) so as to indicate where the new genre makes its departure in terms of relations between minority and mainstream. *The Buddha of Suburbia* and *White Teeth* are about minority cultures but their projected audience is largely white, middle-class and mainstream. This can be witnessed in the strategic exoticism and staged marginality evidenced in both the texts and the paratexts (cover illustrations and jacket endorsements, for example) of these two novels, which imply an audience that is largely unfamiliar with the cultures represented.[2] As well as raising questions of performativity and audience, my reading of the novels demonstrates that relationships with white women function allegorically as the courtship of Britain, which is portrayed as indifferent to the wooing of its immigrant peoples, yet is shown to be encouraging of a self-abasing attitude by buying into consumable ethnic identities when and where there is a market for them.

Where the subcultural urban novel makes its departure, then, is through a change in what I term 'imagined audience' from white majority to subcultural minority, as books are increasingly marketed to subcultural insiders. Furthermore, to talk about subcultures rather than minority cultures involves both a generational shift and a positional shift in terms of attitudes towards the often problematically homogenised mainstream. It also marks a shift towards self-determination as a subcultural member, for those who may have had the labels of 'otherness' or difference thrust upon them (due to ethnic or class allegiances that mark a deviance from the 'norm'). I argue that subcultural affiliation means that these labels can be transformed into a choice or oppositional stance, recasting subcultural members as agents rather than victims. Rather than a fetishised Other (however ironic) as portrayed by Hanif Kureishi and Zadie Smith, I suggest that characters in this new genre of fiction are more concerned with self-fetishisation through the celebration of 'subcultural capital', a phrase that describes non-economic value. These novels use consumerist and sexual desires and systems of value in order to comment upon and critique the construction of multicultural Britain by focussing on the problematic topics of violence, hypermasculinity, gangs and misogyny that are often passed over by more utopian (political and literary) accounts of multiculturalism, such as the representations within and the commentary surrounding Gurinder Chadha's *Bend It Like Beckham* (discussed in the following chapter).

I build upon and extend the work done by Graham Huggan and Sarah Brouillette on the marketing of postcolonial literature, by similarly foregrounding consumerist concerns and extending this criticism to cover authors who have not attained the same commercial or academic prestige to date. Attention to the marketing of postcolonial literature also means focussing upon the outer packaging as well as the inner workings of many of the novels in question. In other words, as well as mapping the various expressions of desire played out *within* the novels, I also consider how the books – and their authors – are advertised and sold to the public. The following extended theoretical introduction outlines approaches to the sexual and consumerist desires that variously define both the inner workings and the (lack of) market success of the subcultural urban novel.

Postcolonialism and the fetish

In this chapter I explore the way that fetishisation, in both the Freudian and the Marxist senses of the term, is used to represent the psychical and economic systems of postcolonial Britain. Laura Mulvey's *Fetishism and Curiosity* (1996) brings together sexual and economic theories in a useful way through her observation that Freudian and Marxist theories converge and diverge around notions of fetishism. This term was historically employed to 'encapsulate the primitive, irrational, beliefs that were associated with Africa' but is used 'ironically' by both Sigmund Freud and Karl Marx to denote 'irrationalities' permeating 'bourgeois economics and its psyche'.[3] For Freud, fetishism is the means by which an object that is 'very inappropriate for sexual purposes' (cited instances including feet, shoes, hair and underwear) becomes the primary sexual object.[4] This suggests that fetishism involves misrecognition of value in terms of what Freud considers the only valid sexual aim (heterosexual intercourse). Marx similarly uses the concept of fetishism to describe the incorrect substitution of value, stating that 'The mysterious character of the commodity-form consists therefore simply in the fact that the commodity [falsely] reflects the social characteristics of men's own labour as objective characteristics of the products of labour themselves'.[5] Marx likens the endowment of autonomy to 'products of labour' to 'the misty realm of religion' in which similar autonomy is granted to what the philosopher (in his typical dismissal of religion) considers to be simply 'the products of the human brain'.[6]

The concept of fetishism is employed by both theorists, Mulvey argues, 'in an attempt to explain a refusal, or blockage, of the mind, or a phobic inability of the psyche, to understand a symbolic system of value, one within the social and the other within the analytic sphere'. Yet, as she remarks, there are important differences between the two approaches, notably that the Marxist approach denotes a 'problem of inscription' in which the exchange value of commodities is hidden, whilst the Freudian approach 'flourishes as phantasmatic inscription' in which 'excessive value' is ascribed to 'objects considered to be valueless by the social consensus'. Mulvey summarises that 'In one case, the sign of value fails to inscribe itself on an actual object; in the other, value is over-inscribed onto a site of imagined lack, through a substitute object'.[7]

The contradictory results of fetishisation are interestingly explored in the following novels, in which shopping and sex, consumerism and consummation, symbolic value and economic value are brought into close proximity. Although the novels do not talk of fetishism explicitly, I demonstrate ways in which they implicitly evoke fetishisation of either the Other (in novels marketed around their exotic qualities) or the Self (in subcultural texts). Fetishisation is signalled by misrecognising the value of objects, or by deliberately over-valuing them in order to create an alternate hierarchy (replacing capital with subcultural capital). I therefore read fetishisation as serving as an index for the values placed on people and objects in postcolonial Britain, which provides the sociopolitical and economic backdrop for the novels considered here.

I demonstrate that in the Marxist sense of the term, real relationships between people(s) are reduced to chains of production and consumption, with products standing in for experiences, lifestyles or values that the consumer may or may not actually possess. Postcolonial Britain itself becomes an idea that can be sold, and greedily consumed or hastily rejected by its subjects. I also invoke a Freudian paradigm, in which excessive value is placed on certain 'ethnic' objects (books themselves, and the collections of exotic paraphernalia that readers come across in the novels) that have no function in uniting the national body politic in a meaningful way. Graham Huggan's analysis of the role of commodity fetishism in the case of marketing postcolonial authors and texts reflects this Freudian language:

> These three aspects of commodity fetishism – mystification (or levelling-out) of historical experience; imagined access to the cultural other through the process of consumption; reification of people and places into exchangeable aesthetic objects – help these books and their authors acquire an almost talismanic status.[8]

Huggan's analysis indicates the problematic way in which certain authors are reified and sold. I suggest that the success of this commodification of imagined access to authors is also dependent on the authors' representation of multicultural Britain, which dictates the extent to which different readers wish to identify.

The postcolonial literary marketplace

Beyond considering the implications of fetishisation and desire in terms of the inner workings of the novels, it is also necessary to consider the literary marketplace in which these desires are staged. Pierre Bourdieu conceptualises the literary arena as a 'Field of Cultural Production' in a critical work of the same name, arguing that each literary work is 'subjectively defined by the system of distinctive properties by which it can be situated relative to other positions'. Bourdieu's analysis situates each literary *oeuvre* in a field determined by the ever-shifting positions of other works in a field organised around 'the structure of the distribution of the capital of specific properties which governs success in the field and the winning of external or special profits (such as literary prestige) which are at stake in the field'.[9] Although convincing in its appraisal of the field, it says little of the roles that authors themselves might play in situating their work or engaging with market forces.

For Michel Foucault, the author has a crucial (but largely incidental/ passive) role to play, his/her 'function' being to 'characterize the existence, circulation and operation of certain discourses within a society'.[10] Although Foucault foreshadows postmodern rhetoric in his assertion that the author is dead, 'a victim of his own writing', he suggests that there is nevertheless an 'author function'.[11] The author as a determining force for deciphering meaning in the text might be dead, but the author as an icon embodying a certain set of discourses and cultural cachet – or, we might say, an author that can be sold to hungry consumers – is alive and well. This perhaps equates to an over-valuation (Freudian fetishisation) of the role of the authors, yet it is incontrovertible that this fetishisation is a crucial tool of the literary market.

Huggan builds on and updates Bourdieu's work (which largely focuses on a history of the literary field of production in France). Despite the criticisms that Bourdieu's model has received for its 'over-schematised distinctions and, in particular, for its attempt to fix the class positions of different consumer publics,' it is, for Huggan, 'useful, nonetheless, in suggesting how postcolonial writers/thinkers operate within an overarching, if historically shifting, field of cultural production'. Huggan explicitly assesses the two 'regimes of value' into which he understands the relevant field to be divided: postcolonialism, which he describes as 'an anti-colonial intellectualism that reads and valorises the signs of social struggle in the faultlines of literary and cultural texts', and postcoloniality, which is 'largely a function of postmodernity: its own regime of value pertains to a system of symbolic, as well as material, exchange in which even the language of resistance may be manipulated and consumed'.[12] The struggle between these 'regimes of value' leads Huggan to question the 'varying degrees of complicity between local oppositional discourses and the global late-capitalist system in which these discourses circulate and are contained'.[13] The distinction that Huggan makes highlights the tensions inherent in the production and consumption of postcolonial literature. Yet to differentiate the two terms serves to valorise and protect postcolonialism at the expense of postcoloniality, by suggesting that the radical politics and reading practices of postcolonialism can act independently of the market system in which the texts and authors circulate. The two terms would be better understood as mutually dependent, as terminology that attempts to divorce the site of production from the site of consumption obfuscates a more complex and nuanced relationship that Huggan himself explores in his analysis of specific texts and the relationships constructed between authors and readers.

In a world in which (postcolonial) authors are increasingly self-conscious regarding the politics of globalisation and market economies, there is a profusion of novels that explicitly engage with motifs of production, desire and consumption, inviting readers to witness and critique the mechanisms of the global capitalist system first hand. Huggan's analysis engages with this booming field in order to interrogate the ironies of the purportedly avant-garde political work of postcolonial narratives that seem at odds with the 'exoticising' marketing engines that produce them, noting that 'a remarkable discrepancy exists between the progressiveness of postcolonial thinking and the rearguard myths and stereotypes that are used to promote and sell "non-Western" cultural products in and to the West'.[14] Huggan's work has proven to be highly influential for conceptualising the strategies that postcolonial authors employ in order to position their works in relation to the market, and I reference some of these strategies in my subsequent discussion of the novels. However, his study focuses only on the 'elite' end of the postcolonial literary market, which, as I outline more fully below, is problematic for itself being dictated by market forces, excluding those authors that have not found such favour with the publishing market, regardless of the comparable literary merit of their work.

Sarah Brouillette undermines Huggan's analysis by contesting that his work is based on a false or unjustified premise: 'His critique of an unspecified global reader in pursuit of exotic access to what is culturally "other" is what allows him to identify, and identify with, an elite group of distinguished consumers said to apprehend texts in a more responsible way.'[15] Brouillette distinguishes her own (ironically similar) study from Huggan's by understanding 'strategic exoticism, and likewise general postcolonial authorial self-consciousness' as evidenced in the novels she discusses, to be based upon a set of 'assumptions shared between the author and the reader, as both producer and consumer work to negotiate with, if not absolve themselves of, postcoloniality's touristic guilt'.[16] Although Brouillette assures readers that she does not subscribe to Huggan's logic 'that separates the authentic from the inauthentic, the insider from the outsider, in an endless cycle of hierarchical distinction and counter-distinction', the literary analysis that she then undertakes is largely dependent on a similar set of tropes and authors to those investigated by Huggan.[17] The reason for this is perhaps that, in the same vein as Foucault, Brouillette understands postcolonial authors to have little hope of 'autonomy from the commercial sphere'.[18] In support of this thesis, she then focuses only on authors who fit the bill of accruing a wide readership whose function is produced through ferocious marketing campaigns. There is not a problem with this recourse to the literary elite *per se*, and indeed much of this book has been concerned with commercially successful authors; however, it appears neglectful when discussing the literary marketplace to consider only the literary equivalents of Harrods. Brouillette's analysis is precise and interesting, but fails in its pretence at describing a general situation when she is in fact discussing merely an elite sector of commercially successful authors who manifest at least partial complicity with their own market positioning, including Derek Walcott, Salman Rushdie and J. M. Coetzee.

The importance of being alert to capitalist mechanisms is highlighted by Neil Lazarus, who raises important questions regarding class and the material, capitalist basis of colonialism. In *The Postcolonial Unconscious* (2011), Lazarus expresses his concern that 'Within postcolonial studies [...] the core concepts of "colonialism" and even "imperialism" are routinely severed from that of "capitalism".'[19] Making the crucial connection, as Lazarus does, between capitalism, imperialism and neo-imperialism means that it is more essential than ever to consider postcolonial novels both as works of ideology and as works of labour, with the capacity both to reflect and to comment upon market systems. For Lazarus, the postcolonial novel is useful for conveying class relations in a number of ways. Crucially, he advocates that we attend to the *ways* in which the social conditions of existence are represented, 'since it is here that writers' own attitudes to what is being expressed come into focus; and here also, therefore, that the nature and level of readers' commitment to the text is negotiated and secured'.[20] As such it is important to attend to narrative distancing, self-irony and strategic exoticism in order to understand the author's own relationship with the system that they (and we as readers) are to some extent inevitably complicit in.

Both Huggan and Brouillette focus on a certain kind of author to make their cases: those that are cosmopolitan, mobile, award-winning celebrities, who speak of global and local politics with the authority attendant upon those that have both attended some of the world's best universities and accrued international stardom (such as Salman Rushdie, Arundhati Roy, J. M. Coetzee and Chinua Achebe). Clearly there is a place for such arguments, but they offer a skewed perspective of the market as a whole, in which the privileged, fund-accruing, celebrity few are taken as representative of what is in fact a far more diverse (and largely less-moneyed) field. In an attempt partially to correct this imbalance, this chapter examines the representation of consumerism and market-driven desires in relation to writers occupying a wider range of positions in the field of literary production, starting with 'celebrity' authors Hanif Kureishi and Zadie Smith, before considering authors that have not (yet) gained such celebrity status or financial independence, namely Karline Smith, Gautam Malkani and Nirpal Singh Dhaliwal.

To open my discussion of Malkani, Dhaliwal and Karline Smith, I consider the books' 'paratexts', that which Gérard Genette defines as accompaniments to the written text that 'surround and extend' the text and ensure its '"reception" and consumption'.[21] These paratextual accompaniments are far from neutral supplements, but instead frame and position the novel, negotiating an intricate web of political, promotional and generic forces. Indeed, for Richard Watts in *Packaging Post/Coloniality*, 'it is in the paratext that the struggle over who has the right to mediate and who maintains the authority to present and interpret this literature is fought'.[22] To cite a British case in support of my concern with the (literal and metaphorical) packaging of texts, Corinne Fowler's 'A Tale of Two Novels: Developing a Devolved Approach to Black British Writing' traces the 'differing fortunes' of Zadie Smith's *White Teeth* and Joe Pemberton's *Forever and Ever Amen* ('also a critical success'), 'examin[ing] the commercial and cultural logic by which novels are coded as worthy of national and international readerships by corporate publishers and high street retail outlets'.[23] Among reasons that Fowler arrives at for the novels' 'differing fortunes,' she suggests that 'literature is frequently co-opted [by publishers] into the project of constructing a national consciousness' and that 'Correspondingly, a novel's ability to conjure up a sense of place in ways that trigger positive cultural associations has important commercial implications'.[24] My response to this is to examine a range of texts, including those that determinedly do *not* paint a happy picture of postcolonial Britain and those that are set outside London's metropolitan centre. In so doing, I echo Fowler's call for academics to maintain 'a critical perspective on the corporate publishing industry'.[25]

Malkani's, Dhaliwal's and Karline Smith's paratexts all point to a different kind of marketing campaign to those provided for Rushdie's, Kureishi's and Zadie Smith's novels. The garish yellow cover, pink font and demotic title of Malkani's *Londonstani* suggests that it is aimed at a younger audience, self-consciously marketed as low-brow with street cred by sporting a single cover image of a young and stylish Asian man, who gazes disinterestedly into the middle distance. Dhaliwal's novel *Tourism* has the kind of front cover that makes the novel embarrassing to read in public, comprising a close-up of a woman's breast exposed in a see-through blouse and an overlaid tag line in red, 'sexy... shocking and touched with genius'. The narrator's commodification of women, which forms a major theme of the novel, is reflected on the cover. Karline Smith's novels *Moss Side Massive* and *Full Crew* appear to be marketed exclusively for urban youth, with cover images that indicate a predominant concern with gang culture (indexed through guns and conspicuously large signet rings). *Moss Side Massive* points to a specific geographic region (an inner-city Manchester district with a large migrant community and a bad reputation for riots and gun crime), while both cover photos are of black men, factors which serve to market the novels along lines of gender, ethnicity and locale. Both of Smith's novels are published by X Press, a press that 'has produced fiction dealing with black street life, marketed to appeal to a youthful, metropolitan black readership' with the 'serious objective' of 're-map[ping] the British inner-city's terrain, focussing attention on black social decay and institutionalized racism'.[26]

In different ways, the marketing for these three authors resists the kind of postcolonial exoticism that Huggan and Brouillette have attributed to the authors they are concerned with: it does not mark them for consumption by a predominantly white, middle-class audience. There is, of course, more than one mode of exoticisation: subcultural urban novels may stand accused of fetishising the violence and misogyny associated with the gangs and subcultures that they take as their focus, and in so doing, of exoticising the subcultural members for a mainstream audience. However, because I go on to argue that the target market for the novels is subcultural insiders, this means that their paratexts can be seen to be less concerned about the exoticisation of the Other, and more concerned with creating an image that is worthy of subcultural capital.

Minority cultures

Staged marginality in *The Buddha of Suburbia*

In an interview with Susan Fischer, Hanif Kureishi describes his last-minute decision to change the title of his first novel from *Streets of My Heart* to *The Buddha of Suburbia*, despite the novel's focus on Karim rather than Haroon, the eponymous Buddha of the title. His choice, Kureishi asserts, is simply because the latter title sounds better; I will leave cynics to discuss the deliberate process of exoticisation that this canny marketing choice entails.[27] Although the given title does not refer to the protagonist, it is, however, metonymic of the novel's main pre-occupations: staged marginality and consumable exotic identities. *The Buddha of Suburbia* belongs to the tradition of the Bildungsroman and follows the protagonist Karim Amir through his negotiation of what it means to be 'an Englishman born and bred, almost'.[28] Oscillating between heterosexual and homosexual relationships, between parents, between locations (the suburbs, London, America and, albeit imaginatively, India), between social classes, between a range of possible self-imposed identifications (including at various points English, French, African American, Indian) and between received labels (black, 'Paki'), Karim learns what it means to adopt or perform an identity. Befitting the novel's concern with performativity, Karim is an actor, an occupation that functions as an enabling device for addressing broader themes of staging, audience and improvisation.

Karim's blossoming acting career sees him in two roles, the first of which is Mowgli, and involves him assuming an Indian accent and sporting 'a loin-cloth and brown make-up, so that [he] resembled a turd in a bikini-bottom' (146). The irony of the faked accent and brown make-up required for Karim to fit the part is that he is ruthlessly informed that he has 'been cast for authenticity and not for experience' (147). Authenticity, it is apparent, is something imposed from the outside as a marker to increase perceived value and to suggest a certain ontological integrity. Problems over the 'authenticity' that Karim brings to the part are exposed as Karim does not understand what is meant when he is asked for an authentic accent, by which the director means an Indian accent, not his native 'Orpington' one.

Karim's performance is shown to collude with and fuel prejudiced attitudes. Aside from the dubious casting, the play is a take on *The Jungle Book*, the author of which is described by Haroon as 'That bloody fucker Mr Kipling pretending to whity [sic] he knew something about India!' (157). This leads Karim's cousin Jamila to describe his performance as 'pandering to prejudices [...]. And clichés about Indians' (157). The episode serves as an example of what Huggan has termed 'staged marginality', described as 'the process by which marginalised individuals or social groups are moved to dramatise their "subordinate" status for the benefit of a majority or mainstream audience' (87). Theatre becomes, in the case of *The Buddha of Suburbia*, an allegory for society, where the processes of casting and staging and the composition of the audience ('four hundred white English people') are writ large (228).

But we should not necessarily take Karim's apparent collusion in racial stereotyping at face value. Indeed, Huggan argues that 'Staged marginality is not necessarily an exercise in self-abasement; it may, and often does, have a critical or even a subversive function' (87). Karim's performance could therefore be read as a parody of audience expectations, working with a series of overblown stereotypes that we must view as ironic. Strategic marginalisation, in this case, reveals more about the desires of the consuming audience than it does about the performer who is 'moved' to re-enact colonial subordination. But if the audience is unaware that they are witnessing a parody rather than an 'authentic' display of Indian-ness (whatever that loaded term might entail), then all the play succeeds in doing, as Jamila recognises, is to confirm preconceptions and to build upon foundations of prejudice. It is only with the extra remove and critical distance that we are granted as readers of the novel that the irony of Karim's performance is made explicit, largely through the motif of performance that runs throughout.

Karim's second acting role, in a play loosely based around class, is arrived at through improvisation, for which he initially takes his Uncle Anwar as inspiration. Anwar had, until recently, been undertaking a hunger strike to cajole his daughter Jamila into an arranged marriage with an Indian man who she had never met. The new approach to acting raises a different set of questions, as the representational onus is now on Karim rather than the director, leading Roger Bromley to suggest that 'Karim [...] embodies mimicry as an active process, not the passivity of tolerated "copies". As an actor he partly reverses the colonial appropriation'.[29] Bromley's use of the modifier 'partly' is integral to the sense of his sentence, however, as Karim's performances are still judged with the colonial audience in mind. Mimicry might be an active process but, as is indicated by the first play that Karim participates in, it is one enacted within the dictates of the pre-existing (post)colonial order, which becomes the interpretational paradigm for minority performances.

The potential for racist/imperialist complicity is made apparent when Karim's mimicry raises problems within the acting troupe. Tracey, a black actress, tries to impress upon Karim the 'burden of representation' that she feels he should share:

> 'Anwar's hunger-strike worries me. What you want to say hurts me. It really pains me! And I'm not sure we should show it! [...] I'm afraid it shows black people – '
> 'Indian people –'
> 'Black and Asian people – '
> 'One old Indian man – '
> 'As being irrational, ridiculous, as being hysterical. And as being fanatical.'
> '[...] It's not a fanatical hunger-strike. It's calmly intended blackmail.' (180)

This section of the novel reads as a metafictional aside regarding the burden of representation perhaps experienced by Kureishi as an author, which he refuses to give in to. As such, the depiction of Anwar in his own artistic work is internally justified and readers are assured that the characters should not be regarded as representative. Karim accordingly becomes little more than a mouthpiece for Kureishi when he answers Tracey's rhetorical question 'We have to protect our culture at this time, Karim. Don't you agree?' with 'No. Truth has a higher value' (181). Despite this protestation, Karim ultimately submits to Tracey's pressure to drop Anwar as his muse and opts instead to draw on Jamila's husband Changez for the part, choosing to betray the wishes of a friend in order to appease the rest of the cast.

The choices that Karim is obliged to make regarding performance magnify the quotidian construction of identity. Karim's professional performances reflect his father's identity construction: Haroon is the self-styled Buddha of Suburbia, visiting suburban households to guide people in 'the Way' through instruction, meditation and yoga (13). Yet whether it is performance or something more ostensibly permanent (history, roots, religion or culture) that is the ultimate determinant of identity is left unresolved in the novel. Karim describes his father as 'a renegade Muslim masquerading as a Buddhist' (16), yet when his Auntie Jean suggests the same, that he has been 'impersonating a Buddhist', Karim retorts that 'He is a Buddhist' (44). A tension between whether Haroon is a Buddhist because that is how he chooses to construct his identity, or whether he is a Muslim because he was born one is left to play out, as Kureishi refuses to close down the debate.

What is certain is that the identity that Haroon constructs is a marketable one for which he finds a ready audience. Unlike the practising Muslim characters of the novel (Uncle Anwar, Auntie Jeeta, and to a certain extent Changez), who are financially poor and struggle with racist hostility and physical abuse, Haroon is socially mobile and financially relatively well-off (although this is largely the result of his extra-marital affair with the socially ambitious Eva). Furthermore, descriptions of Haroon focus on his exotic dress, his 'red and gold waistcoat and Indian pajamas' (31), whilst suburban homes that he visits are depicted in terms of their material products, in rooms cluttered with 'sandalwood Buddhas, brass ashtrays and striped plaster elephants' (30). Unlike one's inherited cultural, religious or national identity, a performative construction of identity is presented as something that money *can* buy. James Procter notes the shifting ontological paradigm that this represents: 'the suburban interior [...] crammed with material goods [...] distinguishes the semi-detached from the stark basements and bedsits of early postwar fiction where acts of production (work and the search for it) overshadowed rituals of consumption'.[30] In Kureishi's narrative, people define themselves by products that they consume: identity becomes a costume that can be donned, whilst lifestyle can be found in the pages of a magazine.

A consumable identity has national ramifications. Just as Charlie – son of Eva and lover of Karim – goes to America and sells 'Englishness, [...] getting a lot of money for it' (247), the marketing of marginality has implications for Britishness (or perhaps Englishness, in the terms of the novel) itself. Consumer goods are often self-consciously marketed for their 'exotic' qualities, and as Huggan asserts, 'Marginality [...] is a primary strategy of commodity culture, which thrives on the retailing of cultural products regarded as emanating from outside the mainstream.'[31] This could be read as reinforcing a hierarchy whereby margin dwellers are producers ripe for exploitation by mainstream consumers. Such an unequal relationship between exotic 'product' and mainstream consumer is also played out in the novel's romance plot in which ethnic minority characters themselves become the subjects of desire precisely for their purported exotic qualities.

Karim's romantic undertakings often reflect his vexed relationship with the British body politic in a manner reminiscent of the national romance, a genre of literature that Doris Sommer defines as performing 'the marriage between Eros and Polis'.[32] For Sommer, the paralleling of erotic and political desire that she finds in Latin-American literature means that readers are situated to desire the unification of the diverse political factions represented by the lovers as they will the happy resolution of the romance plot. Although national romance has the potential to bring together otherwise disparate elements of society, it has not always been seen as a particularly revolutionary genre of literature. Further to Sommer's criticisms as to its 'culturally hegemonizing' and 'bourgeois' tendencies,[33] Mary Louise Pratt's work on imperial literature and travel writing figures 'transracial love plots' as a form of neo-colonisation or enslavement, in which 'romantic love rather than filial servitude or force guarantees the wilful submission of the colonized', and the 'allegory of romantic love mystifies exploitation out of the picture'.[34] While the historical context outlined here is distinct from the postcolonial present, imperial legacies are long-lasting and Pratt's study outlines a history of racism played out in sexual intercourse that has uncomfortable parallels with *The Buddha of Suburbia*.

Kureishi's novel interweaves the political and the romantic (and I use that term here in the loosest of senses) not to paper over inequalities with romantic platitudes, but to expose the transactions involved in various sexual affairs throughout the novel and to expose ways in which they reflect wider social disparities. Karim, for example, is exploited whilst participating in an orgy with his girlfriend, his director Pyke, and his director's wife. Pyke, who occupies a position of authority over the young actor, 'insert[ed] his cock between [Karim's] speaking lips' without so much as asking (203) and 'virtually ruptured' him during anal intercourse (219). Karim's traumatic sexual encounter is not dwelt upon in any significant manner, other than as a signal that 'the fucker was fucking [him] in other ways' (219). To a certain extent *The Buddha of Suburbia* has a similar function to Kureishi's earlier screenplay, *My Beautiful Laundrette* (1985), which employs romance as a means of imaginatively removing borders between classes and ethnicities in order to posit a more utopian future and can therefore be read as a national romance in the sense laid out by Sommer.[35] The film enables the temporary suspension of Thatcherite social norms of homophobia and racism by allowing second-generation Pakistani migrant Omar to be both the boss and the lover of the white, working-class, ex-National Front supporter, Johnny. However, the novel is far more complex than the film in terms of the workings of desire, as in *The Buddha of Suburbia* a complex nexus of relationships does not allow the reader simply to will one relationship into being and in so doing identify with a national project.

Changez summarises the novel's philosophy accurately when he avows that 'in this capitalism of the feelings no one cares for another person' (215). Rather than relationships naïvely imagined to allegorise the happy coming together of disparate social entities, *The Buddha of Suburbia* instead uses sexual relationships to describe a set of transactions that are rarely equal, whether explicitly financial (as in the case of Changez and his favourite prostitute, Shinko), commoditised (with the use of dildos), or exploitative (Karim's encounters both with Pyke and with a rather enthusiastic Great Dane). The link between erotic desire and national politics is writ large in Karim's assessment at the end of his failed relationship with Eleanor: 'And we pursued English roses as we pursued England; by possessing these prizes, this kindness and beauty, we stared defiantly into the eye of the Empire and all its self-regard – into the eye of Hairy Back, into the eye of the Great Fucking Dane' (227). It follows that, far from using relationships to present unification and provide a utopian reflection of the nation, sexual union is portrayed here as a form of (post)colonial revenge; rather than writing back, Kureishi's characters fuck back, using sex as a weapon to turn back on those that have formerly 'fucked' them.

National bromance and triangular desire in Zadie Smith's *White Teeth*

I turn now to Zadie Smith's *White Teeth*, a novel in which the anticipated representation of a celebratory image of multicultural relations was expressed in the financial and media investment in the work before its completion. 'The hype began in the autumn of 1997. Zadie Smith was 21 and just down from Cambridge when her first novel was sold on a mere 80 pages for an advance rumoured to be in the region of £250,000'.[36] Zadie Smith, described in this article's title as 'young, black [and] British', was sold to the public in advance of her novel, with the desire for the author's success illustrating a contemporaneous millennial desire for a new voice for British multiculturalism.

This mediation of desire, in which desire for a utopian national future is projected onto an upcoming novelist, is reflected in tropes of the novel itself. *White Teeth* has roots stretching historically from the Indian Mutiny of 1857 into the present day and geographically between Bangladesh, Jamaica and Britain. The action largely revolves around the tragicomic lives of three families: Bangladeshi Samad and Alsana Iqbal with their twins Magid and Millat; white British Archie and Jamaican Clara Jones with their daughter Irie; and Jewish Marcus and Joyce Chalfen with Joshua, the eldest of four sons. In order to illustrate the marketability of certain modes of identifying and relating in postcolonial Britain, I focus predominantly on the novel's portrayal of male homosocial bonds and the white femme fatale after returning briefly to the subject of performative identity.

In Kureishi's novel, the performance of identity is seen as a potentially liberating and elastic process offering a means of resistance to categorisation from the outside, despite its usual recuperation within a consumerist, capitalist world. By contrast, *White Teeth* pushes against the limits of hybridising, performative or discontinuous constructions of identity by restoring a sense of (predominantly colonial) history that cannot be so easily forgotten. Millat Iqbal, 'Social chameleon', constantly reconstructs his identity to fit in with different social situations.[37] His first serious social allegiance to a 'Raggastani' group follows what is by now a familiar model, characterised by consumable items such as films and music, and 'Naturally there was a uniform' in which 'everything, everything, everything was *Nike*™.; wherever the five of them went the impression they left behind was of one giant swoosh, one huge mark of corporate approval' (231–2).

Millat ultimately realises, however, that despite his efforts at performing a particular identity, there are stronger forces at play:

> He knew that he, Millat, was a Paki no matter where he came from; that he smelt of curry; had no sexual identity; took other people's jobs; or had no job and bummed off the state; or gave all the jobs to his relatives; that he could be a dentist or a shop-owner or a curry-shifter, but not a footballer or a film-maker; that he should go back to his own country; or stay here and earn his bloody keep; that he worshipped elephants and wore turbans; that no one who looked like Millat, or spoke like Millat, or felt like Millat, was ever on the news unless they had recently been murdered. (233–4)

Millat eventually eschews a marketable identity, instead joining a group with the unfortunate acronym KEVIN (Keepers of the Eternal and Victorious Islamic Nation) and going to Bradford to burn a (persistently unnamed) book. This marks the failure of identity as defined by consumable products and effective performances; if identity is performed, then the roles available for ethnic minority characters are limited and the only remaining way to assert an identity is to burn those products in a performance of resistance.

White Teeth constructs desire as imitative in the Girardian sense, not moving directly from subject to object, but mediated through another desiring subject, who becomes the mediator of said desire, and often the 'rival'.[38] Although René Girard's definition refers to romantic triangles of desire between characters, it is equally applicable to an analysis of consumerist desires, in which products, lifestyles and personal grooming are sold via their mediation in advertising. Here, the triangle could be expressed as the desire for an object as mediated by advertising, which leads to more desire in a perpetual cycle. *White Teeth's* Irie reverses the desire for the exotic we saw enacted in *The Buddha of Suburbia*, in a process that Philip Tew describes as 'domesticat[ing] the exotic [...] through the comic cruelty of self-knowledge'.[39] Finding no reflection in England, the 'gigantic mirror' that she looks into, Irie can only see herself as abnormal, whilst desiring to be 'the same as everybody else' more than anything (266, 284). When Irie goes to have her hair 'fixed' and is asked what she requires, the answer she gives illustrates her mediated desire: she wants 'Straight hair. Straight straight long black sleek flickable tossable shakeable touchable finger-through-able wind-blowable hair. With a fringe' (273). The excess of adjectives used to describe the hair that Irie desires reads like an advertising campaign, suggesting that Irie's desire for straight hair is mediated through the fetishisation of a lifestyle that such beautiful hair might offer.

Triangulated and mediated desire is also reflected in the novel's relationships. Although *White Teeth* portrays a range of heteronormative marital, extra-marital and teenage relationships, I would suggest that the novel's great romance is between Archie Jones and Samad Iqbal, two old friends who are brought together through military service during the Second World War. The bond between Archie and Samad is the novel's strongest: they make decisions together, meet and eat together on a daily basis and share with each other what they will never share with their wives, forming a close homosocial bond. Archie reminisces: 'Sounds queer. But it's the truth. Always Sammy. Through thick and thin. Even if the world were ending. Never made a decision without him in forty years' (532). Eve Kosofsky Sedgwick builds on Girard's notion of triangular desire to theorise the bond formed between two men in their rivalry over a woman in order to 'draw the "homosocial" back into the orbit of desire', desire being 'an affective or social force'.[40] However, the homosocial bond in Smith's novel is not created over a shared object of desire; rather the two men play the key roles of a national romance by bringing together disparate elements of the community through a bond apparently stronger than romantic love: 'bromance', in today's parlance.

'Bromance' played a key role in the 2012 TV series *Make Bradford British*, a reality show designed to bring different communities together by forcing a select group of people to live together.[41] Although the

programme has been justly criticised for its 'obsession with racial tension' that obscures other issues such as poverty, effectively turning
Bradford into a 'single-issue city', what is potentially useful for my
purposes here is the question of what the series posited that it would
take to make Bradford British.[42] The answer to this seems to present
itself in the blossoming bromance between Rashid, a devout Muslim
who prays at the Mosque five times a day, and Damon, a skinhead who
goes into the project thinking that Mosques are 'terrorist centres'. The
programme's most compelling moments are constructed through a
relationship between these members of what are presented as Bradford's
two most antagonistic groups. The couple find mutual respect, sharing plenty of back-slapping man-hugs, and the programme's debrief
predominantly focuses on their story and their shared construction of
Britishness as something vaguely connected to heteronormative family values and respect. The somewhat idealistic implication is that if
these men – symbolically bearing the burden of representation for their
respective communities – can find mutual friendship and respect, then
so too can the wider community. This is what I mean by 'national bromance': a genre with the same national agenda as national romance,
but operating through the homosocial bond between two men.

    If Archie and Samad are to be understood in the same light as Damon
and Rashid, it is necessary to consider what the two characters bring
to the table and how they negotiate their views to fuel the 'bromance'.
Archie's initial opinion of Samad and Alsana is that they are 'not *those*
kind of Indians (as, in Archie's mind, Clara was not that kind of black)'
(54). Although Archie does not articulate exactly what 'those kind' of
Indians (actually Bangladeshis) would be, it is apparent that his friends
are somehow distinguished and considered to fall under a certain norm
from which 'others' deviate. He falls foul of the tendency that Kathryn
Perry has observed in her analysis of interviews with interracial cou-
ples, in which 'charm functions as a denial of blackness, reinvesting
the interracial relationship with the same normalising invisibility of
colour that white people believe their own whiteness to represent'.[43] In
choosing to befriend Samad, Archie also denies his friend's difference.
Samad has an opposing understanding of relationships between his
children and the white majority; he is such a stickler for tradition that
he refuses to see the younger generation's 'assimilation' as anything
other than 'corruption' (190) but is nevertheless blind towards his own
alcohol-consuming, adulterous hypocrisy. Unlike Damon and Rashid
who develop positions of mutual respect to accommodate the other's
beliefs, Archie and Samad change very little: this is a national bromance

that operates with a mutual blindness rather than the mutual exchange of ideas and values.

A problem with the homosocial bonding, or bromance, enacted within the novel and beyond is its exclusion of women, especially when this bromance has wider social or national implications. This is apparent in the misogynist overtones evident in Smith's novel, in which Britain is portrayed as a wanton temptress. Poppy Burt-Jones – a caricature of a naïve liberal white woman with a predilection for the exotic – is portrayed as representative of white women in general, and also with the corrupting tendencies of Britain as a nation. During his brief infatuation and fling with Poppy, Samad complains: 'I have been corrupted by England, I see that now – my children, my wife, they too have been corrupted. [...] And now it seems this final temptation has been put in front of me. To punish me, you understand' (144). Corruption at the hands of the nation and temptation at the hands of his sons' music teacher are pushed into close proximity, suggesting their similar aims.

Using a single woman to represent an entire nation has a long (and problematic) literary tradition, though this woman is more frequently placed in the role of mother. Elleke Boehmer describes gendered politics involved in the representation of the (post)colonial nation as follows: 'In practice, [...] and certainly in the operation of its iconographies and spectacles of power, nationalism operates as a masculine *family drama* [...], based on [...] gendered and unequal images of family roles' (emphasis in original).[44] Samad's trajectory 'from one brown mother country into the pale, freckled arms of an imperial sovereign' traces the shift from family romance to national romance, drawn along the lines of sexual rather than familial love with an allusion to 'pale, freckled arms' that suggests intimacy and embrace (162). I support Maurice Godelier's argument that 'Sex-related differences between bodies are continually summoned as testimony to social relations and phenomena that have nothing to do with sexuality. Not only as testimony to, but also as testimony for – in other words as legitimation.'[45] By equating Poppy with a national body politic, the novel effectively legitimises the misogynist dismissal of (white) women as corrupters and temptresses.

My analysis of Samad's legitimising misogynist tendencies might seem a little hard given that he is frequently parodied and revealed to be a hypocritical character. However, where Samad is redeemed in the novel through his good intentions, there is no redemption for the two-dimensional Poppy. The trope of the seductive and corrupting white woman is one that also plays out in a number of Kureishi's works, including *The Buddha of Suburbia*'s Eva Kay, *The Black Album*'s Deedee

Osgood and Rachel, Nasser's mistress in *My Beautiful Laundrette*. Reading *White Teeth* largely against the grain has enabled me to foreground some of the more problematic relationships and modes of identifying in postcolonial Britain that have frequently been lost in celebrations of the novel. I have demonstrated how erotic and economic desires are mediated in the novel in ways that indicate the mutual blindness or ignorance central to constructions of national identity and that show how postcolonial Britain is structured around commodifiable means of identifying to the exclusion of uncommodifiable identity positions. I return to the representative burden of the white woman again in my analysis of *Tourism* at the end of this chapter, but for now I turn to the new intervention into relationships between mainstream and minority made by subcultural urban fiction.

Subcultures

This chapter has thus far dealt with markedly mainstream texts, in terms of the novels' wide appeal and considerable commercial success. One way to conceptualise the move that I make in the second half of this chapter is to phrase it in terms of a shift from novels about characters from ethnic minorities that have been targeted at and consumed largely by mainstream audiences, to subcultural novels that are written about and marketed for subcultural consumers. To talk about subcultures rather than minority cultures involves both a generational shift and a positional shift in terms of attitudes towards the mainstream. *The Buddha of Suburbia* and *White Teeth* might be considered novels of (white) seduction, using romance as a trope to signify the (at times messy) union of disparate social factions. By contrast, subcultural studies and texts frequently focus on 'resistance' as a group's defining logic. By tracing this shift, romance is replaced by conflict as the ruling metaphor for relationships in the latter half of this chapter.

For Ken Gelder, in his seminal work on *Subcultures* (2007), resistance is employed as a subcultural strategy for '"winning space" back from the ruling classes', either in terms of territory or of style ('by using commodities, the signs of "dominant culture", differently').[46] Reading texts with an eye to subcultures therefore enables an understanding of Britishness defined from the bottom up, rather than the top down (for John Clarke et al., subculture is always 'subordinate and subordinated' in relation to the 'dominant culture').[47]

A key difference in studying subcultures as opposed to minority cultures is that the former are defined in opposition to both the 'dominant' culture and to their parents' culture. Clarke et al. define this 'double articulation' of youth subcultures in terms of class, arguing that sub-cultural members' lives are determined by a shared class position, but that they also 'project a different cultural response or "solution" to the problems posed to them by their material and social class' through their subcultural styles and activities.[48] Though I posit ethnicity and colonial legacies (rather than class) as the predominant defining characteristics of experiences of Britishness today, parallels with the 'determining matrixes' of class are apparent. Like the working-class youth that Clarke and company take as their subjects of scrutiny, the characters that populate the novels discussed subsequently also confront many of the same social problems as their parents (racism, alienation and disenfran-chisement), yet simultaneously define themselves against their parents in a way that is more collective and structured than individual teenage rebellion.

Subcultural affiliation treads the line between social exclusion and a self-imposed choice to distance oneself from society. Unlike parents in the novels by Malkani and Karline Smith, who frequently advocate cooperation and compromise across lines of religion and ethnicity despite experiences of racism, younger characters repeatedly reject such advances as the actions of 'coconuts' (brown on the outside, white on the inside). They prefer to adopt stances of hostility and self-elected removal from society that nevertheless index social alienation as a defining condition. Sarah Thornton summarises such a tension as fol-lows: 'Subcultures, in other words, are condemned to and/or enjoy a consciousness of "otherness" or difference.'[49] This construction also illustrates the *potentially* liberating aspect of subcultural affiliation for those who may have had the labels of 'otherness' or difference thrust upon them (due to ethnic or class allegiances that mark a deviation from the 'norm'). Subcultural affiliation means that these labels can be transformed into a self-imposed choice or oppositional stance, recasting subcultural members as agents rather than victims.

The representation of subcultural identities often hinges upon the two activities outlined in the introduction to this chapter as synony-mous with constructions of urban spaces: sex and shopping. To take the latter term first, the very title of Dick Hebdige's influential work on British subculture – *Subculture: The Meaning of Style* (1979) – suggests the crucial function of clothing in the construction of subcultural identity. For Hebdige, patterns of consumption are crucial to the construction and display of subcultural identity, as he argues that 'it is through the distinctive rituals of consumption, through style, that the subculture at once reveals its "secret" identity and communicates its forbidden meanings'. He concludes that it 'is basically the way in which commodities are *used* in subculture which mark the subculture off from more orthodox cultural formations' (emphasis in original).[50] This logic implies that subcultural consumption is deviant consumption, using products in unconventional or unintended ways. Objects are fetishised (ascribed excessive value) in subcultural circles, which shifts and modifies the way in which capital is conceived. For Hebdige, this deviance is embodied in the self-reification of subcultural members, as by 'Converting themselves into objects, those youths immersed in style and the culture of consumption seek to impose systematic control over the narrow domain which is "theirs" [...]. The posture is auto-erotic: the self becomes the fetish'.[51]

Another way of thinking through the relationship between subculture and consumerism is to consider 'subcultural capital', a phrase that describes non-economic value in monetary terms. The majority of subcultures considered in Gelder and Thornton's *Reader* are from working-class backgrounds, and for Thornton, 'Subcultural capital is the linchpin of an alternative hierarchy in which the axes of age, gender, sexuality and race are all employed in order to keep the determinations of class, income and occupation at bay.' She highlights the inherent paradox of the term 'subcultural capital', which 'reveals itself most clearly by what it emphatically isn't'.[52] However, the subcultural groups to be found in the literature analysed here are from moneyed backgrounds, as oppositionality itself is commoditised. The conspicuous consumption of luxury items begins to tally with subcultural capital, as the term returns to its economic roots.

Another defining feature of subcultural identities as represented in the novels considered here is their relationship with sex, and more often than not, sexism. In all of the novels that I subsequently analyse, the subcultural groups described are incredibly male-dominated and often overtly sexist. This is not an unusual charge to be levelled at subcultures, the accounts of which often orbit around young men. Angela McRobbie and Jenny Garber account for the apparent invisibility of girls' subcultures by suggesting that 'the very term "subculture" has acquired such strong masculine overtones'.[53] Malkani's and Karline Smith's novels are preoccupied with male gangs, with female characters playing only peripheral roles as wives, girlfriends or mothers without any comparable female grouping. However, the novels are internally critical of the homosocial relationships created within the gangs, as the peripheral female characters stand for alternative (af)filiations (familial, romantic) that are detrimentally impacted by the privileged subcultural alliances between the young men. The male and often misogynist perspective voiced in the texts regularly conflates erotic and consumerist desires as women are objectified, consumed and discarded, while products are described in sexualised language.

'I'm gonna make your heart and your profits rise': subculture and parody in Karline Smith's Moss Side novels[54]

Smith's *Moss Side Massive* is firmly situated in the gang culture of Manchester's most infamous neighbourhood. The scene is set as Fluxy – leader of the Piper Mill Posse – is shot dead by an unseen assassin, which serves as the trigger for the subsequent rise in gang warfare between his old posse and the rival Grange Close Crew, who they believe to be responsible for Fluxy's murder. Taking control of the Piper Mill Posse, Fluxy's brother Jigsy vows revenge-at-any-cost and the remainder of the novel traces the downward spiral of attack and counter-attack, while the wives, girlfriends and mothers of the men involved can do nothing but watch on as their loved ones pursue this nihilistic course of action. The final showdown sees a car full of Piper Mill members and associates shot off the road, with only Easy-Love Brown emerging from the wreckage. Piper Mill's own Easy-Love turns out to have been the puppeteer pulling the strings that dictated the gang warfare, having ordered the hit on Fluxy so as to stir up rival antagonisms, with the ultimate aim of claiming leadership of the group for himself. Although the police cannot accrue enough evidence to convict Easy-Love of murder, he is arrested for taking policemen hostage.

Full Crew takes up the narrative four years later at the early prison-release of Easy-Love. Back on the streets he used to rule, he is promptly beaten within an inch of his life and returned to hospital. Faced with the demise of his old crew, he realises that he will quickly have to organise himself a new one for protection against the gangs that have evolved in his absence. But it is a tough network that he must negotiate, requiring new allegiances and carefully chosen loyalties. Teenager Danny Ranks, ruthless, violent, and a strong believer in retribution whether the offence is accidental or intentional, heads up the new Worlders Crew and sets out to destroy Easy from the moment of his release, determined not to lose his place at the top as the ex-con returns. Danny's main rival is Yardie Godmother Miss Small, who heads up the Dodge Crew. Her devoted gang of men provide her with protection and wealth, and in return become a kind of extended family, living, cooking and sharing together. But readers should not be tricked by the family dynamic of the gangs; in this money and status-driven world, the business-like and corporate enterprises entered into mark a dog-eat-dog world where loyalty, trust and filial bonds are employed as bargaining tools in ruthless yet fragile hierarchies.

These novels map a Manchester (or 'Gunchester' in Smith's own terminology, 260) that is intensely local, moving the reader through familiar sites and streets, but they also push out towards wider affiliations as Jamaican gangs and IRA members weave through the subplots. While gang warfare is not carried out across ethnic lines, the novel makes it explicit that the gang culture has historical roots, drives and explanations in the disenfranchisement and attendant alienation of migrant groups, as the black DI Edwards recognises the historical legacy of a city that still has only four black students in its best school and whose residents view him as a traitor for choosing a job in the police force and becoming a 'beast bwai'.

Moss Side Massive comes equipped with its own detailed subcultural geography and history; DI Edwards recalls his father telling him about the early stages of Commonwealth immigration in the 1950s and 60s, at which point young immigrants formed gangs to defend themselves from the 'teds and rockers [who] spent their time threatening their new black neighbours. [...] When the teds and rockers faded out [...] the fighting became intra-racial', with rivalries forming between 'Africans, Jamaicans and "Smallies"'.[55] Continuing to outline the specific local geography of the areas affected by these gangs, Edwards concludes that although only 'rubble' remained of the old gangland hotspots, 'their legacy lived on amongst the sons of those first immigrants' (253). However, today's youth are distinguished from their parents in the novel by being more 'ruthless' and wanting more, 'much more' (253). What is significant about the subcultural geography described is that it situates the contemporary gangland scene in a very locally specific and historical way in terms that relate to other subcultures, without commenting on any mainstream or normative culture that the gangs might be responding to. This suggests that there are many modes of opposition to the mainstream, of which the gangster subculture that is the focus of the novels is just one.

Lynne Pearce discusses Karline Smith's novels under the generic conventions of crime fiction. For Pearce, the novels participate in the Manchester crime genre, in which writers show a keen awareness of the way that 'historical and institutional forces have materially shaped city-space and frequently highlight the link between present crime and the social and cultural violence done to the region in the past'.[56] Pearce is careful both to distinguish and to illustrate the interdependence between social realism (as a literary mode) and social reality, stating that Smith's characters occupy a space that is at once 'historical *and* hyperbolic, material *and* aesthetic'.[57] The novels lend themselves to the generic conventions of crime fiction, and as Lee Horsley argues of the genre, 'The investigative structure provides a ready-made instrument for unearthing the previously invisible crimes against a people.'[58] However, reading with this set of genre tools risks obscuring relationships between subcultural groups and between participants in each subculture. It is therefore vital to examine characters in the novels in terms of style, performative identity and modes of opposition, rather than criminality and deviance. The gangland scene that I focus on here offers a very different mode of resistance to the mainstream to other subcultural groups mentioned but not explored in detail during the novels, such as identification as a Rasta, which has a subcultural as well as a spiritual element, marked by its style and modes of consumption.

The gang scene described in Smith's novels is one of conspicuous consumption in which luxury items are an index of power and status. Brand names ('Moschino, Armani, Klein, Versace, Rockport, Nike' (*FC* 249)) litter the text, and work as signifiers of wealth and power for their owners. This pursuit of luxury and excess as a stylistic marker of subculture might be dismissed as a simple case of greed on the part of the gangsters, but the social backdrop of the novels is one in which the characters are taught to prize monetary wealth, yet are excluded from the means of attaining such wealth legally, so consumption develops a performative and oppositional aspect in relation to mainstream modes of consumption. The case of three brothers in the novels is illustrative of this plight, as there seems to be no middle ground between poverty and wealth attained through gang affiliation and drug peddling. The eldest brother, Storm, gets involved in 'a little hustling', which escalates uncontrollably, for the simple reason that 'being broke was embarrassing' (*MSM* 218). Blue, described as a 'smart kid [who] had done well at school', is nevertheless 'bombarded with reminders of the materialistic world that didn't form part of his existence' and also begins to sell drugs as a child in order to attain the only marker of status that is meaningful amongst his peers (*MSM* 9–10). Zukie is the only one of the brothers who refuses to get involved with the gang scene, identifying instead with the spirituality and music of Rastafarianism, but he is faced with the serious problem of unemployment in the area, especially among blacks. Arriving at the Job Centre, Zukie finds that the only job that does not require previous experience – a job as a handyman paying a mere £120 per week – has already been filled, two hundred applications having been received. Zukie succeeds in remaining outside of the gang circles until he is reluctantly drawn in through association with his brother, but his story illustrates that there is very little (legal) opportunity to 'mek it in this white man's world' (*MSM* 38). I follow Horsley's assessment, that 'Yardie [West Indian] fiction [...] implicitly demands a re-assessment of the postcolonial economic and cultural circumstances that made the Yardie underworld possible [...]. Yardie fiction exposes the economic *need* that underlines the apparent *greed* of the gangland members.'[59]

This paints a very different picture to the image of cosmopolitan London evoked in novels like *The Buddha of Suburbia* in which ethnic products are consumed to lend a touch of the exotic. It renders increasingly apparent the need for a devolved approach to literary studies, as advocated by critics such as Pearce, Fowler and Crawshaw in their *Postcolonial Manchester: Diaspora Space and the Devolution of Literary Culture* (2013), as the representation of black identities, aesthetics, experiences and social mobility from novels written just four years apart is so markedly divergent. To privilege certain experiences of blackness through selective publication (normally those that are cosmopolitan, London-centric and paint a happy picture of multicultural Britain) serves implicitly to create a homogenous norm and repeat acts of exclusion already committed in the socio-economic arena.

The subtitle of this section brings together subcultural performance and parody, two elements that I use in order to conceptualise the way that the gangs are structured in the novels. Gangs function in a way that explicitly mimics legitimate businesses and companies. The following scene shows Miss Small allocating positions in her crew:

Michigan and Ranger are still in Sales and Debt Recovery. Hatchet and Slide are Security. Trench, I want you to be the crew's main Security Consultant and Easy I waan you to be Co-Director with myself as Company Director until I decide to evaluate certain positions in de near future. (*FC* 98)

The formal terminology and strict hierarchy that the gang adheres to parallels companies on the right side of the law and in so doing forces a comparison with these companies. Each member of the crew is effective in their allocated role, displaying skills that would be enviable in a different setting. In a similar instance, Storm's mother is proud of her son's success as a salesman, oblivious to the fact that his products are drugs. Discussing common conceptions of subcultures, Gelder states that 'their relation to labour might be understood as parasitical, or as a kind of alternative "mirror-image" to legitimate work practices (so that one might even speak, in a certain sense, of a subcultural "career")'.[60] Yet the fact that the labour practices might be considered as the illegal reverse of 'legitimate work practices' raises the question of why the subcultures have, as such, been forced underground: it is hard to see where a self-imposed choice to remove from society ends and social alienation begins in this scenario.

Opposition to the mainstream is indexed not just through criminality, but through musical preference in Smith's novels. The musical preference of those identifying with the gangs is distinguished both against 'mainstream' musical consumption and against that of Rastas: 'Vegas wasn't a reggae super star whose lyrics ostracized gangs or violence. His lyrics were born strictly out of the dog-eat-dog world, ghetto-heart streets of Kingston Jamaica. To poor afflicted yout' he was a super-cult hero' (*FC* 169). Gelder defines gansta rap music as occupying a '"post-protest" position' that nevertheless helps to demonstrate that 'racial discrimination remains a fact of [...] daily life'.[61] Unlike *The Buddha of Suburbia*, in which minority identities are performed for the eager (if patronising) consumption of a white audience, the consumption of dissenting music that documents a history of racism paints postcolonial Britain in a rather different light. For characters in Karline Smith's novels, being black – associated in the novels with hypermasculinity and deviance – is a badge of honour and a source of subcultural capital, with each character introduced along with a reference to the precise shade of their skin colour. To be black and not to conform to this subcultural type (privileging hypermasculinity, street credibility and West Indian inflected argot) is to be held as a traitor, as implied when the novels' black detective is told to pronounce something 'like a true-born nigga instead of some wanna be middle-class white man' (*FC* 236).

In Karline Smith's novels sex, like consumerism, is also portrayed as providing a mode of resistance to – rather than collaboration with – mainstream culture. If the romance plots in Hanif Kureishi's and Zadie Smith's novels are concerned with the doubling of desire at personal and political levels as versions of national romance, Karline Smith's novels might be read as a critique of the desire for power that expresses itself in the domination of women.[62] Women occupy peripheral roles in the novels, excluded from the homosocial bonds that unite the gang members; they are frequently referred to as 'bitches' and 'hos', and a man's ability to 'manners his woman' stands as a marker of pride (*MSM* 267). Easy-Love Brown is the series' worst manipulator of women, seducing two women simultaneously but to different ends. The quotation that stands as the subtitle for this section is taken from Easy's seduction of Vaniesha (the notorious Miss Small), whose gang he subsequently plans to usurp. His promise to make her 'heart and [...] profits rise' shamelessly conflates sexual and materialistic desire in a way that cheapens any illusion of romance that might otherwise have been claimed, cheesy lines aside (68). Sex, for Easy, is just another means of manipulation or asserting his authority. His other girlfriend – an Irish woman with IRA links who goes by the name of Chris – is equally seduced by Easy's money and she consents to have sex with him in a bed covered in paper bills. The crass and uncomfortable equation of sexual and material desire (another classic line includes Easy's request that Chris join him to 'make a baby in our money bed' (*FC* 116)) foregrounds the problematic paralleling of these desires perhaps better hidden in more sanguine romance plots.

Moss Side Massive and *Full Crew* might initially seem like straightforward subcultural novels, written and marketed for subcultural consumption and for an implicitly male audience. However, even if this is the case, the novels internally critique the subculture, largely through their casts of female characters, who represent the world of filiative relationships that the men sacrifice for their affiliative subcultural ones. The first few sections of *Moss Side Massive* are focalised through members of the Piper Mill Posse following their leader's assassination, meaning that from the outset, readers are encouraged to identify with the gang. But the subsequent introduction of female voices (those of partners and mothers), of policemen, and of men from the rival gang, serve to challenge this identification and critique the subculture internally. Characters are called by different names according to which group they are operating within at the time (Storm is called Clifton by his family at home). This is a means of defamiliarisation that illustrates the characters' multiple and often conflicting responsibilities, and it indicates the men's complete departure from familial or relational ties when operating within the gang.

In conclusion, Smith paints an alternative view of postcolonial Britain by locating her characters amidst the poverty and social alienation of Moss Side, Manchester. By taking as her muse a subculture that values conspicuous consumption and hyper-masculine assertions of power, Smith is able to provoke a consideration of the social situation that has provided a fertile breeding ground for gang culture. Though she depicts her characters as products of circumstance, Smith does not entirely excuse them. The novels' dialogism and multiple points of focalisation function to offer explanations for the subculture's stance, whilst also internally critiquing it through the string of broken families that the men leave in their wake. Smith's novels engage a side of multicultural Britain that is not marketable to a mainstream audience and that completely resists the tendency to exoticise minority identities for profit. Instead, Smith's imagined audience is of subcultural insiders to whom she presents both the allure of and the problems entailed by this mode of identification as gangster.

Failing the authenticity test: subculture and performativity in Gautam Malkani's *Londonstani*

Where Karline Smith's novels foreground the socio-economic backdrop of poverty that drives her characters to identify in opposition to a mainstream culture that excludes them, Gautam Malkani's *Londonstani* has a very different social backdrop, in which opposition to the mainstream is far more an active and performative choice than one dictated by social circumstance. This section details the altar of conspicuous consumption at which the characters worship, before moving on to the unusual marketing of the novel and the authenticity test at which the author claims repeatedly to have failed. In so doing, it will become clear that the novel raises questions concerning the imagined audience(s) of postcolonial British novels and considers how far readers are prepared to accept the performativity of identity.

The novel centres on a group of young men who self-identify as 'desis', using a modernisation of the Sanskrit word for 'countryman' to mean 'homeboy', and to identify a group that has previously been labelled, as the novel itself puts it, 'rudeboys, [...] Indian niggas, then rajamuffins, then raggastanis, Britasians, fuckin Indobrits'.[63] Protagonist Jas is a 19-year-old from Hounslow who is retaking his A-Levels along with his desi friends. In order to make money and purchase the luxury items worshipped by their subculture, the boys have a business unlocking mobile phones, which – tax evasion aside – is just about above board until they break one of the phones they have been given and are forced to steal a new one. They steal the phone from their teacher Mr Ashwood, who finds out and tries to set them on a better path by introducing them to his model ex-student, Sanjay, in order to give the boys something to aspire to and work for. However, Sanjay quickly decides to turn the boys into assets for his own illegal business and they begin to make more money by selling on their unlocked (and presumably stolen) mobile phones. Besides the unconventional business mentoring that the boys receive from Sanjay, Jas himself is secretly mentored by him in the ways of seduction, in order that he might try his chances with the beautiful, but Muslim, Samira. To date a Muslim girl, Jas realises, is a crime for which his friends would definitely disown and possibly kill him. A downward spiral of events, in which Jas loses his friends, his money, his girlfriend, and his Dad's business, leaves him lying in a hospital bed at the end of the novel. It is only then that readers learn what Jas is short for: not Jaswinder, like his friend, but Jason, or more precisely 'Jason Bartholomew-Cliveden: aged nineteen, white, male' (340). The novel's deliberate red herring forces a retrospective reading of the subculture as one based on the performance of identity, despite its apparent affiliation to an ethnic group.

Like the gangs of Karline Smith's novels, the desi boys in *Londonstani* style themselves in the most expensive of designer clothing and drive the fastest, newest, flashiest cars; as Sanjay reminds them, 'Conspicuous consumption, luxury brands, immediate gratification and nice things are much too important to you, that much at least you guys have already decided' (167). Yet this is where the similarity with Smith's gangs ends: the desi boys of *Londonstani* are from middle-class backgrounds with two-parent families and a much wider array of life choices. Their decision to adopt a 'street' argot and an illegal livelihood is a freely made choice to reject the mainstream, not one that is engendered by a background of poverty and associated social alienation. The stylistic choices that the boys make to surround themselves in the most luxurious of items are self-consciously articulated as an economic ideology by their mentor, Sanjay: 'there's no Marxist alternative any more. The fall of communism, the rise of bling' (168). Employing quasi-religious terminology, Sanjay explains to Jas and his friends that 'You will forever be judged and judge yourselves by your luxury consumerist aspirations, your nice stuff' (167–8).

The ideological/religious nature of Sanjay's explanations amasses extra significance if we consider that the boys' parents' culture is defined along religious lines, all (with the exception of Jas) coming from Hindu or Sikh backgrounds. Their parents' generation is shown to discriminate according to ethnicity or religion, with Ravi's Mum telling him 'she'd die if he ever went out with a BMW (by which she meant black, Muslim or white)' (335). The desi boys adopt the prejudices of their parents, but are shown to have little care for religious practices unless they concern the machismo of family honour or can be incorporated into their clothing style. We are told that 'Hardjit always wore a Karha round his wrist an something orange to show he was a Sikh' (9), for example, and they all wear rakhis until Diwali to show how many girls they are bound to protect (175). The incorporation of religious symbols into desi clothing illustrates the shared culture with their parents, but with material goods replacing religious gods as the key marker of identity, a subcultural turn is evident. In an interview, Malkani states that 'Hardjit might pretend that he's sourcing his identity from his ethnic roots or whatever, but he's not. He's sourcing it from Hollywood, Bollywood, MTV Base and ads for designer fashion brands'.[64] It is this issue of 'pretence' and the loaded language of (in)authenticity that, as demonstrated below, is central to an understanding of the novel as a whole.

As this tendency towards re-appropriation implies, this urban subculture has quite a different relation to the mainstream than many of the subcultures that have previously received critical attention (punks, mods, rockers, hippies and skaters, for example), because it has such a consumerist pull as to tend towards the mainstream itself. In Hebdige's assessment of subcultural style, he suggests that mainstream consumption signals the collapse of a subculture, citing *Cosmopolitan*'s embrace of punk style in its pages as 'presag[ing] the subculture's imminent demise'.[65] Yet Sanjay, the novel's spokesperson for the ideology of urban youth culture, argues that although 'more and more people subscribe' to the subculture (170), 'This isn't about society becoming more affluent, this is about a subculture that worships affluence becoming mainstream culture' (171). According to Sanjay (and perhaps it is worth bearing in mind in this context that Gautam Malkani is also a journalist for the *Financial Times*), this should change the way that the economy itself functions, as this subculture 'operate[s] at a much higher level of inflation' (171). What is significant is that the wealth required to support this lifestyle cannot be attained through legal means by the boys. This implies the increasingly criminal means required to support an unsustainable level of spending. Malkani's economic mapping of the subculture that is tending towards the mainstream might, therefore, be read as a wider and more disturbing social forecast and critique, and indeed we are already seeing the increasingly criminal economics of the country's wealthiest politicians and business leaders in the repeated revelations of tax evasions and expenses scandals.

Alongside its luxury-branded stylisation, this urban subculture is also characterised by interplay between ideas of ethnic authenticity and the performance of a subcultural identity. Like the gangsters of Karline Smith's novels, the urban desis identify against 'coconuts,' who are portrayed as complicit with white, middle-class values. Pulling up alongside an Asian man's car, they cruelly observe:

> You could tell from his long hair, grungy clothes, the poncey novel an [sic] newspaper on his dashboard an Coldplay album playin in his car that he was a muthafuckin coconut. So white he was inside his brown skin, he probably talked like those gorafied desis who read the news on TV. (20–1)

His choice not to live the same lavish lifestyle as the urban desis causes them to write him off as 'some gora-lovin, dirty hippie' (22). Whiteness, or 'gorafication' is frequently used as an insult in the novel. However, the line between whites and Asians, goras and desis, is not as clear-cut as readers might initially surmise, as illustrated by Jas's desi pretence/ performance throughout the novel.

Londonstani's structure is designed to trick readers into believing that, like his friends, Jas is also from an Indian background. The 'we' of the novel appears to be drawn along ethnic lines, explicitly so at points. Hardjit, in the process of beating someone up, turns to Amit, Ravi and Jas for confirmation of his threats, shouting 'Call me or any a ma bred-rens a Paki again an I'ma mash u an yo family. In't dat da truth, Pakis?' (3). Their uniform response – 'Dat's right [...] dat be da truth' (3) – serves to align Jas with Amit and Ravi. None of the boys are actually from Pakistani backgrounds, illustrating both the conflation of Indians and Pakistanis in racist abuse and the desire of the boys to appropriate or perform a subordinated status. Jas's refusal to reveal his surname is also put down to it being 'one a them extra long surnames that nobody'd ever pronounce proply', citing a problem more typically associated with South Asian names (24). Even his girlfriend, Samira, describes him as 'just another straight-off-the-boat possessive desi guy', equating his (increasingly misogynist) attitude with those of a first-generation migrant (294). Malkani disperses red herrings like this throughout the novel in order to fuel assumptions that Jas shares his friends' Indian 'roots' (a word that I use here in the loosest of senses).

Initially marketed for consumers of Zadie Smith's *White Teeth* and Monica Ali's *Brick Lane*, *Londonstani* quickly fell under the critical radar when it became apparent that the novel was not courting favour with the traditional market for multicultural fiction. In an article questioning if the British novel has lost its way, Robert McCrum cites the book's mis-marketing as the reason for its lack of commercial success, arguing that 'if it had been published, as its author once intended, as a teen novel, it might have found a secure place as a contemporary classroom classic'.[66] However, following a £300,000 cash advance from Fourth Estate, 'the die was cast' and 'Like a Fiat Uno entered for Formula 1, after a squeal of brakes and a loud bang, *Londonstani* was reduced to a stain of grease, and some scraps of rubber and tin, on the race track of the 2006 spring publishing season.'[67] An examination of the various covers in which the novel has been packaged give an idea of the way that the projected market has evolved. The hardcover versions offer a choice of a pink tiger on a pale patterned backdrop, which serves to exoticise the novel, or of a tube sign, reinforcing its status as a London text; the paperback options add two further covers, one showing a hooded boy on a backdrop of grey paving slabs with a union jack flag in the corner, painting a rather more dismal image of Britishness, and the other capturing an image of a desi rudeboy on a backdrop of yellow with garish pink font and a London skyline shadowing the title. It is the latter cover – most conspicuously marketed for an urban teen audience – that has been selected for subsequent paperback reprints and the Kindle edition of the novel. McCrum's rather patronising assessment of the novel seems to imply that its status as teen fiction only suits it for the classroom, or more problematically, that teen fiction more generally is only suited for the classroom. But this is clearly not the case, and Malkani's novel deserves critical attention for its alternative perspective on urban culture in multicultural Britain and for the important questions that it raises regarding identity and authenticity.

In an article on the market for London's multicultural fictions, James Graham puts the unfavourable early reception of the novel down to the fact that, unlike the earlier 'multicultural fictions,' it refused convincingly to make 'knowable' the communities that it represented.[68] 'This is because', Graham argues, '*Londonstani* self-consciously mimics the way subculture is *performed*, rather than representing the way religious, racial or ethnically defined communities live'.[69] However, the novel's playful performativity of identity is a common feature of novels representing multicultural Britain, and should not therefore be seen as mapping out a new direction in the oeuvre. As illustrated previously, *The Buddha of Suburbia* abounds with themes of performativity and staging precisely in order to show the 'lie' of authenticity. Creating a binary, as Graham does, between performing and being resurrects the very barrier that Malkani's fiction works to dismantle.

Graham's dubious reading of earlier multicultural fiction aside, *Londonstani* undoubtedly grapples with authenticity in a way that has not been palatable to some audiences. My conviction is that the novel itself establishes an imagined or implied audience that is different from that of the 'minority' novels discussed in the first half of this chapter. Returning to Huggan, we might recall that he describes the identity performance as witnessed in novels such as *The Buddha of Suburbia* and *The Satanic Verses* as 'staged marginality', which is the 'process by which marginalised individuals or social groups are moved to dramatise their "subordinate" status for the benefit of a majority or mainstream audience'.[70] The difference with Malkani's novel to Huggan's formulation, I would therefore argue, is that although it similarly revels in performative identities and a (sub)culture defined by what it consumes, the imagined audience implied by the text (if not by the original paratext) consists of subcultural insiders, *not* the 'majority' audience suggested by the texts that Huggan examines.

I coin the term 'imagined audience' as a critical framework for considering to whom the novels appear to be talking. Taking *The Buddha of Suburbia* as a case in point, Kureishi's novel appears to be addressing a white, mainstream audience; if it were not, his critique of white middle-class 'exotic' consumerism would be pointless, and it would be unnecessary repeatedly to represent the diegetic audiences as predominantly white. Similarly, the hype surrounding the publication of Zadie Smith's debut novel launched her into the mainstream. By contrast, *Londonstani* is a text that seems to speak to itself. Our narrator, Jas, slips between first and second-person narration and in so doing, generalises his own situation, assumes the audience's similar experiences, and creates a conversational relationship. Jas frequently slips out of the first-person 'I' and begins to extrapolate more generally: 'In the end you ignored everyone. The whole fuckin lot. The problem for you was that the situation with Samira was different' (145). Sometimes Jas also talks to himself explicitly in moments of self-loathing, where different factions of his personality go to war, leaving him stammering and helpless in front of his friends. The only audience that Jas cares about is his friends, who – despite Jas's devotion to 'MTV Base an Juggy D videos' – seem to possess a superior level of 'rudeboy authenticity' (6).

However, authenticity is not something that Jas is alone in lacking. By situating a number of the scenes in various parents' houses, Malkani is able to illustrate that the boys *all* behave differently at home to on the streets or with friends, replacing their 'desi rudeboy' postures with polite and respectful exchanges with parents and aunties. Malkani himself has been plagued by assumptions surrounding authenticity with regards to his British Asian identity. He is justifiably annoyed at the 'authenticity hurdle that reviewers have required [him] to jump', which 'implies that there's a single authentic British Asian experience and that authentic experience can't be shared by someone who went to Cambridge and works for the FT'. He states that 'The whole point of the book was to look at the construction and performance of inauthentic identities among young people today regardless of race.'[71] The presence of the novel's deliberate red herring (in the form of the white narrator) in part contradicts Malkani's own assertions, as race is deliberately foregrounded as an important feature in the performance of identity by being hidden until the end. However, Jas's performance provides the key for understanding the inherently performative nature of all of the characters that populate the novel.

Although I have argued that the novel speaks to itself, this is not to say that it fails to exercise any criticism of the behaviour it depicts. It is ultimately the boys' greed and desire for luxury that proves to be their fatal flaw, leading to their involvement in Sanjay's scam, a scam that results in Jas being attacked by three unidentified thugs as he attempts to set fire to his father's business in order to cover up the robbery that he has just committed. Malkani also highlights the misogyny present in the desis' treatment of women. Although Jas starts promisingly – defending Samira's honour as his friends accuse her of sluttishness – he assumes an increasingly misogynist perspective as the novel progresses. Following Sanjay's formula for 'Cross-Cultural Chirpsin' (or chatting up a Muslim girl) to the letter, Jas demonstrates an increasing tendency to treat Samira like an object to be controlled and possessed, to the extent that he begins to utter the same crass misogyny for which he had earlier berated his friends. The novel is not afraid to engage with the problematic side of multicultural Britain, addressing issues of greed and misogyny head-on.

It follows that though *Londonstani* talks to itself – and by that I mean to subcultural insiders, not to an imagined white and/or mainstream audience – it is nevertheless self-critical. Malkani's novel both celebrates a subcultural world in which all identities are performative *and* critiques problems of misogyny and greed that have been levelled at desi rudeboys. It has not, to date, received the critical attention that it deserves, because it has been crucially misunderstood in relation to its multicultural predecessors and presents a vision of multicultural Britain that has a problematic relationship with money and hypermasculinity, making it unpalatable to the market at which it was initially directed.

'I'm just a fucking tourist ... I just look at the view': post-subcultural identity and the order of money in Nirpal Singh Dhaliwal's *Tourism*[72]

The final novel to which I turn in this chapter could be considered post-subcultural: whilst subculture has been called 'a response to the individualisation and alienation of modern life', post-subcultural commentary holds that 'individualisation is modern life's logical and desirable conclusion'.[73] Bhupinder ('Puppy') Singh Johal, the narrator of Nirpal Singh Dhaliwal's *Tourism*, is a perennial outsider. Barely recognising social ties or responsibilities, he adopts the detached gaze of the perpetual tourist, which is removed at once from 'mainstream' values and from relations to work and consumerism, yet also fails to acknowledge subcultural ties with other outsiders. Puppy has left his Southall childhood home to mix with London's multicultural elite, and shamelessly seduces rich-girl Sophie in order to live off her wealth and get closer to Sarupa, fiancée of Sophie's cousin. The narrative takes us through a host of graphically detailed sexual encounters, climaxing at Puppy's eventual seduction of Sarupa. Yet this does not signal a romantic resolution to the novel, as Sarupa (though pregnant with Puppy's child) soon goes back to her fiancé and leaves Puppy to indulge in a downward spiral of unhealthy eating, smoking marijuana and watching daytime television. Puppy finally gets his break by stealing £20,000 from his only close friend and escaping to Europe in order to shed any remaining ties and to indulge his touristic predilection more seriously.

Although this novel has a different relationship with subculture, it provides an interesting counterpoint to the literature discussed previously in terms of its engagement with sex and capitalism as the main factors driving the novel's ideology (or collapse of ideology). Similar to the novels discussed in the first half of the chapter whose narrative motors came from romantic relationships linking different ethnic groups, *Tourism* represents a number of interethnic relationships; however, these relationships are viewed from a cynical distance as comical stereotypes of desire, resounding with political incorrectness and louche irreverence. The novel is littered with soundbites on the narrator's opinion of the 'miscegenist heaven' that is London: 'white women clung to well-wrought ethnic studs who pushed tricycle pushchairs laden with fat brown babies; demure young white men guided Asian girlfriends through stalls selling hookahs, avant-garde sneakers and sun-dried tomatoes'; 'in his grab for wealth, Whitey created the body his women want to fuck the most'; 'white chicks love dark cock [...]. Even Princess Diana was crazy for it', and so on (52, 62, 160).

Yet a novel so immersed in sex in all of its lurid detail is profoundly unerotic, as Puppy describes the various sexual acts in clinical detail and in so doing removes any illusion of emotional attachment or desire. Recounting his experience with a prostitute (Luca), Puppy recalls: 'She closed her eyes and slid a firm grip up and down my erection, winding her hips while I fingered her' (15). This scene – reminiscent of a Mills and Boon novel by virtue of its explicit erotic language – is deflated by the remarkably anti-climactic addendum: 'This continued for some time' (15). His longer-term relationships hardly fare better, as a series of bathetic plunges from the artificial heights of soft-core prose deny sexual climax. Descriptions of sex are brief and mechanical, ending with distraction or disinterest:

> My prick stiffened. I held her buttocks; I gripped one and she moaned, moving her head back and forth, sucking my tongue. I fingered her arsehole; she liked it and pushed her hips back, easing it in further. I dug my finger in deep, pulled her close and sucked her mouth hard. I thought about fucking her again, but saw no reason to spoil her. I drew my face away and nodded to the bowls of coffee, the two slices of toast lying on the work top. 'I've made breakfast.' (49)

Scenes such as the above serve to highlight the emotional detachment of the narrator, placing him as a voyeur rather than an agent in the world that he inhabits.

Puppy's emotional detachment confirms his overriding anti-ideology. As the subtitle states, Puppy considers himself a 'tourist', an answer that he gives in response to Sarupa's bemused questioning: 'So you're not a socialist, or an anarchist or anti-globalist, even though you think capitalism is mediocre and paranoid?' (85). His sense of alienation is not only self-imposed, however, as he argues that he would 'have to feel [...] relevant to the world in order to care about it' (85). The self-perception of his own irrelevance to the society contributes to his decision to remove himself from the logic of its workings. Puppy understands that money is the only thing that counts in the social milieu that he wants to occupy, and this is something that he unfortunately lacks.

Sarupa is the only woman with whom Puppy is emotionally involved, but she moves in social circles that Puppy cannot properly enter. Her dismissal of him in favour of her rich but uninteresting fiancé serves to highlight the novel's ideology: it is not romance that has the power to unite different social factions, but money. As Puppy observes, 'Money alchemises people, the mere suspicion of it changes *everything*' (52).

For people like himself and his black friend Michael, who are both financially excluded from London's elite circles, the only hope is 'Knowing
what white people want' and selling it to them, which is Michael's
philosophy for 'making it' in Britain (159). The only way that they
can subvert the hierarchy is to ridicule consumers with the products
that they 'sell'. Growing tired of an undistinguished career in journal-
ism, Michael decides to produce some artwork, for which he receives
lottery funding. His concept is a 'multi-screen video installation: called
Niggers, it involved images of everyday white people – plumbers, bank
clerks, taxi drivers – dancing the running-man to Vanilla Ice's 1990 hit
single "Ice Ice Baby"' (159). When questioned on the rationale behind
the piece, he answers 'I wrote about how this idea deals with the white
paradigm, and its appropriation of the black subject. [...] Fuck knows
[what it means]. Evie told me to write it. But they fell for it. Can you
fucking believe that?' (159). Selling crazy products to a hungry, white,
consuming public is a way of ridiculing a society built on the hierarchy
of who has the capacity to consume the most.

Romance fails as an alchemical agent for disparate social factions in
Tourism; however, Puppy uses sex as another way of reversing the ruthless capitalist hierarchy by placing himself as the consumer of white
bodies. Described as so much meat on a shelf in acts of disinterested
appraisal, white women are frequently subjected to Puppy's cruel gaze:
'The blonde [...] was sexy, but wasn't the prettiest girl around; her face
was wide, her teeth a little crooked. I didn't mind; I wouldn't have to
put in too much work' (221). This reverses a hierarchy that Felly Nkweto
Simmonds identifies in her article 'Love in Black and White', in which
she argues that in 'sexual relationship[s] between Black and white [...]
the white body is ascribed the status of consumer... of Black bodies', citing historical and contemporary examples in support of this.[74] This article was published nearly two decades ago, and I would hope that were
it written again today the prospects for interracial relationships would
not look so bleak. However, the article has contemporary relevance in
terms of its emphasis on the interconnected history of sexual and racial
politics, which necessitates the inclusion of the 'public/political' as well
as the 'private/personal' in the theorisation of 'interracial romances'.[75]
Rather than simple and generic misogyny, Puppy's denigration of
women is limited to those who are white, creating an alternate hierarchy in which capital is not supreme and in which those without it do
not have to pander to the consumerist desires of the white majority.
I do not valorise this viewpoint, but I would argue that it engages with

a problematic side of interethnic relationships in postcolonial Britain shied away from by more sanguine accounts.

This paints a rather bleak picture of contemporary postcolonial Britain, but in so doing it reveals and challenges the capitalist logic and blinkered devotion to the economy that increasingly defines British politics. Gelder's analysis of the post-subcultural trend illustrates that it is the perfect model for Dhaliwal's social critique: 'All that this post-subcultural picture of heterogeneity is left with here is a benign and docile expression of capitalism's primary ideological fantasy, the "individual's freedom of choice".'[76] Puppy stands as an outworking and (due to his cruel character traits) implicit critique of capitalist logic. Denied the freedom of choice granted by financial wealth, the narrator instead exercises his freedom of choice on the sexual market, expressly grateful that he 'didn't have to strive for wealth to avoid a life of substandard sexual partners' (139). In so doing he replaces a financial hierarchy with a sexual one and becomes a representative of the ruthless detachment of market forces.

This chapter has illustrated how the subcultural urban novel foregrounds the interrelated consumerist and sexual desires underlying social relations in contemporary Britain. The genre presents an uncomfortable picture of multiculturalism defined by conflict, economic struggle and gang culture that the biggest and most affluent publishers are not willing to endorse. By engaging with these novels it becomes possible to create a critical vocabulary for approaching these frequently maligned texts and to expose the politically motivated marketing prejudices that inform publishing choices, so as to ensure that the academy does not fall into the trap of replicating these acts of exclusion. This chapter has also mapped a change in the imagined audiences of postcolonial British fiction from mainstream majority to subcultural minority, by comparing the subcultural novel to more mainstream fiction that has posited romance rather than conflict as the ruling metaphor for social relationships. The novels discussed here, spanning two decades, illustrate a changing cultural and literary landscape with a shifting relationship between minority and mainstream, producer and consumer. Each novel considered here offers a challenge of its own as to the way that postcolonial Britain might be imagined, but shared concerns of performativity and audience, sex and sexism, fetishisation (of the Other, or of the Self), mainstream and minority (or subculture) unite these novels as workings out of the sexual and consumerist desires that lay behind interpersonal and intercultural relationships in contemporary Britain.

4
Multicultural British Comedy/The Comedy of Multicultural Britain

Comedy has been employed in the service of a number of masters, politically ranging from the reactionary and conservative – ridiculing cultural outsiders to preserve the status quo – to the radical and revisionary, challenging stereotypes and disrupting the status quo. Historically, constructions of Britishness have relied upon assumptions of inclusion and exclusion, superiority and inferiority and a series of hierarchies, which have been reinforced through complementary forms of comedy. Comedy has both a political role – mimicking, commenting on, or transparently embedded in hierarchical structures of power – and a psychological one, giving voice to taboo subjects and revealing socially repressed desires or fears.

This chapter focuses upon two waves of postcolonial British comedy in film, identifying ways in which they challenge or support the contemporaneous zeitgeist. A first generation of comedy pursues a happy, multicultural idyll through the use of gentle and inclusive comedy. Although this type of comedy allows for the subtle undermining of stereotypes, I argue that its utopian tendency relies on the repression of social challenges that would threaten its potential harmony. A second generation of comedy employs laughter as an alternative response to fear, centring on the socially ostracised figures of the suicide bomber and the gangster repressed by the previous generation's idealism. Postcolonial comedy seeks to challenge the residual stereotypes and hierarchies of the colonial era, but as the social dominant shifts according to government, international affairs and new modes of exclusion, the types of comedy and subject matter must also evolve in order to remain socially relevant. Outlined below are the critical frameworks that are pertinent to postcolonial comedy.

Superiority theory

Comedy's power to exclude, commonly understood as the 'superiority theory', is theorised by Thomas Hobbes, who states that 'Laughter is nothing else but a sudden glory arising from some sudden conception of some eminency in ourselves, by comparison with the infirmity of others'.[1] Hobbes's definition of comedy relies upon a hierarchy: we laugh at difference in those considered inferior, and for this to be effective there must be a clear distinction between (as Hobbes terms) 'others' and 'ourselves'. What is concerning about this type of comedy is the slippage between normativity and superiority: we might rephrase Hobbes's definition of comedy as equating difference with inferiority and therefore laughing at difference. The elision of superiority and normativity is made apparent in Northrop Frye's ethical analysis of satire, an aggressive comical technique that serves to ridicule individuals or social groups and is often employed in the service of social critique. Frye argues, 'Of course a moral norm is inherent in satire: satire presents something as grotesque: the grotesque is by definition a deviant from the norm: the norm makes the satire satiric.'[2]

In postcolonial terms, comedy employed in such a manner is clearly problematic, essentially laughing at difference, associating difference with inferiority and revolving around a set of hierarchised binary identifications. But what is of more interest are the particulars of the Others chosen and the 'threat' that they represent to the 'dominant group that constructs them'. As Susan Purdie reasons, 'there is no point in "othering" people who have no claim to the identity space you are trying to occupy'.[3] As such, comedy based on superiority inadvertently exposes the imagined power of the Othered group and reveals underlying social fears.

Purdie posits three positions adopted during a joking exchange that are crucial to understanding the mechanisms of comedy. These are the Teller, the Audience and the Butt, all of which can at times be embodied by one person.[4] Purdie defines the relationship between the three available positions: 'the "Butt" [...] is constituted by the joking exchange as excluded from the Teller-Audience relationship and, in being so, reciprocally confirms the collusion of these two positions as masterful jokers'. The Butt of the joke can also be the Teller, the Audience, or both when the joke is self-ironising. However, Purdie clarifies that when the Butt 'involves actual targets, joking constructs these as not fully members of the community of proper speakers, and this involves complex and often strong feelings towards them'.[5] According to Purdie's definition, comedy based upon a sense of superiority could be aggressive and hostile, but equally it could be self-ironising.

I return to self-ironising comedy in the 'Laughing through the tears' section, in which the Butts of the jokes are often also the ethnic minority Tellers, mocking themselves to create what Purdie describes as a resultant 'delicious intimacy' between Teller and Audience.[6] This 'gentle' comedy begins to open a gap between the normativity and superiority that threaten to overlap in racist and/or sexist comedy. Marie Gillespie indicates the community-building potential of jokes by suggesting that 'those who share a joke belong to a community, however temporary, of people alike enough in outlook and feeling to be joined in sharing a joke'.[7] This demonstrates why comedy is invaluable for redrawing boundaries of inclusion and exclusion involved in notions of Britishness. But no matter how momentarily unifying a joking exchange can be, we should not pretend that cultural self-mockery and the exploitation of stereotypes is unproblematic. Using features of one's identity drawn from ethnic difference or stereotype as the Butt of a joke is a problem of 'gentle' comedy that I return to in my critique of the first wave of comic films.

Incongruity theory

Comedy based on incongruity is used to undermine orthodoxies and upturn hierarchies. John Morreall sees comedy arising from incongruity as the result of living 'in an orderly world, where we have come to expect certain patterns among things, their properties, events, etc. We laugh when we experience something that doesn't fit into these patterns'.[8] Mikhail Bakhtin's theory of carnival highlights the political implications of this form of comedy. In *Rabelais and his World* (1965), Bakhtin states that 'carnival is the people's second life, organised on the basis of laughter'.[9] This 'second life' – comparable to the medieval Feast of Fools or modern-day Mardi Gras – is one of overturned hierarchies, celebration, and the suspension of rules and social conventions. Bakhtin understands carnival as celebrating 'temporary liberation from the prevailing truth and from the established order' and 'mark[ing] the suspension of all hierarchical rank, privileges, norms, and prohibitions'.[10] This suggests that the laughter provoked by carnival has a purpose, as boundaries between the sacred and profane are (temporarily) removed and institutions lose their power.

The political reasons for laughter induced in this manner are decidedly ironic: the existence of a 'second life' implies a 'first life' – of toil, hardship or enslavement – that the 'people' must be reconciled to (we might think of laughter as a kind of soma).[11] But although this suspension of social norms might be temporary, the psychological effects are more enduring, as once something has been degraded through laughter it somewhat loses its semblance of power. Comedy does not pave the way for any real political revolution and I would argue that the carnivalesque is rather more placatory than Bakhtin suggests. Yet as outlined above, it does have the capacity to change *conceptions* of power and hierarchical social norms, a distinction to which I return later.

I cannot analyse the films using the same understanding of carnivalesque incongruity as Bakhtin. For him, carnival laughter is inclusive: it 'expresses the point of view of the whole world' and 'he who is laughing also belongs to it'.[12] There is no outside to carnival laughter and, as such, everyone is implicated in the ridiculous world with its laughable hierarchies. Film audiences, however, are not necessarily implicated in the incongruities that take place on the screen, meaning that laughter can be potentially more hostile. This chapter therefore foregrounds where the viewer is being placed in relation to the spectacle on screen, so as to consider whether the laughter engendered is inclusive – laughing at a shared and ineffective political system or putative national ideal – or exclusive, laughing from a particular side of a constructed hierarchy.

Furthermore, it is important to note that incongruity is not always a cause for laughter. To clarify why this is the case it helps to consider comedy's traditional counterpart: tragedy. Andrew Stott defines the two genres via reference to the audience's required emotional attachment: 'If it is generically appropriate for tragedy to ask us to be sensible of human suffering, then comedy [...] allows us to stand back and look upon human misfortune from an emotional distance, sometimes even deriving great pleasure from it.'[13] This suggests that the potential for humour is a matter of perspective rather than an essential quality of events. In their introduction to *Cheeky Fictions: Laughter and the Postcolonial*, Susanne Reichl and Mark Stein suggest that one of the most pertinent examples of incongruity failing to equate to comedy is the case of postcolonialism itself, arguing that 'The relationship between the former coloniser and the former colonised is [...] an example of a fundamentally non-humorous disparity', being 'fundamentally inequitable'. They conclude that a range of postcolonial comic modes variously 'reflect a struggle for agency, an imbalance of power, and a need, a desire, for release'.[14] The 'release' that the critics refer to is presumably release from the legacies of the colonial period, although it may also refer to the cathartic release achieved through laughter, as I go on to consider in the next section.

Whilst I would argue that postcolonial comedy does indeed have the potential to encourage laughter at residual incongruities of the colonial period by mocking ridiculous stereotypes that bear little or no resemblance to reality, the postcolonial comedies considered in this chapter go further than this. They also question more recent fears and stereotypes that have arisen out of specific political 'events' such as 9/11 and 7/7, or out of classist anxieties about risks associated with deprived socio-economic groups. Constructions of otherness shift to reflect current concerns (of the suicide bomber or the gangster, for example) rather than being perennially embedded in former colonial ties. This attests to the adaptability of postcolonial texts and criticism for challenging neo-imperialism as well as its colonial counterpart.

Relief theory

The final and most relevant theory of comedy for the purposes of this study is constructed around its function as relief or release. Over a century ago, Sigmund Freud articulated his belief in joking as the momentary overcoming of inhibitions in *Jokes and their Relation to the Unconscious* (1905). The connections that Freud makes between the teller and the recipient of jokes are crucial, as the latter 'must be able as a matter of habit to erect in himself the same inhibition which the first person's joke has overcome, so that, as soon as he hears the joke, the readiness for this inhibition will compulsively or automatically awaken'. Drawn to its logical conclusion, this implies that in order for a joke to provoke laughter the audience must be familiar with the inhibitions that are being overcome, or the taboos that the joke gives voice to. An effective joke is, in Freud's terms, 'evidence of far-reaching psychical conformity'.[15] Similar to theories of comedy based on superiority or incongruity, relief theory also implies a relationship constructed between teller and audience through shared laughter at a joke.

However, Freud's analysis of the relationship between teller and audience has further implications when he goes on to consider the structure of irony, the essence of which lies in 'saying the opposite of what one intends to convey to the other person'. He goes on to emphasise that 'Irony can only be employed when the other person is prepared to hear the opposite, so that he [sic] cannot fail to feel an inclination to contradict.'[16] Therefore, when irony is employed a certain audience is assumed, and for the irony to function the audience must also have certain preconceptions about the teller of the joke. This joking paradigm is frequently deployed in postcolonial comedy: in the mouths of actors from ethnic minority backgrounds, stereotypes become absurd and audiences are forced to interpret performances drawing on cultural stereotypes as ironic. Yet this highlights why irony may have a problematic basis in postcolonial comedy as it has the potential too easily to conflate a worldview with a dress code/skin colour and thereby work to homogenise a particular religious or ethnic group.

The connection that Freud makes between joking and taboo is also significant as the implication is that comedy can speak volumes about what is socially or politically constructed as 'correct' and trace a shifting zeitgeist as it evolves to reflect a changing set of taboos. The recent rise in comedy that engages with the representation of British Muslims, for example, can thereby be read as evidence of a society grappling with the implications of extremist approaches to Islam whilst also being wary of allegations of Islamophobia.[17] Similarly, films such as Joe Cornish's *Attack the Block* that deal with hypermasculinity and gang culture index an unwillingness to openly discuss the alienation and socio-economic deprivation that represent the dark side of British multicultural reality. Suicide bombers and gangsters are taboo topics when it comes to an idealised vision of British multiculturalism that sits uncomfortably with multicultural realities; comedy has the power to expose these taboos and draw uncomfortable topics into the arena of debate. Addressing the problematic and ironic ways in which the term 'multiculturalism' has been employed, Alana Lentin and Gavan Titley state that 'In an era where the concept of race is taboo and the charge of racism diluted, contested and inverted, multiculturalism provides a discursive space for debating questions of race, culture, legitimacy and belonging.'[18] In addition to framing contemporary debate as one that is opportunistically presented as concerning 'multiculturalism' rather than race and racism, as do Lentin and Titley, I would add that comedy is the ideal arena for debating these questions, as taboo topics are foregrounded as a convention of the genre.

Unlike the national media, which largely conforms to culturally accepted notions of political correctness, films discussed at the end of this chapter (*Four Lions* and *Attack the Block*) deploy offensive language, trade openly in stereotypes and encourage laughter at minority groups. This conversely serves to highlight the hypocrisy of the media by revealing what is obscured by politically correct language. Following a convincing discussion of comedy's 'double-edged' expression of both desire and derision, Virginia Richter argues that:

> The function of laughter cannot be subsumed exclusively either under the heading of transgression nor under the heading of social control: it serves to stabilise the hierarchy between different social groups – black/white, middle-class/poor, doctor/patient, university educated/uneducated, but it is also transgressive since it discloses the aggressive desires habitually glossed over by politically correct language.[19]

Her argument makes it apparent that whilst comedy can only ever reproduce hierarchies, however ironically, it does enable the revelation of the 'aggressive desires,' or fears, which are linguistically repressed. No matter how controversial the films might seem, they only expose stereotypes and prejudices that must already have currency in contemporary discourse in order for audiences to appreciate their irony.

Whilst Freud's notion of joking is flawed insomuch as it relies wholly upon a supposedly 'involuntary' nature that he likens to dreaming – thereby crucially failing to consider occasions when jokes are deliberately constructed – his groundwork on the social and psychological function of jokes remains relevant. The way that multicultural politics and its taboos are addressed in comedy and differently inflected according to socio-political zeitgeist and the dynamics of the 'psychic conformity' between teller and implied audience are particularly pertinent to this study.

Postcolonial comedy

Although all of the above theories of comedy can be related to postcolonial theory, Homi Bhabha goes further in explicitly conceptualising the ambivalent uses of comedy for colonial and postcolonial purposes. Bhabha highlights the importance that comedy has had for advancing and justifying the progress of colonialism, stating 'If colonialism takes power in the name of history, it repeatedly exercises its authority through the figures of farce.'[20] Yet he goes on to illustrate methods for comically undermining colonial authority, through both an engagement with stereotypes and via the subversive use of mimicry. Bhabha's theorisation of the stereotype regarding its relation to gothic and modes of Othering has been outlined in Chapter 2, but here I focus on the importance of engaging with stereotypes rather than simply dismissing them as false. For Bhabha, 'To judge the stereotyped image on the basis of a prior political normativity is to dismiss it, not to displace it, which is only possible by engaging with its *effectivity*.'[21] It is only through understanding the workings of stereotypes that they might be displaced or lose their power. An engagement with the effectivity of stereotypes is enabled in postcolonial comedy as the stereotypes are employed reflexively in order to provoke ironic laughter. A comical engagement with stereotypes also has the potential to unmask the lack on which Bhabha suggests that they are constructed, unveiling fears or anxieties that are simultaneously contained and revealed by the anxious repetition of the stereotype.[22]

Bhabha also discusses mimicry as an ultimately ineffective strategy that has nevertheless been employed to fix images of the Other in colonial discourse. The desire for colonised subjects to mimic their colonising counterparts stems from 'the desire for a reformed, recognizable Other, *as a subject of a difference that is almost the same, but not quite*' (emphasis in original). This means, for Bhabha, that 'the discourse of mimicry is constructed around an *ambivalence*; in order to be effective, mimicry must continually produce its slippage, its excess, its difference'.[23] As such, mimicry spills over into mockery, 'which in disclosing the ambivalence of colonial discourse also disrupts its authority'.[24] Mimicry belies the authenticity and authority assumed by colonial rule, as the (former) colonial centre sees its image distortedly reflected and thereby undermined.[25]

Yet there is a problem of agency in Bhabha's construction, as it suggests that the mimicking/mocking subject is the inevitable result of colonial discourse. Whilst this deftly exposes the inherently flawed means employed in the service of colonisation, it also colludes with colonial discourse by ignoring any agency on the part of the colonised subject. By contrast, the mockery and parody enacted in the films examined below is self-aware and often self-reflexive. Contemporary postcolonial comedy is able to hold British ideals up to a mirror and show them lacking, but asserts the agency of minority characters, rather than figuring them as passive outworkings of a postcolonial condition.

Laughing through the tears

This chapter focuses on films as opposed to novels for the purpose of considering postcolonial comedy, first and foremost because film is the most frequently consumed medium of enjoying it. Yet there are also stylistic motivations for prioritising a discussion of film. Stereotyping is largely involved in the *spectacle* of difference, as racial stereotypes are often attached to physical markers – what Frantz Fanon describes as being 'overdetermined from without' – making visual media a more appropriate forum.[26] Mimicry and mockery are similarly matters of performance, better suited to visual media. Finally, positionality and audience are important factors pertaining to an understanding of comedy, and directorial choices made in the production of film, such as camera angles, framing and perspective, are useful means of judging the way that audiences are being positioned.

In a letter to Gurinder Chadha, former prime minister Tony Blair proclaimed his love for the film *Bend It Like Beckham* (2002), 'because it represented his Britain, a very diverse, multicultural Britain'.[27] As such this film (and its enthusiastic mainstream reception) is emblematic of a Blairite political climate that ostentatiously claimed to celebrate multiculturalism. Alongside *Bend It Like Beckham*, this section will discuss *Bhaji on the Beach* (1993) and *East is East* (1999) as films that encourage what I have termed 'laughter through the tears'.[28] By this I refer to a type of emotive 'feel good' comedy that is based around inclusivity and purportedly universal ideals.

I understand multiculturalism, as does Anne-Marie Fortier, 'not so much [as] a policy and governing response to the "realities" of cultural and ethno-racial pluralism, as [...] an ideal aimed at the achievement of well-managed diversity'.[29] Fortier's assessment of the slippery nature of the term indicates the tensions embodied between the simple fact of cultural diversity and ways of approaching and/or managing this diversity, which leads to its interpretation as an ideal, or point of aspiration. It is this blurring of reality and ideal that renders it a problematic term, because when multiculturalism is understood as an ideal set of relationships in a diverse society then there is a burden to represent these relations in a positive light. What is more problematic is when the ideal is taken for the reality, as is exemplified in Blair's statement, cited above. By taking an ideal representation of multicultural Britain for a straightforward mirror on society, as Blair does, then it serves to exclude any people, cultures or events that could taint the utopian picture created. If multiculturalism is taken to mean the best possible managing of relations between a culturally diverse nation then those that might already suffer exclusion at the hands of racism, disenfranchisement and alienation are doubly excluded through a political ideal that cannot face up to social realities. It is for this reason that the turning point in this chapter hinges on interpretations of multiculturalism, from films discussed in this section that celebrate an ideal but necessarily exclusive picture of Britain to those discussed in the next section that engage the hidden realities of multicultural Britain.

As opposed to the shocking or satirically astute comedy of the films that I discuss in the next section, the comedy examined here is comparatively gentle. The comedy does not present a controversial object of attack, but instead displaces social inequities to the recent past or prioritises 'universal' issues of inter-generational strife or sexism. Any sense of contemporary inequality or prejudice is papered over in the name of a multicultural ideal, to the extent that although they are postcolonial comedies by virtue of challenging colonial legacies and stereotypes they have often done more to offend the migrant communities concerned than to critique racially motivated injustice in contemporary society. I do not want to critique the utopian *vision* of a society with no outsiders that the comedies attempt to create, but rather to draw attention to those that *are*, by necessity, excluded from the vision.

One means of portraying a more inclusive contemporary society is to displace racist attitudes onto the past and thereby find comedy in a bygone way of life. Damien O'Donnell's *East is East* (1999) – based on a play by Ayub Khan-Din – is set in 1971. This temporal remove potentially weakens the relevance of any social critique enabled by the film, although by satirising Enoch Powell and his supporters the finger is clearly pointed at those who still harbour racist prejudices. O'Donnell's film is set in Salford, and takes as its focus a Pakistani immigrant, George Khan, with his white British wife and their seven children. George Khan ('Genghis' to his children, on account of both the shared name and his authoritarian tendencies) faces an uphill battle trying to force his children to conform to his traditional Pakistani/ Muslim values, as his wife watches on and intercedes on their behalf when she sees fit. The plot revolves around a spectrum of culturally stereotypical family dramas, which leads Ali Nobil to claim that '*East is East* invites us to enjoy a film about Asians in Britain in terms of what it likes best: arranged marriages, domestic violence and oppression'.[30] However, whilst the film may use dubious means to draw an audience (during the marketing phase 'the distributor refrained from depicting Asian characters on the major promotion posters in anticipation that such "obvious" ethnic labelling might limit the film's audience appeal'), it does invite a criticism of overtly racist figures like Powell.[31]

Although many of George's efforts to bring his children up in the Muslim faith are mocked or undermined, his reminder to Tariq that in Islam everyone is equal, 'no black or white' resounds as a happy alternative to the backdrop of politically endorsed intolerance that is evident in their surrounding Salford estate. The majority of intercultural friendships and relationships that the film presents are shown to be happy, mutual and tolerant but Mr Moorhouse plays the part of neighbourhood representative for Powellite ideology. This is most evident in a scene during which the tomboyish Meenah Khan kicks a football through a window that displays a poster of Powell himself. As the children run away with screams and laughter, Mr Moorhouse's face appears at the window in the space previously occupied by Powell's head. A timely close-up reveals his futile anger. The shot that frames the poster visually resembles a childish 'your face here' attraction to be found in fairgrounds, comically undermining the anger expressed by Mr Moorhouse via the incongruity of the juxtaposed images of childish amusement and adult rage; he is rendered incapable of achieving his intended effect. Furthermore, the switching of Powell's head for Mr Moorhouse's visually marks him as Powell's (lone) stand-in on the street. The image effectively blurs the boundaries between mimicry and mockery that Bhabha identifies as pertinent to challenging authority, by replacing Powell's face with its comically ineffectual representative.

Powell's impotence is further demonstrated by the Khan children's refusal to take his message seriously, thereby undermining his assumption of power. Whilst watching a televised racist speech by Powell with his siblings, Saleem jokes, 'we can have a whip round and get Dad repatriated', and in so doing reinterprets Powell's words as comical opportunity rather than intended threat. In another instance, Earnest Moorhouse embarrasses his grandfather by innocently greeting Mr Khan with a 'salaam alaikum' within the former's earshot whilst he is sermonising on the detrimental effects of immigrants ('You let one of 'em in, and the whole fuckin' tribe turns up'). This has the effect of exposing Mr Moorhouse's views as archaic and outdated. His own teenage granddaughter is having a relationship with Tariq Khan, whilst Earnest is friends with Sajit and infatuated with Meenah, illustrating that for the younger generation (even twenty-eight years before the film is released) the norm is tolerant multiculturalism rather than intolerance and racism.

However, *East is East* is often problematic in its use of comedy in relation to other values that emanate from outside white majority culture. Religion (specifically Islam) is figured as a concern solely of the older generation, through the presentation of a purely superficial Muslim identity for all but one of the Khan children and a lot of screen-time devoted to the spectacle of watching them unwillingly dress up for Nazir's wedding. Their traditional Muslim dress is depicted as masking their chosen identities: Meenah pulls off her headscarf every time elders' heads are turned in a comically child-like act of disobedience, and Sajit is never seen without his Parka which, unlike the *taqiyah*, is seen as an integral part of his identity. The fact that the children largely opt for different lifestyles to their father is not problematic in itself. However, the representation of George as violent, hypocritical and bigamous – often shot from low angles to show him looming over his cowering wife or beaten children – serves to demonise George's religious views by association with their tyrannical and ruthless practitioner.[32]

Furthermore, *East is East* presents racism itself in a curious way, as both Tariq and Sajit refer to Pakistani friends and relatives as 'Pakis' in a derogatory manner that constitutes a form of othering. It is clear when they make these proclamations that they do not include themselves in the term, with Tariq explicitly identifying as British *not* Pakistani. This could be read as an implicit critique of a society that encourages the internalisation of racist values among migrant communities, pro-voking laughter at the strange incongruity of a Pakistani-British boy appropriating the term. But the way that other Pakistanis in the film are constructed – through dress, ideals and often accent or language – as different to the Khan children, actually encourages superiority-induced laughter at the Other who has not assimilated in the same way.

The film's later partner-piece, *West is West* (2010), will not be discussed at length as it is largely set in Pakistan rather than Britain, but it does take up Sajit's internalised racism in a noteworthy manner.[33] After calling his father a 'Paki', Sajit is taken to Pakistan to learn respect for his father's country and culture; however, the film fails to address the root cause of the racism, which lies in the bullying that he under-goes at school. As such, Sajit's internalised racism is seen as a problem to be dealt with in the individual rather than the society. Sajit learns about Pakistani culture so that he can be proud of it, but the bullies go unpunished.

The two films are problematic in their call for assimilation by migrants rather than a mutual process of becoming that also involves work on the part of white British culture(s). However, the films do enable a criti-cal reflection on processes of ethnic commodification and exoticisation. *East is East* reaches a climax when the Shahs (with whom marriages have been furtively arranged) visit the Khans. As the door is shut to the Khans' residence, Earnest Moorhouse is shown peering through their window before the camera cuts to a scene in the living room, implicitly positioning the audience as nosey white spectators.

Similarly, in *West is West* the tendency to exoticise is parodied as Tariq plays up stereotypes of Pakistan by talking about his father's spirituality ('he's practically Gandhi)' in order to chat up a white girl and sell her his wares. Made up words like 'transen-tit-ises', accompanied by the mixing of religious signifiers (his father is Muslim not Hindu) trigger laughter at Tariq's failure to conform to an exotic, Orientalist stereotype, when he is exposed as a fraud by his laughing younger brother. This also implicitly serves to mock those that seek to exoticise the East, such as Sajit's school teacher, Mr Jordan, who is the embodiment of academic Orientalism in the film.

Whilst O'Donnell's film mocks racist ideologies, Gurinder Chadha's *Bhaji on the Beach* depicts a gentle self-mockery of the South Asian community represented. During the film, a traditional English holiday to Blackpool is given a subcontinental twist as the Saheli Women's Group take a minibus from Birmingham to the tune of a Punjabi version of Cliff Richard's 'Summer Holiday'. Through the course of the day a number of the women have their views challenged or comically undermined.

Much of the film's comedy relies on undermining prejudiced characters by suggesting that they have lost a grip on reality. This means that audiences are positioned to laugh at anything the prejudiced characters say. The film opens with a very realist establishing sequence, during which the camera pans slowly down a graffitied and rundown street. Mysterious music then serves to offer an alternative to the realist image, as the camera appears to enter the dark void of a shop door. The scene cuts to an image of the Hindu god Ram shot from a low angle to signify his power, followed by a shot of Asha from the point of view of Ram, illustrating her comparative submission. A sequence of brass interjections accompany a series of jumpy camera cuts and lend a sense of drama as Asha flounders at the series of visions presented to her. An aerial shot shows her turning confusedly down a corridor walled with oversized images of Hindi film posters and western consumer products like Coca Cola, Cadburys and Golden Wonder, ending with Ram and the contrapuntal sound of a voice saying 'Asha! Know your place!' At this point, the vision ends and Asha is left standing in front of a dropped tray of food and incense sticks that she was about to place in front of the image of Ram in her shop. The bathetic plunge from the spiritual to the mundane tasks of running a shop and preparing breakfast serves to poke fun at a woman who seems ill equipped to deal with her quotidian reality. By highlighting Asha's loose grip on reality, she is undermined in her subsequent efforts to castigate the younger generation for their worldly ways. Indeed, immediately following the opening scene with Asha, the camera cuts to Ginder, who is shown reading the divorce papers that serve as an index of her practical response to situations.

Asha's visions are used to portray her construction of the world through stereotypes, but playing these images in a non-realist dimension conflates prejudice with madness. Upon finding out that teenage Hashida has become pregnant outside of marriage, Asha has a vision in which the girl is a wanton blonde smoking a cigarette and wearing a revealing outfit. This stands as a metaphor for Asha's warped perspective, as in reality Hashida conforms to none of the older woman's stereotypes. The extent of Asha's dislocation from reality is marked by her being unaware of where she is when she comes around from her visions. She is often drenched in the interim, from walking into the sea or standing under a sprinkler. Her stereotypes are thereby relegated to a fantastical world that does not correspond with the way things really are, yet they also serve as comical hiatuses from an otherwise fairly gritty feminist plot revolving around sexism, domestic violence and prejudice amidst a nexus of social factors including ethnicity, gender and class. As such, the visions comically mirror the real events of the plot but from an adjusted comical perspective. By viewing social and familial dilemmas in the contrasting dimensions of gritty realism and farcical comedy it serves, controversially perhaps, to suggest that overcoming these issues can be reduced to a matter of perspective.

Comedy in *Bhaji on the Beach* is also derived from self-mockery within the migrant community. In Blackpool, two of the teenage girls on the trip, Ladhu and Madhu, have an argument over Madhu's tendency to 'let these white prats do it to [her]'. To bring about reconciliation with her friend afterwards, Ladhu begins to mimic the older women on the trip. Dropping her usual Birmingham accent in favour of the Indian accent of a non-native speaker, she begins her speech in the same way as Pushpa did earlier: 't'irty years I have been here and I have never seen such a thing, getting stupid I-love-you you-love-me loving bites'. Her mimicry of the older women's accents and syntax slips into a mockery of their melodramatic approach to problems as the two girls end the scene in mutual laughter raising their hands in mock despair and exclaiming 'Hai Ram! Hai Ram!' (Oh Lord!). The film could, as such, be seen as pandering to stereotypical preconceptions about (particularly older) Asian women; however, it would be patronising to suggest that migrant communities should not laugh at themselves in the same way as any other does. As Rainer Emig asks: 'Why should ethnicity (and minority status) condemn people to a Puritan sobriety?'[34]

Bhaji on the Beach does distinguish self-abasing migrant comedy from white racism in one of its more sober scenes. Whilst sitting in a café, Hashida can hear two of the older women on the trip gossiping about her intercut with the racist observations of the white woman serving at the counter. In response to this, Hashida throws a hot drink at the older woman, before messing up the café counter and telling the waitress that she can 'fuck off too'. This illustrates that even though what the older women are doing is hurtful, it does not excuse the white woman's racism, and both are duly scolded (or scalded). By the end of the film, a new female solidarity is evident in the group of subcontinental women, as they defend Ginder against her violent husband and are brought together in laughter at a novelty boob-cake supplied by the Mumbaite Rekha.

A decade (and one American film) later, Chadha returned to Britain in order to make *Bend It Like Beckham*. Her motives were explicit: 'I set out to [...] make the most commercial, mainstream, wide-appealing, multiplex movie I possibly could – with an Indian girl in the lead'.[35] The result is a classic 'feel-good' film based around the parallel plights of Jesminder (Jess) Bhamra and Juliette (Jules) Paxton, who are passionate and driven when it comes to football, much to the distress of their respective families. Writing about late eighteenth-century British comedy, Jean Marsden asserts that 'English comedy does indeed become a representation of national character – at least as the British would like to see themselves'.[36] Over two centuries later and the same can be said of Chadha's film, which effectively represents Britain as a multicultural utopia. Chadha is happy being described as a British film-maker, saying that 'because I have redefined what Britain means in my work, I'm comfortable with British, because I know British also includes me'.[37]

In order to create her happy, multicultural British society, Chadha pictures concerns associated with race, religion and ethnicity as part of a more universal problem of sexual discrimination. This is enabled by constructing an essentialist image of femininity encoded through shopping, materialism, physical appearance and ostentatious heteronormative sexuality that Jess and Jules must battle against. This outdated, pre-feminist construction of femininity is primarily represented by the girls' mothers. Whereas Jules's mother wants to enhance her daughter's sexual desirability with a pump-up bra, Jules chooses a sports bra for practicality. In a parallel scenario, Jess undergoes a sari fitting prior to her sister's wedding; although Jess would prefer the sari to be looser, the fitter pulls the tape measure tighter, whilst joking with Jess's mother that 'even these mosquito bites will look like juicy juicy mangoes,' provoking the mirth of both Jess's mother and sister.

By concentrating on the sexual desirability of their daughters' bodies, the mothers are shown to be furthering patriarchal ideals via comparisons to male responses. When Jess is playing football with her male friends, they imply that her body makes her less suited to the sport, by taunting her to 'chest it'. Instead, she hurls the ball at one of the boy's groins, doubling him over in pain and deconstructing the culturally encoded stereotype about the fragility of women's bodies. The parallel nature of these scenes, all concerned with the girls' chests, illustrates that the older women occupy a similar role to men through their pre-feminist sexual stereotyping that serves to further patriarchal ideals. Justine Ashby remarks that the mothers' 'limited ambitions for their daughters are coded as trivial and laughably *pre*feminist. Rendered comic, their misgivings can be swept away with relative ease'.[38] Set amidst the cultural thrall of the Spice Girls and declarations of 'girl power', the film can easily laugh off the ideals and traditions of an older generation as outdated.

The generation gap is captured through the aesthetic juxtaposition of two sequences. First, a montage of scenes shot in the centre of London using natural lighting and bright colours shows Jess buying football boots to the tune of former Spice Girl Mel C's 'Independence Day'. A cut to the beige and brown colours of the Bhamras' living room, with artificial lighting and near-static characters appears by comparison to be set in the past, suggesting a bygone and claustrophobic way of life. The incongruity of the two images creates a comical gap between the parallel lives that Jess leads. Audiences are positioned to laugh at the scene within the Bhamras' household, because it does not seem to have a place in the world that has been depicted during the immediately preceding exterior montage.

Another effect of prioritising gender battles in the film is that concerns raised by Jess's family regarding cultural and religious values about the role of women are viewed in the light of a more universal problem (regarding the role of women in society and/or the family). Although Jess might receive a particularly hard time from her family in respect to her wishes to play football, there are comparisons made throughout to the similar plights of both Jules and her coach, Joe, who has a fraught relationship with his father. By focussing on universal topics like family dispute, patriarchal attitudes and the place of women in society, this film gently undermines stereotypes and questions an inclination to Other according to cultural difference by creating parallels between different cultures. As a result, when Jess faces a wall of footballers blocking her penalty kick and imaginatively substitutes them for family members, it is the fact that they are *female* family members rather than Sikhs that poses the greatest threat to Jess reaching her 'goal' in the context of the film.

Chadha's film integrates difference by utilising a multidirectional satire that weakens any specific site of attack and ensures that overall the comedy prioritises inclusion above subversion. I borrow the term 'multidirectional satire' from John Clement Ball, who asserts that the 'concept of satirical multidirectionality [...] works against the binary model of norm and deviation and offers one in which oppositions may be set up without either side being endorsed'.[39] This is effected during *Bend It Like Beckham* by gently poking fun at a number of characters, whether it be Paula Paxton (Juliette's mother) who misreads Jules as a lesbian, Mrs Bhamra who is frequently duped by her daughters, or Tony's family, who believe that their homosexual son is hopelessly in love with Jess. During a scene at the end of Pinky Bhamra's wedding, Jules is dropped off to the celebrations by her mother. When Mrs Paxton steps out of the car and sees Jess wearing her shoes she reads this as confirmation of her suspicions that Jess is involved in a lesbian relationship with her daughter, shouting 'Get your lesbian feet out of my shoes!' However, this misreading is met with equal confusion, as Jess's relatives do not understand what is meant by 'lesbian' and counter her attack with 'She's not Lebanese, she's Punjabi.' In a farcical progression, this is topped with 'I thought she was a Pisces', thereby misinterpreting 'lesbian' as a star sign. This scene encourages laughter at a number of different characters who are unable to read the situation correctly, and in turn ensures that a satirical attack in any specific direction is weakened. If the misreading had been voiced by Mrs Paxton alone, then she would be the sole butt of the joke and the full force of the laughter would be directed against her, but a collection of misreadings serves to democratise the laughter and thereby weakens its blow.

Chadha's film presents a happy and hopeful version of multicultural Britain. However, this kind of representation has not been exempt from criticism, due to its tendency to turn a blind eye to political realities of the day. Ashby summarises the political zeitgeist:

> Given that *Bend It Like Beckham* was released in the context of racially motivated public disorder in northern English towns and cities in 2001, the election successes of the explicitly racist British National Party in 2002, and the widespread victimization of British Muslims following 9/11, it is difficult not to conclude that this choice of an ending provides a highly selective, even utopian view of Blair's Britain.[40]

Chadha's portrayal of Britain reads as a cover-up that sweeps social problems under the carpet. In keeping with this evasion of contemporary social issues, Chadha resorts to archaic British Others in order to perform Jess's integration. Following a football match against a German team, Jess is consoled by her teammates that she's now part of a tradition for losing a penalty shoot-out to the 'Jerries', invoking Britain's former Others (exemplified in the football chant 'Two world wars and one world cup').

What is more problematic is that the comedy's happy resolution is only possible if ethnic minority characters conform to western values of freedom above other (conflicting) cultural values such as respect for elders or religious duties.[41] For Heinen, the cultural hierarchies embedded in the film are more problematic than its naïvely utopian ending: 'in *Bend It Like Beckham* [...] Western values are in the end the only common ground on which the two cultures can meet'.[42] This problem is apparent when Jess expresses concern at having to bare her legs to play football and requests to keep her tracksuit bottoms on, but Joe unquestioningly replies in the negative. However, when she lurks in the spectator stand rather than warming up, Joe comes to see what is wrong, and it is revealed that Jess is embarrassed about a burn that has disfigured her leg. After a short conversation Jess's embarrassment is comically deflated: when Joe says he's sorry, Jess replies, 'I know; put me off beans on toast for life.' What is problematic about this scene is that Jess's mother had previously expressed concern at her daughter revealing her legs during a daydream at the film's opening, so reasons for keeping her legs covered have been foreshadowed. The fact that Jess's reasons for covering are different to her mother's does not change the fact that Jess is given no option *but* to wear shorts before Joe has even allowed her to explain. In this manner, the film assumes unquestioning submission to values coded as modern and western, suggesting that traditional, cultural or religious concerns are archaic and irrelevant to the younger generation.

Overall, the 'gentle' comedy employed in the above films has both its strengths and its limitations. In terms of spectatorship, these films have all achieved mainstream success, something that Chadha explicitly strives for, having turned her back on 'films that only academics are going to see and appreciate', an accusation she levels at Black Audio and Sankofa Film Collective.[43] However, 'mainstreaming' may also be understood negatively as 'a "streamlining" of culture, as a subordination of cultural specificity to one hegemonic cultural strand'.[44] Problematic subordination to cultural hegemony is indeed something that is evident in the above films, largely due to their tendency to pander to a utopian view of multicultural society.

Laughing through the fears

The final section of this chapter removes us from the celebration of multiculturalism and generously inclusive laughter enacted in the previous films. Historically speaking, the official party-line of multiculturalism introduced with the Labour government in 1997 has soured. Following 'race riots' in Oldham, Burnley and Bradford in the summer of 2001, political rhetoric surrounding multiculturalism shifts and is increasingly constructed as a failed experiment rather than an ideal or aspiration. The Cantle Report, published in December 2001, is commissioned to 'seek the views of local residents and community leaders in affected towns [...] on the issues which need to be addressed to bring about social cohesion'. The report lays blame upon the 'parallel lives' lived by communities in the towns affected by the riots.[45] Home Secretary David Blunkett's speech reflects this view and heralds the failure 'to produce cohesive communities and common citizenship in the UK'.[46] For Alana Lentin and Gavan Titley, 'The vision of community cohesion, in turn, marks the emergence of integration discourses explicitly predicated on the failure of multiculturalism, and instigates a lingering tendency to reduce the politics of race to the problem of community.'[47] This is problematic, as it allows for institutionalised racism by another name. Shortly following the riots, the terrorist attacks of 11 September 2001 act as a further catalyst for constructing multiculturalism as a failure, and British Muslims are increasingly policed, interrogated and suspected as the 'enemy within', a situation foreshadowed in the aftermath of the 'Rushdie affair' outlined in the introduction to this book.

I do not intend to suggest that the riots, 9/11, or any other tipping point engendered a sudden shift in Britain's multicultural reality, or to suggest that multiculturalism had never before been critiqued, as it had, largely by the right, for many years before 2001. However, what did occur at this point was a shift in official rhetoric, as the word 'multiculturalism' came to be constructed discursively as a failed ideal. I do not wish to fall into the trap of tracing the ascendancy and fall of multiculturalism, but to consider ways in which multiculturalism has been presented in changing political rhetoric and how this is reflected or refracted in postcolonial British comedy. Lentin and Titley's *The Crises of Multiculturalism: Racism in a Neoliberal Age* (2011) offers an insightful account of the ways in which 'iterations of multiculturalism have been used to argue for, legitimize and position new formations of the problem of difference'.[48] In light of this, I focus in the following not on how multicultural realities may have shifted, but on how filmmakers begin to tease out the ambiguities and elisions of multicultural dis-course, bringing forth the hidden realities that multicultural discourse frequently works to obscure.

The two films that form the focus of the remainder of this chapter concern themselves with disenfranchised communities within British society, directly addressing the way that the ideal of multiculturalism serves to repress the dark side of Britain's multicultural reality. Chris Morris's *Four Lions* (2010) and Joe Cornish's *Attack the Block* (2011) focus on the culturally and politically stigmatised figures of the suicide bomber (in the case of the former) and the gang member (in the case of the latter). However, by including figures that are often excluded from benign representations of multicultural Britain in a comic man-ner, the films do not reinforce patterns of exclusion and encourage laughter at the outsider. Instead, they parody media constructions of fear and undermine us/them affiliations encouraged by a form of Britishness that expresses itself in relation to culturally subordinated and 'extreme' Others. These dark and satirical films undermine com-edy's generic convention of providing a happy and mutually satisfying ending for all of the characters. In this sense, the films could be con-sidered comical in mode rather than in genre: this is comedy in spite of itself, relentlessly funny yet refusing to offer comic appeasement as a solution to social ills.

Four Lions is the first feature-length film by Chris Morris, a director notorious for his dark humour and outrageous satire. This notoriety stems from work such as *Brass Eye*, a televised series of mockumentaries that take the media frenzy surrounding controversial topics such as drug addiction and paedophilia as their inspiration. In *Four Lions*, the focus of hysteria that he brings to light surrounds a group of 'jihadis' from South Yorkshire as they plan and carry out a suicide mission. The group of men – comprising Omar, Barry, Waj, Hassan and, prior to his untimely demise, Faisal – spend the majority of their time in-fighting, which enables Morris to find humour in the frequently hyperbolised threat of the suicide bomber.[49] Also a first-time film director with TV credits, Joe Cornish interweaves a sci-fi alien-invasion plot with comedy in *Attack the Block*. The film takes a Brixton gang and their fight against aliens as its focus, largely deriving comedy from the gang's discourse.

Attack the Block and *Four Lions* work to subvert stereotypes by includ-ing stock 'types' (the gang member, the student and the nurse, for example) but fleshing them out in order to create rounded and com-plex characters. By using these stock 'types' it is possible to assume certain preconceptions or associations; however, by making characters emotionally complex and therefore believable, they are not constrained to re-enacting a series of stereotypes. As such, any stereotypes that are engaged in the films are done so ironically. This ensures that audiences are forced to analyse how and why the stereotypes have gained such currency.

In order to challenge diminishing stereotypes, *Attack the Block* draws on some common associations made with black cultures via references to music, drugs and violence and undermines these associations through the plot and characterisation. Brewis, for example, is the film's most dependent consumer of marijuana and is always introduced by a diegetic soundtrack of black rap or reggae music playing in his headphones. However, his white, middle-class status destabilises associations between the music or marijuana as solely emanating from black cultures. The film also portrays black characters as inherently British rather than Britain's Other, as racist rhetoric attempts to. An emblematic image towards the end of Cornish's film shows the hero, Moses, hanging out of a window and only prevented from plummeting to his death by the Union Jack flag that he clasps.

Four Lions tackles stereotypes alternatively by employing tropes of surveillance and thereby drawing attention to the way that material is framed and presented to viewers. The ringleader, Omar, is himself a security guard, which works as an enabling trope for meta-cinematically foregrounding processes of observation and representation, whilst questioning who is controlling the camera's gaze and to what end. Like Morris's earlier work, *Four Lions* plays with the documentary format through the use of handheld cameras and a plot-line driven around the build-up to a climactic event. In some senses it parodies 'ethnographic' documentaries by taking a marginalised group as its object and working on the basis of grass-roots research.

However, rather than presenting the material as scientific and/or objective, the film is shot in a manner that Fatimah Tobing Rony would describe as employing the 'third eye', evidencing a 'sensibility to Subject and Object double-consciousness'.[50] By means of bringing the camera to the forefront and exposing viewing perspectives as constructed by the camera, this manner of filming challenges 'popular and scientific conceptions of the Ethnographic' in which, 'With the presence of the camera obscured, the viewer is meant to observe and experience the film as if he or she had been there, from a "fly on the wall" perspective.'[51] Tobing Rony speaks of the 'third eye' predominantly in terms of 'a person of colour growing up in the United States', for whom 'the experience of viewing oneself as an object is profoundly formative', which renders the term inapplicable to Morris as a white man filming a group that is frequently presented as the Other of British culture. But the director is nevertheless sensitive to the danger of presenting the camera's gaze as objective by constantly drawing attention to it. Whilst films like *East is East* have been criticised for their tendency to reproduce a spectacle of the Other that was easily consumable by a mainstream audience, the self-reflexive camera work of *Four Lions* assures that the gaze is also turned back on audiences.

Perhaps one of the reasons why the latest wave of comedy is so much more aggressive than its forebears is down to the fact that, as white directors, Morris and Cornish are entirely unconcerned with challenging or offending white audiences. Rather than gently pursuing what Emig terms the 'integration of difference' in an inclusive and benevolent manner, these directors unflinchingly pose critical questions as to the social conditions (of poverty, exclusion) that must be present for the rise of gang culture or Islamism to occur, as well as interrogating the function of media representations in exacerbating the state of affairs.[52] This is not to suggest that white directors have sole access to the luxury of indifference to challenging or offending white audiences, but it is the case that Cornish's and Morris's films suggest a new trend in postcolonial British cinema, that has until now been rather more placatory.

The opening scenes of Morris's film foreground concerns of observation, representation and performativity in order further to subvert the conventions of traditional ethnography. During the shooting of the initial home video – intended as an explanation of the suicide mission the bombers intend to carry out – cuts between POV shots through a handheld camera and a high-angle, seemingly omniscient shot, foreground the manipulation of perspective. The third important viewing perspective is introduced later in the film via CCTV and night-vision cameras that imply the aspect of surveillance to which characters are subjected. Concerns over providing a convincing performance are expressed during the shooting of this video; Waj's comically small (toy) gun raises questions of performance and the (thwarted) desire to be taken seriously, while Faisal refuses to take a box off his head, illustrating his intent not to be watched but also rendering futile any attempts to be taken seriously. Showing characters as explicitly *acting* and responding to the presence of a camera works to subvert the conventions of traditional ethnography, in which 'the individual "native" [or in this case, character from ethnic minority background] is often not even "seen" by the viewer but is taken for real'.[53]

Four Lions portrays characters with an extreme paranoia of being observed that is ultimately shown to be warranted, as it becomes increasingly apparent that the characters *are* being watched. This is registered by including integral scenes that are focalised through a CCTV lens, or through extra-diegetic camera clicks that do not visibly originate in the scene being shot. The comedy works in a curious way in this situation, as methods of avoiding observation are shown as increasingly farcical and overblown, yet the reason behind the lions' actions is ultimately justified both within the film and without in skewed media representations that tend to present a one-sided, monologic view of Islam and its adherents. Peter Morey and Amina Yaqin argue that what we see in the western media today 'is the distortion of particular features of Muslim life and custom, reducing the diversity of Muslims and their existence as individuals to a fixed object – a caricature in fact'.[54] They suggest that this 'distortion' is brought about through 'framing structures' that 'rather than being descriptive and neutral [...] are defined by questions of belonging, "Otherness," and threat."'[55] This signals the importance of critically challenging the representation of Islam perpetuated by the media.

Internal conflict and contradiction assures that in Morris's film Muslim characters are not taken as representative, meaning that Islam cannot be homogenised and fixed as Other. Among various anti-observation tactics employed in the film, some of the bombers take to shaking their heads in order to blur any images that are captured. When he notices this, Omar observes, 'CCTV's a video, you're just gonna look like a load of Sufis on speed!' This scene deconstructs monolithic representations of Islam by performing an internal Othering of Sufi Muslims and comically debasing the mystical element of Sufism by associating it with drug abuse. Ella Shohat and Robert Stam discuss the danger of characters from ethnic minorities becoming 'allegorical', arguing that 'within hegemonic discourse every subaltern performer/role is seen as synecdochically summing up a vast but putatively homogenous community', whereas 'Representations of dominant groups [...] are seen not as allegorical but as "naturally" diverse, examples of ungeneralizable variety of life itself.'[56] By focussing the entire film around a group of suicide bombers and their internal nexus of relationships rather than having a lone or token character, Morris assures that diverse and conflicting personalities and belief attitudes are shown, and individual characters do not become allegorical or representative.

Morris's film separates surface signifiers of Muslim identity and actual belief attitudes (defined by Giovanna Borradori as 'the way in which we believe rather than what we believe in'),[57] in order to challenge media stereotypes dependent on stock images. The most powerful example of this occurs during a parallel montage of scenes. Images shot in the flat where the group discuss plans to take their suicide mission to the marathon are alternated with images shot from a shaky handheld camera somewhere outside, with green lighting used to suggest night-vision. Progressively shorter intervals between cuts bring the montage to a climax as the flat is surrounded by police. At a climactic point the flat that has been shot from outside is forcefully entered by the police. Inside – rather than the anticipated group of suicide bombers – are a group of older Muslim scholars, who had previously been ridiculed by the bombers for their peaceful and cerebral interpretation of Islam. The comedy climaxes as the police read the wielding of a water pistol by Omar's brother, Ahmed, as signifying violent intent. The dramatic irony is that the audience will recognise the 'weapon' as the same water pistol that Ahmed had previously refused to use when pro-voked by Omar's wife, Sofia. The construction of this scene suggests that popular understandings of Islam depend on surface signifiers of Muslim identity – the beards and traditional dress sported by the older scholars – rather than actual belief attitudes. As such, the plot justifies the farcical anti-observation efforts of the bombers, as Muslims *are* being targeted for observation, just the wrong ones. In this case the extreme actions of the four lions are portrayed as a response to the society that they live in; their fears are justified in the context of the film, putting the critical onus on damaging misrepresentations and superficial stereo-types rather than the bombers as a serious threat.

Morris both finds humour and combats fear in the portrayal of suicide bombers that are hopelessly inept. Rather than an organised network of cold killers, Morris's film presents us with an absurdly disorganised array of characters, demonstrating traits of kindness, brotherhood and comic ineptitude alongside their desires to fight the *kafir* (unbelievers). This goes against the grain of representations of terrorists in previous Hollywood-produced films, integral to which is what Carl Boggs and Tom Pollard have described as a 'monolithic culture of thuggish male warriors who relish violence, directed mostly against innocent civilians, and who lack motives beyond hatred and jealousy'. Boggs and Pollard highlight the inherent contradiction of this, as 'Despite their lack of intellectual sophistication and political strategy [...] such warriors are depicted as a grave threat to the very foundations of civilized society.'[58]

Four Lions exposes discrepancies in the representation of terrorism by aligning the end result more closely to the haphazard strategies adopted by the characters throughout. The name that the group of bombers give themselves – the 'four lions' – serves as a further means of tempering serious intent with farcical actions. Their chosen moniker connotes both Osama bin Laden, also known as 'The Lion,' and *The Lion King*, a story that Omar renarrates in order to explain his actions to his young son metaphorically. As well as complicating a picture that would be easier to fear in its simple singularity (the suicide bomber as pure evil), the juxtaposition of bin Laden and *The Lion King*'s Simba also serves to deflate the perceived power of the former Al Qaeda leader.

A further source of comedy that Morris derives from the figure of the suicide bomber is the uncertainty surrounding the concept of *jihad* in Islam, along with the associated matters of martyrdom, terrorism and suicide bombing.[59] Much of the film's comedy originates in arguments over how the group should be training and what would be the best target for attack. The wide array of beliefs surrounding what *jihad* means and how it should be exercised are stretched to ridiculous proportions in Morris's film, in which Barry (the group's white convert and the most illogical and aggressive figure in the group) advocates bombing a mosque to radicalise the moderates, whilst Faisal wants to 'bomb Boots' for selling condoms that 'make you wanna bang white girls'. When Faisal comes to an unfortunate demise (caused by tripping over with a bag of explosives) Barry believes that he is a martyr for damaging the infrastructure by simultaneously blowing up a nearby sheep. However, Omar's question as to whether Faisal is 'a martyr or [...] a *fucking* jalfrezi?' illustrates uncertainties in interpretation even from those committed to a suicide mission. Violent understandings of *jihad* are contrasted with the comically pacifist Ahmed, who is so stringent in his non-violent beliefs that he even refuses to engage in a water fight, preferring to quote opinions than squirt water. This illustrates that devoted Muslim belief can, and usually does, *preclude* violence, giving voice to a dominant understanding of *jihad* that prioritises inner struggle over armed fighting.[60]

However, there is a more sinister undertone to this proliferation of sentiments regarding *jihad*, as its violent interpretation is shown to thrive only in certain circles; in the case of the film it is the young, disaffected men rather than the older scholars who interpret *jihad* in a violent way. Indeed, the DVD version of Morris's film includes a documentary entitled 'Lost Boys' made by *Four Lions'* Associate Producer, Afi Khan, which focuses on the alienation and hostility experienced by young Asian men from Nelson, Lancashire, at the hands of BNP members. Humayan Ansari discusses interpretations of *jihad* in Muslim communities following a survey of British Muslims in the wake of 9/11 (although prior to the 7/7 London bombings). He notes that inter-pretations of *jihad* have tended to emphasise either its peaceful or its violent nature, positing personal understanding as well as circumstance as influential factors.[61] So perhaps what is being mocked in the film is the uncertainty surrounding such a crucial point of belief, but I would suggest instead that the film exercises the critique of a society that pro-duces the 'circumstances' in which people choose to interpret *jihad* in a violent way; as is voiced in the film, 'why shouldn't I be a bomber if you treat me like one?'

The way that the film operates dares members of the audience to make judgements about characters in order to illustrate that it is just such pre-judgements that create the right atmosphere for previously peaceful characters to radicalise. During a scene at a public debate Hassan wants to test people's reactions to him as a Muslim. He stands up and starts rapping: 'I'm the Mujahideen and I'm making a scene, now you gonna feel what the boom boom means; it's like Tupac said, when I die I'm not dead; we are the martyrs, you're just squashed tomatoes. Allahu akbar!' At this point he sets off a line of party poppers that are strung around his waist and designed to look like bombs. In response to the screams and shocked faces that a wide shot of the audience captures, he responds 'Just cos I'm Muslim you thought it was real?!' During this scene the diegetic gaze of the audience responding to Hassan acts as a foil for cinema audiences, assuming a certain kind of subject: these are people attending a talk panel entitled 'Islam: Moderation and Progress'. This talk apparently draws a similar mix of middle-class liberals and students that Film4 marketing hopes to attract, by producing films that are 'alternative' and aimed at 'an intelligent audience'.[62]

By challenging the response of this audience, the film attacks the insidious prejudice disguised in the politically correct language of the middle class, rather than explicit racist abuse. To do this, Morris cre-ates the circumstances in which prejudgements about previously non-violent Muslim characters engender violent reactions, rather than the reverse; Hassan is recruited by Barry at a later stage in the film. As such, fear creates its object, and by comically undermining the way that fear of suicide bombers engenders a response in the film, Morris stays true to form by attacking the media that create such hysteria around the threat of suicide missions. When Hassan's party poppers go off the audience is granted comic relief that ridicules any prejudiced preconceptions that may have been harboured. To laugh at something reduces its power to induce fear; in pursuit of this, Morris provokes laughter at sites of excess (as in the tension built up during Hassan's rap) as a way of *combating* the production of cultural fears.

Scenes such as the above illustrate the real work required to rethink the complexities of terrorism and its relationship to national politics and the media. With considerable foresight, Jean Baudrillard argued (in 1993) that 'the violence of old was more enthusiastic and sacrificial than ours', whereas now we are faced with 'a simulacrum of violence, emerging less from passion than from the screen, a violence in the nature of the image'.[63] Understanding acts of terrorism in this manner highlights the self-perpetuating nature of violence and its media-generated image; violence does not beget violence *per se*, but by means of the repetition and spectacle of its reproduced image. The cycle feeds off itself. Boggs and Pollard similarly argue that terrorism on film would be better understood as 'a mode of political activity that both *reflects* and helps *create* a violent society of the spectacle where pervasive feelings of fear, anxiety and paranoia are reproduced daily'.[64] Working against this cinematic trend, *Four Lions* serves to challenge monolithic perspectives on terrorism, calling into question the interrelated domains of media and national politics and their complicity in creating and perpetuating instances of the terrorist subject.

Four Lions mixes the sacred and the profane so as to depict characters as humanly flawed individuals, without passing judgement on the religion itself. Dialogues containing quick switches from 'salaam aleikums' to crudely scatological comments and insults illustrate the hypocrisy of ordinary characters that want to bring about shari'a law but cannot control their own profanities, encouraging laughter at the faithful rather than the faith. By presenting flawed individuals, the film encourages audiences to refrain from homogenising religious believers under simplifying ideological banners.

Waj is the film's main example of a flawed and confused believer; he is portrayed as child-like throughout, with a prayer bear to say his prayers and books like *The Camel that went to the Mosque* that serve as indexes of his immature approach to Islam. The extent to which his religious belief is divorced from any real understanding becomes apparent when he and Omar go to a training camp in Pakistan and are preparing to pray: Waj cannot understand why the rest of the men are praying towards the West rather than the East, despite repeated insistences that they have flown over Mecca. His farcical confusion illustrates his child-like devotion to religious practices without comprehending the meaning behind them.

Furthermore, a series of stories that Omar offers to Waj as justifications for what they are doing mimic the bedtime stories that Omar tells his young son. This internal parallel means that Waj's absurd repetition of 'rubber dingy rapids bro' (after Omar's analogy for the joy of the afterlife), is filled with pathos as it becomes clear how theologically confused he is and how much he clings onto this childish metaphor for Paradise. Ultimately it is Omar's trickery of Waj – confusing him and thereby denying him the free choice of martyrdom – that engenders the pathos of the ending; the comedy turns sour and Waj is left sitting in a kebab shop about to blow himself and the Muslim owner up, surrounded by armed police and helplessly questioning whether he'll still get points for taking the Muslim man with him, 'like Nectar card'.

Whereas *Four Lions* challenges the media hype and exacerbation of fear surrounding suicide bombing, *Attack the Block* takes representations of the postcolonial city as its comic and critical focus. When writing on 'postcolonial London', John McLeod prefers to prioritise fictions that imagine London in utopian terms. Whilst he allows that 'Cultural creativity should not be considered outside London's insoluble and unforgettable social conflicts', he nevertheless focuses on texts that seek to 'daringly imagine an alternative city in which divisive tensions are effectively resisted'.[65] The aim of his project is 'to suggest that [...] projective, utopian impulses possess a transformative potential which contributes to and resources the changing shape and experiences of London's "facticity"'.[66] It is apparent that McLeod's critical agenda is comparable to Chadha's fictional one: imagining a utopian space into being. However, just as Chadha's utopian imaginings work unwittingly to efface those who do not comfortably fit the benignly multicultural picture, critical paradigms that work around such visions arguably aid the same process.

In response to this I step away from visions of the middle-class idyll of a multicultural city, frequently expressed in terms of flaccid political correctness or according to utopian aspirations of 'progression' and 'transformation'.[67] Instead this chapter examines the alternative critique offered by *Attack the Block*, which depends on a *dys*topian, rather than utopian vision of the city and does not pretend to re-imagine London in any 'progressive' or 'transformative' way. The film centres on the Brixton neighbourhood, an area long defined by the media and popular culture as synonymous with riot, poverty, gang culture, violence, drugs and its Afro-Caribbean community. Historically the area has been home to heavy-handed policing ('Operation Swamp 81'), witnessed riots in 1980, 1985, 1995 and 2011, and has been bombed by a neo-Nazi in 1999. Culturally it has been referenced in James McTeigue's *V for Vendetta* as the place where riots first break out and in The Clash's 'The Guns of Brixton' as a place of resistance to unjust policing. In such narratives, Brixton represents the multicultural reality too often repressed by ideals of multiculturalism.

Cornish's film draws on the genres of dystopia and visceral horror accompanied by stylistic tropes of the noir thriller, as it plunges the viewer into Brixton amidst an alien invasion that is ignored by the media and police alike. The establishing shot is a pan of a bustling London city amidst the spectacles of Firework night; the camera then zooms down to capture a white woman (Sam) leaving Oval tube station and moving away from the bright lights of the city into graffitied streets with lower lighting and in which people cast elongated shadows, echoing conventions of the noir thriller. The way that Sam exits the open frame of the shot as she walks down the shadowy street suggests that there is something that we should be aware of outside the frame. Sure enough, against the exposed backdrop of the graffitied wall, another silhouette enters the frame, heightening the tension. A series of shots and reverse-shots in rapidly increasing cuts reveals that she is surrounded by a gang, who proceed to rob her of her purse and ring. As yet, there is little cause for laughter. However, the tone soon changes from gritty realism to farce, as the gang who 'merk' Sam are subsequently confronted with an alien invasion: 'That's an alien bruv. Trying to take over the Earth. Believe it. But it ended in the wrong place. The wrong place.'

London is a city trapped in its symbolism, with even the names of streets or small districts suggesting a chain of significations and associations, well known even to those who have not visited the area. Cornish's film at once plays upon this symbolic over-determination and simultaneously defamiliarises the area, stripping it of its usual associations. *Attack the Block* defamiliarises Brixton by means of a generic shift. Aesthetic signifiers of the noir thriller employed in the tense and shadowy opening sequence – perhaps suited to an area (imaginatively) associated with drugs, gangs and violence – are displaced to accommodate the aesthetics of science fiction. Using familiar sci-fi effects the film is tinged with a green light, with all of the action revolving around a tower block that is illuminated to look like a space ship, both stylistic choices serving to create a sense of otherness.[68]

The film's sci-fi elements also relate to the comic aspects of the film, because the character arc of the aliens parodies the history of Brixton's migrant communities and their (problematically termed) 'reverse colonisation' of the area. From the first sighting of the alien, cited above, assumptions are made about their intentions to violently colonise; in response, the gang kill the first alien that they find and carry it around as a trophy. Like the majority of the gang members, the aliens are black; this is discussed by the gang, when one of the members observes that the alien they are studying is 'blacker than my cousin Femi'. Parallels between the reception of the aliens and of predominantly black neighbourhoods in Britain are not subtle, hidden behind social niceties or politically correct language: they are black, alien and by settling in the neighbourhood are perceived to pose a threat to the 'indigenous' community. Foregrounding race, as the film does, highlights the colonial heritage of racism and disenfranchisement often experienced by migrant communities in Britain at a time when multicultural discourse attempts to cloak discussions of race under talk of communities or cultures. Lentin and Titley go so far as to say that 'renditions of multiculturalism provide a space for the redrawing and laundering of contemporary racisms'.[69] Taking their lead, I would argue that by re-centring discourses of race, Cornish's film returns what multicultural discourse attempts to repress.

As in *Four Lions*, fear creates its object, and at the end of the film it is revealed that the gang have brought the attack on themselves by killing the first alien and unwittingly covering themselves in the female's pheromones, designed to attract subsequent male aliens; there is no indication that the aliens would have attacked otherwise. Simon Dentith argues:

> All parody refunctions pre-existing text(s) and/or discourses, so that it can be said that these verbal structures are called to the readers' minds and then placed under erasure. A necessary modification of the original idea is that we must allow the act of erasure to operate critically rather than as merely neutral cancellation of its object.[70]

As such, Cornish's parody of migrant 'aliens' (one need hardly mention that this is a term also applied to foreigners), requires that the audience critically reconsiders early responses to British immigration, and whether, as is suggested by the barely disguised parody, subsequent unrest is not also the result of migrants' hostile receptions upon arrival to the country.

However, the film's critique is not limited to paralleling us/them relationships between migrant and native communities, but also challenges binaries *per se*. References to 'the beast(s)' signify three different groups operating in the film: the aliens, the gang and the police, all of whom are referred to as beasts or monsters within the first ten minutes. Upon discovery of the first alien the gang terms it the 'Beast of Brixton', whilst both Sam and an older lady who comforts her after her attack refer to the gang as 'fucking monsters', a statement that syntagmatically connotes the aliens by means of a swift camera cut to the image of the alien. In a less apparent but undeniably present reference, the first song played on the film's soundtrack is KRS-One's 'Sound of da Police', which lyrically links the police with the beast.[71] Similarly, when Moses risks his life to rid the block of the aliens the camera follows the alien pursuit accompanied by a soundtrack of police sirens, once again casting the police and the 'beasts' in the same role, as predators preying on their mutual target.

However, the destabilisation of binaries enacted in *Attack the Block* does not pave the way for a 'productive' and culturally hybrid space as envisioned by Bhabha in his construction of the 'Third Space of enunciation'.[72] Neither does it fall into the trap of the kind of banal multiculturalism that frequently focuses on sites of affluence and in so doing simultaneously represses alternative (maybe less celebratory) stories. Instead, the film explores networks of local affiliations, with the looming tower block representing the focus of identification for characters. This is cinematically represented by the way that characters are introduced in the film, a tool that is often employed to convey important or defining characteristics: their beauty, malice or occupation, for example. Close-ups of the face might suggest the focus on a character's psychology, whilst long shots might prioritise setting or location as a way of defining the character. Cornish, however, opts to introduce his characters with shots of their feet, showing little more than their shoes and the streets that they are treading. This prioritises local identity as the most important means of understanding a character, the only other signifiers that the audience can glean from the shot being vague indications of class or (lack of) vocation according to the choice and condition of the footwear.

The significance of (extremely) local affiliations, at points not seeming to extend beyond the block itself, is depicted as simultaneously liberating and entrapping. Although local affiliations cut across borders erected by class, ethnicity, gender and vocation, they do not have the power to combat national institutions, represented in this film by the police. The importance of local identity is comically conveyed in the film through a dialogue between two white characters, Brewis and Sam, in which Brewis assumes that Sam shares his desire to flee the building (to go to a house party in Fulham), whilst Sam is determined not to be chased out of her home. This flouts his assumptions of a shared identity presumably drawn from ethnicity and/or perceived class and instead prioritises her local neighbourhood as a point of identification. In a similar instance, Moses explains to Sam that they wouldn't have 'merked' her had they known she lived in the block, showing the gang's purported local integrity. However, the block – besides being the site of an alien invasion – is often visually represented as a place of entrapment, with the foreground of shots of the characters often sporting bars that mimic incarceration in a prison.

The opposing tropes of liberation and entrapment within local affiliations climax at the film's denouement, where Sam's protestations about the gang that 'I know them, they're my neighbours, they protected me' are ignored, as the bars of the police van close over Moses's face. The neighbourhood's celebration of Moses's heroic triumph over the aliens – echoed in chants of his name that penetrate the walls of the prison van – are ultimately futile, as Moses's fate lays in the hands of a national institution, not a local community. The comedy is not parochial – unduly prioritising the local at the expense of the global – but instead offers small glimmers of provisional resistance to national powers that are unique to local communities drawn together in perceived neighbourly affiliations.

The film also comically challenges multicultural rhetoric that is based in the assimilation of minority communities. This is again achieved on a local level, where Brewis – a middle-class student living at home and off his parents' wealth – represents a minority in the film due to his elevated class status. Whilst all of the members of the gang speak in London Jamaican, whether they are Caribbean in origin or not, the dialect is presented as organic and unaffected in this circumstance; however, when Brewis attempts to adopt the dialect he is cast as Other, an uninvited outsider to the linguistic group. When Brewis switches from an RP accent whilst talking to his Dad on the phone to London Jamaican when he meets the gang, he is shown as trying to perform certain cultural signifiers to assimilate to the group. Brewis changes his grammar to include double negatives and words like 'shizzle' as an attempt to assimilate, but his failure to master the discourse marks him as an outsider and at the same time the awkward silences following his contributions render him laughable.

One such scene involves the gang discussing what they should do with the alien that they have captured and killed, joking about calling Simon Cowell regarding a potential 'Alien's Got Talent' show, whilst passing around a spliff and laughing at each other's jokes. Brewis, previously at the edge of the scene, enters the room saying 'Jokes man, jokes' to be greeted by a group of hostile faces. A low-angle shot is used to look up at Brewis, but rather than showing the usual power associated with the shot, it suggests dislocation, as he is being judged by the group sitting at the eye-level of the shot. This shot shifts the social norm, as we look with the gang up at Brewis, symbolically indicating that cultural and linguistic norms are created by the majority, and in Cornish's film, unlike the outside world, Moses's gang forms the majority. When Brewis drops the affected accent and pretences of poverty he is taken more seriously and incorporated into the group. Cornish's comedy of reverse assimilation (from the mainstream to the minority) foregrounds the farcical performance required in efforts to assimilate.

Attack the Block strives to make gang members the subjects rather than the objects of representation by bringing to the forefront processes of observation and representation. As with *Four Lions*, Cornish's film also plays with the construction of fear, distinguishing between perceived and actual threat. Comedy is evoked by means of a change in discourse: as the gang runs out of Ron's apartment shouting 'Let's get tooled up blud!' he observes 'Quite sweet really, ain't they?' thereby associating their acquisition of weapons with childish play rather than violent threat. Regarding the gang members as children foregrounds their innocence and vulnerability, something that is highlighted after this comic precursor by focussing on the young ages of the gang members. Moses – who is portrayed as the leader and the most experienced – is only 15 and still owns a Spiderman duvet.

Both the film's comedy and its pathos serve to refocalise the way that gangs are considered, undermining essentialising discourses. Whilst the process of undermining is sometimes transparent and a little heavy handed ('This ain't got nothing to do with gangs. Or drugs. Or violence in rap music. Or video games'), at other times it is more subtle, with Sam acting as a foil for stereotypes about gangs. Whereas Sam swears frequently and is told off for having a 'potty mouth', members of the gang use bad language rarely and their discourse downplays the seriousness of events, for example saying 'The man's a sausage' of drug dealer Hi Hatz, who has just pointed a gun at them. Dialogue like the above also serves comically to deflate the threat that is posed: calling a man a sausage as opposed to swearing refuses to give credit to threat, even when the threat is (diegetically speaking) real. Stephen Hessel argues that 'Despite [...] openness to the incursion of fear, the expectation of laughter postpones the very same anxiety that produces it.'[73] It can similarly be argued that Cornish, like Morris, *deliberately* offers laughter as an alternative response to cultural anxieties, thereby reducing the propensity for fear.

By way of conclusion I will make reference to both *Four Lions* and *Attack the Block* in order to consider exactly how this recent wave of postcolonial comedy differs from what went before. Although this recent wave of postcolonial comedy is far more daring when it comes to representing the realities of multicultural Britain often obscured or omitted by more celebratory accounts, there is, however, a sudden scarcity of the strong female characters that populated the previous generation of comedy. Omar's wife, Sofia, has the largest female role in *Four Lions*, but she still has very little screen-time and reasons for her support for Omar's suicide mission are left frustratingly unarticulated throughout. Meanwhile, androgynously named Sam is the only female character to accompany the gang in *Attack the Block*, and she mainly occupies the role of victim by aligning herself to a gang that has previously mugged her for the sake of her own protection against the aliens. Rather than undergoing a satisfying character development of her own, she serves as a foil for the development of the protagonist, Moses, who moves from gangster to hero in the space of the film. This marks a change in focus from the decidedly more universal, and somewhat less controversial 'battle of the sexes', which warranted the plethora of strong female characters, to culturally specific manifestations of issues related to class, violence and religion in the most recent films.

What we are witnessing through the marginalisation of women in this recent generation of comedy is an increasing focus on young men, who have a well-documented history of stigmatisation and disenfranchisement from society. The homosocial bonds created between the men in these films therefore offer an alternative site of power in the face of economic recession, prejudice, and in the case of *Four Lions*, Islamophobia. As I mentioned in the introduction to this chapter, Purdie's psychoanalytic exploration of joking suggests that sharing in a joke creates a reciprocal collusion of the teller and the audience as masterful jokers, the Butt of the joke being excluded from this relationship.[74] This suggests that joking can form the basis for a sense of power or superiority. The men's socio-political impotence, signified by their exclusion and alienation, is thus partially compensated by the linguistic prowess that drives their witty repartee. The marginalisation of women in recent multicultural British comedy therefore seems, if not inevitable, then at least comprehensible in the context of the increased media stigmatisation and disenfranchisement experienced by young men. This has warranted a form of comedy that belatedly and partially compensates for the experience of social impotence and alienation by means of a focus on homosocial bonds that are strengthened through the linguistic power granted by the successful telling of jokes.

Another way in which the later wave of films differs is in the foregrounding of religious modes of affiliation. Unlike the first wave of films considered, in which religious values are pushed to the margins and/or associated with an older generation, Morris's film reinstates religion in comedy, with a religious belief – however confused – being the key point of affiliation and identification for the majority of the characters. This marks a shift in contemporary society, where especially since the 9/11 and 7/7 bombings there has been an increased pressure on British Muslims to articulate precisely their national and religious affiliations, with high-profile commentators like Ziauddin Sardar bemoaning the 'constant requirement' to provide explanations for incidents such as 7/7.[75] Sardar roots the increased publicity and politicisation of British Muslim citizens in a number of causes, from the politicisation of Pakistani Barelvis at the end of the twentieth century that was eventually paralleled in Britain's (majority Barevli) Muslim population, to the 'toxic environment' created by British foreign policy.[76]

Yet, in the very year of the 7/7 bombings, Avril Horner and Sue Zlosnik suggest that 'loss of transcendence [...] characterises the modern [presumably western] condition'. They argue that this loss of transcendence can inspire both comedy and terror as a Manichean view of good and evil collapses, leaving uncertainty in its place.[77] It might, therefore, be argued that because of the seemingly 'modern' use of comedy that derives humour from what could otherwise be terrifying, the intended audience is not religious, and might as such view religion ironically or as posing a subjective rather than objective perspective on the world. This would tie in with what Horner and Zlosnik argue is the telos of the comic: 'throw[ing] the frames of social reference into doubt and mak[ing] moral judgement appear a matter of relativity'. In this manner they suggest that 'the comic can function as intellectually liberating, despite closures that appear to be conservative in restoring the individual to society'.[78]

However, it is at this point that that both Morris's and Cornish's films differ from Horner and Zlosnik's definition of 'modern' comedy and enable a social challenge: they do not have conventionally happy endings and as such do not serve to return the individual to society. I support Umberto Eco's view that 'carnival can only exist as *authorized* transgression' (emphasis in original) through which the individual is sated (or sedated) and returned to society for the remainder of the year.[79]

Morris's and Cornish's films bring the dominant society into question by refusing to provide comic resolution. Whilst *Four Lions* finishes with all four of the 'lions' having blown themselves up, *Attack the Block*'s protagonist – Moses – is taken away in a police van, despite the neighbourhood's vocal support of him. As such, transgression is not 'authorized' in the films and their uncomic endings make them modally rather than generically comic.

All of the films considered within this chapter are works of postcolonial British comedy, yet what this has meant for each generation has shifted according to contemporaneous social prejudice and political ideals. The overriding desire expressed by the first wave of films is for a happily multicultural society facilitated through an ostensibly inclusive form of comedy. These films are sometimes problematic for their inclination to repress social problems in pursuit of a utopian ideal and for subordinating to a white mainstream hegemony. However, without the work achieved by this first wave of postcolonial British filmmakers, later cinematic output – with its darkly ironic tone that assumes the luxury of stereotypes not being taken at face value – may not have been possible. The later films diverge from their predecessors by addressing what (and who) is repressed in such utopian multicultural desires, focussing on fears exacerbated through hysteric media that affect particular migrant groups. These films posit laughter as an alternative response to a sense of threat, and in so doing critique a society driven by the production of cultural fears. In previous decades, perhaps it was more conceivable, or indeed helpful, to invest cinema with transformative and utopian potential, but in the throes of an increasingly right-wing and nationalist politics, it is more important to be able to laugh at and thereby potentially undermine ways in which cultural fear is relentlessly constructed and disseminated.

Conclusion: Genre Revisited

This study has identified and explored four new genres that have evolved to accommodate and negotiate the changing face of postcolonial Britain since 1990. It has focussed on the way that notions of Britishness are challenged and rewritten in genre fiction that operates on the borders of mainstream literary fiction in terms of both market consumption and critical attention. I have illustrated ways in which the new genres identified simultaneously challenge and reinscribe both national and generic borders by opening up to postcolonial topics, authors and contexts. British Muslim Bildungsromane, gothic tales of postcolonial England, the subcultural urban novel and multicultural British comedy have been explored as four new genres that interrogate both their generic forebears and traditions and the representations of Britishness that they are generically bound or designed to perpetuate.

Chapter 1, centred on British Muslim Bildungsromane, argued that in the wake of the 'Rushdie affair' Hanif Kureishi, Robin Yassin-Kassab and Leila Aboulela have rejected the allure of hybrid identities celebrated in *The Satanic Verses* and instead adopted the Bildungsroman form as an apposite space in which characters can negotiate affiliations and reach a stable sense of identity. As I have shown, British Muslim Bildungsromane explore networks of affiliations, representing the desire for a fixed mode of identifying by engaging with the trauma of its absence. Moving away from overly sanguine or optimistic accounts of hybrid identities, this chapter foregrounded readings of painful processes of transformation or conversion that bespoke the desire for a stable identity and belief system that would reinvest the world with meaning and the possibility of communal identification. I have suggested that the re-centring of religious (as opposed to national, racial or ethnic) identities in recent British Bildungsromane should serve as a challenge to postcolonial theorists to open up to religious topics. Furthermore, I have argued that postcolonial writing in contemporary Britain entails a concern for decentring ideas of nationhood as the only – or the primary – source of identification, instead opening up the 'imagined community' to multiple sources of affiliation that the authors variously demonstrate do not have to be mutually exclusive.

Chapter 2 turned to gothic tales of postcolonial England, a new subgenre that I have identified as negotiating postcolonial gothic concerns within the former colonial centre in order to give voice to the traumas of racism and alienation that cause ethnic minority characters to experience themselves as Other. As I have shown, this subgenre marks a departure from existing criticism on postcolonial gothic that tends to locate it elsewhere, in countries that were formerly colonis*ed* rather than colonis*ing*. I argued that this new subgenre has three crucial functions: it challenges imperial gothic in which alterity is often equated with monstrosity so as to voice perceived threats of foreign invasion of the self/nation; it appropriates familiar gothic tropes and repurposes them to express fears and traumas associated with migration, alienation and racism from the perspective of ethnic minority characters; and it sometimes (although not always) posits ways of dealing with the legacies of colonial trauma. Engaging with novels by Meera Syal, Nadeem Aslam, Hanif Kureishi and Helen Oyeyemi, I suggested that a division emerges in this diverse body of literature between novels that seek to foreground the lingering and insurmountable effects of colonial trauma by denying closure or resolution, and those in which a perverse desire for trauma is appropriated as a means of generating a sense of collective heritage.

In Chapter 3, I argued that the subcultural urban novel radically shifts the conventional paradigm of postcolonial fiction, as rather than 'writing back' to the (former) colonial centre, it is produced for the consumption of a community of insiders. As I have demonstrated, the subcultural urban novel makes its departure from more mainstream novelistic representations of minority cultures (as explored via Hanif Kureishi's *The Buddha of Suburbia* and Zadie Smith's *White Teeth*) through a change in what I have termed 'imagined audience' from white majority to subcultural minority, as books are increasingly marketed to subcultural insiders. I have suggested that the reframing involved in talking about subcultures rather than minority cultures involves both a generational shift and a positional shift in terms of attitudes towards the mainstream. It also marks a shift towards self-determination as a subcultural member, for those who may have had the labels of 'otherness' or difference thrust upon them (due to ethnic or class allegiances that mark a deviance from the 'norm'). I have argued that subcultural affiliation means that these labels can be transformed into a choice or oppositional stance, recasting subcultural members as agents rather than victims. Novels discussed as part of this new genre – by Karline Smith, Gautam Malkani and Nirpal Singh Dhaliwal – used consumerist and sexual desires and systems of value in order to comment upon and critique the construction of multicultural Britain by focussing on the problematic topics of violence, hypermasculinity, gangs and misogyny that are often passed over by more utopian (political and literary) accounts of multiculturalism. This chapter raised important questions regarding the responsibility of postcolonial academics not to repeat acts of exclusion already performed in corporate publishing preferences.

The final chapter tracked the evolution of multicultural British comedy through two distinct phases, the first of which was defined by a desire to represent a happy multicultural society with inclusive laughter as its aim, whilst the second of which was defined by the use of comedy as an alternative response to media constructions of fear. Shifting attitudes towards 'multiculturalism' structured my readings of the films, as I moved from those that celebrated a (problematically exclusive) multicultural Britain to those that took the hypocrisies of multicultural politics *as* the source of comedy and satirical attack. I suggested that comedy has an ambivalent potential for both radical social critique and inclusive humorous appeasement, taking into account both the political and the psychological effects of laughter that are harnessed by the comedies under consideration here. Postcolonial comedy seeks to challenge the residual stereotypes and hierarchies of the colonial era, but as the social dominant shifts according to government, international affairs and new modes of exclusion, I have traced ways in which the types of comedy and subject matter must also evolve in order to remain socially relevant.

This study has been contained to the discussion of four new genres that have emerged to accommodate the changing face of postcolonial Britain since 1990. This list of new genres is not exhaustive, however, and there are obvious areas for expansion to take into account other genres (including crime, sci-fi and the noir thriller) that have similarly evolved to reflect the desires and fears of postcolonial Britain. Each time genres expand to include postcolonial topics the boundaries of genre are redrawn and postcolonial theory must adapt to address questions raised therein. Focussing on the postcolonial sci-fi, for example, might lead to questions over the representation of aliens, the politics of fantasy or the kinds of social critique enabled through the portrayal of dystopian worlds. The postcolonial noir thriller might engender discussion around constructions of criminality, morality, deviance, exclusion, social injustice, and so on. So there is no tidy way of concluding the story of postcolonial British genre fiction, as the parameters constantly shift and change in order to encompass new ways of desiring, new objects of fear and new fashions in the production and consumption of literature. The intention of this work has been to raise the profile of postcolonial genre studies by indicating ways in which British identity is approached, shaped and critiqued from the margins. In turn, I hope that this work will open up the field of postcolonial genre studies to academics researching other locations and histories.

Notes and References

Introduction

1. Gurinder Chadha, cited in Ben Quinn, 'Bend It Like Beckham to be made into musical', *The Guardian*, 31 October 2014, http://www.theguardian.com/stage/2014/oct/31/bend-it-like-beckham-musical (accessed 5 January 2015).
2. See 'About', Bend It Like Beckham: The Musical, http://www.benditlikebeckhamthemusical.co.uk/about/ (accessed 31 January 2015).
3. Gurinder Chadha and Sonia Friedman, 'Exclusive: A new British musical about where we are now: Gurinder Chadha and Sonia Friedman on what inspired them to tackle Bend It Like Beckham the musical', *Bend it Like Beckham: The Musical*, http://benditlikebeckhamthemusical.co.uk/?gclid=Cj0KEQiAiamlBRCgj83PiYm6--gBEiQArnojD8OY81uGgNtQDEKMgO7m0SJ1xzV4U4wR0S-J-Tpx7AYaAqiL8P8HAQ#content (accessed 5 January 2015).
4. Benedict Anderson, *Imagined Communities* (London: Verso, 1991), p. 4; Homi K. Bhabha, 'Introduction: Narrating the Nation', in *Nation and Narration*, ed. by Homi K. Bhabha (London: Routledge, 1990), pp. 1–7 (p. 1).
5. Homi K. Bhabha, 'DissemiNation: Time, Narrative, and the Margins of the Modern Nation', in *Nation and Narration*, ed. by Homi K. Bhabha (London: Routledge, 1990), pp. 291–322 (p. 297).
6. Angela Carter, cited in Anne Hegerfeldt, 'The Stars that Spring from Bastardising: Wise Children Go For Shakespeare', *Zeitschrift Für Englische Philologie*, 121 (2003), 351–72 (p. 371).
7. Bill Ashcroft, Gareth Griffiths and Helen Tiffin, *Key Concepts in Post-Colonial Studies* (London: Routledge, 1998), p. 150.
8. Peter Brooks, *Reading for the Plot: Design and Intention in Narrative* (London: Harvard University Press, 1992), p. 37.
9. Brooks, *Reading for the Plot*, pp. 90, 91.
10. Mark Currie, *About Time: Narrative, Fiction and the Philosophy of Time* (Edinburgh: Edinburgh University Press, 2007), pp. 12, 18.
11. I borrow Brooks's terms here (p. 77).
12. Peter Morey and Amina Yaqin, *Framing Muslims: Stereotyping and Representation after 9/11* (Cambridge, MA: Harvard University Press, 2011), p. 36.
13. Rick Altman, *Film/Genre* (London: BFI Publishing, 1999), p. 198.
14. Altman, *Film/Genre*, p. 195.
15. Altman, *Film/Genre*, pp. 204–5.
16. Vron Ware, 'The White Fear Factor', in *Terror and the Postcolonial*, ed. by Elleke Boehmer and Stephen Morton (Chichester: Wiley-Blackwell, 2009), pp. 99–112 (p. 106).
17. Fredric Jameson, 'Magical Narratives: On the Dialectical Use of Genre Criticism', in *Modern Genre Theory*, ed. by David Duff (Harlow: Longman, 2000), pp. 167–92 (p. 168).
18. Jameson, 'Magical Narratives', p. 175.

19. David Duff, 'Introduction', in *Modern Genre Theory*, ed. by David Duff (Harlow: Longman, 2000), pp. 1–24 (p. 2).
20. Vladimir Propp, 'Fairy Tale Transformations', in *Modern Genre Theory*, ed. by David Duff (Harlow: Longman, 2000), pp. 50–67.
21. Bill Ashcroft, Gareth Griffiths and Helen Tiffin, *The Empire Writes Back*, 2nd edition (London: Routledge, 2003), p. 2.
22. John McLeod, *Postcolonial London: Rewriting the Metropolis* (London: Routledge, 2004), p. 14.
23. McLeod, *Postcolonial London*, p. 15.
24. James Procter, 'General Introduction', in *Writing Black Britain 1948–1998*, ed. by James Procter (Manchester: Manchester University Press, 2000), pp. 1–12 (p. 7).
25. Charlotte Williams, *Sugar and Slate* (Aberystwyth: Planet, 2002), p. 175.
26. With reference to the 'Parekh Report' of 2000, Anne-Marie Fortier argues that 'Because of [the] association [of Englishness] with white supremacy, white privilege, imperialism, and its historical position at the centre of British political and cultural life, [the report] rejects Englishness as an appropriate label for the re-imagined multi-ethnic nation'. Anne-Marie Fortier, *Multicultural Horizons: Diversity and the Limits of the Civil Nation* (London: Routledge, 2008), p. 25.
27. Amin Malak, *Muslim Narratives and the Discourse of English* (Albany: State University of New York Press, 2005), p. 7.
28. Kobena Mercer, 'Back to My Routes: A Postscript to the 1980s (1990)', in *Writing Black Britain 1948–1998*, ed. by James Procter (Manchester: Manchester University Press, 2000), pp. 285–93 (p. 287).
29. James Procter, *Dwelling Places: Postwar Black British Writing* (Manchester: Manchester University Press, 2003), p. 171.
30. Chris Allen, 'From Race to Religion: The New Face of Discrimination', in *Muslim Britain: Communities Under Pressure*, ed. by Tahir Abbas (London: Zed Books, 2005), pp. 49–65 (p. 54).
31. Allen, 'From Race to Religion', p. 55.
32. Paul Weller, *A Mirror for our Times: 'The Rushdie Affair' and the Future of Multiculturalism* (London: Continuum, 2009), p. 2.
33. Homi Bhabha, *The Location of Culture* (London: Routledge, 2000), p. 6.
34. Gayatri Spivak, 'Reading *The Satanic Verses*', in *What is an Author?* ed. by Maurice Biriotti and Nicola Miller (Manchester: Manchester University Press, 1993), pp. 104–34 (p. 126).
35. Tariq Modood, *Multicultural Politics: Racism, Ethnicity and Muslims in Britain* (Edinburgh: Edinburgh University Press, 2005), p. 106.
36. Modood, *Multicultural Politics*, pp. 106–7.
37. Modood, *Multicultural Politics*, p. 111.
38. Salman Rushdie, *The Satanic Verses* (London: Vintage, 2006), p. 102. All further references shall be given parenthetically in the text.
39. Salman Rushdie, *Imaginary Homelands* (London: Vintage, 2010), p. 394.
40. Bhabha, *Location of Culture*, p. 6.
41. Rushdie, *Imaginary Homelands*, p. 394.
42. In her poem 'So you think I'm a mule?' Jackie Kay dismisses terms such as 'hybrid', 'mulatto' and 'half-caste' for carrying connotations of impurity and miscegenation. Jackie Kay, 'So you think I'm a mule', in *Writing Black Britain 1948–1998*, ed. by James Procter (Manchester: Manchester University Press, 2000), pp. 202–4.

43. Rushdie, *Imaginary Homelands*, p. 394.
44. Salman Rushdie, *Joseph Anton: A Memoir* (London: Jonathan Cape, 2012), p. 177.
45. Rushdie, *Imaginary Homelands*, p. 376.
46. The 'Parting of the Arabian Sea' section recounts the Ayesha *Hajj* in which a village is led into the Arabian Sea. The narrative leaves it ambiguous as to whether the pilgrims drown or walk along the bottom of the ocean to complete their *hajj*. Other non-realist elements revolve around ghosts, Mephistophelean narrators and characters with an angel/devil complex.
47. John Erickson, *Islam and Postcolonial Narrative* (Cambridge: Cambridge University Press, 1998), p. 142.
48. Rushdie, *The Satanic Verses*, p. 37.
49. Ian Baucom, *Out of Place: Englishness, Empire and the Locations of Identity* (Princeton: Princeton University Press, 1999), p. 204.
50. Joyce Wexler, 'What is a Nation? Magic Realism and National Identity in Midnight's Children and Clear Light of Day', *Journal of Commonwealth Literature*, 37 (2002), 137–55 (p. 138).
51. Rushdie, *The Satanic Verses*, p. 174.
52. This paradigm was famously propounded in Ashcroft, Griffiths and Tiffin's seminal work *The Empire Writes Back*.
53. See V. S. Naipaul, *The Mimic Men* (London: Vintage, 2001).
54. Graham Huggan, *The Postcolonial Exotic: Marketing the Margins* (London: Routledge, 2001), p. 93.
55. Rushdie, *The Satanic Verses*, p. 3.
56. Tariq Modood, 'British Asian Muslims and the Rushdie Affair', *Political Quarterly*, 61.2 (1990), 143–60 (p. 154).
57. See further Rushdie's essays 'In God We Trust,' 'In Good Faith,' 'Is Nothing Sacred' and 'One Thousand Days in a Balloon' in *Imaginary Homelands*, pp. 376–92, 393–414, 415–29, 430–39.
58. Bhabha, *Location of Culture*, p. 86.
59. Lindsey Moore, 'Special Issue: Glocal Imaginaries: Preface', *Postcolonial Text*, 6.2 (2011), http://www.postcolonial.org/index.php/pct/article/download/1323/1169 (accessed 18 November 2012), 1–7 (p. 4).
60. Bhabha, *Location of Culture*, p. 66.
61. Mikhail Bakhtin, 'Rabelais and His World', excerpt in *The Bakhtin Reader*, ed. by Pam Morris (Edward Arnold: London, 1994), pp. 194–244 (p. 206).
62. John Clement Ball, *Satire and the Postcolonial Novel: V. S. Naipaul, Chinua Achebe, Salman Rushdie* (London: Routledge, 2003), pp. 13, 120.
63. For further discussion on fears projected onto Black masculinity, see Frantz Fanon's chapter on 'The Negro and Psychopathology' in *Black Skin, White Masks*, trans. by Charles Lam Markmann (London: Paladin, 1972), pp. 100–48.

1   British Muslim Bildungsromane

1. See Eric Pickles, 'Letter to Muslim leaders: The text in full', *The Independent* (19 January 2015), http://www.independent.co.uk/news/uk/eric-pickles-letter-to-muslim-leaders-the-text-in-full-9987249.html (accessed 15 February 2015).

The Charlie Hebdo shootings took place on 7 January 2015, when Saïd and Chérif Kouachi, identifying as members of Al-Qaida, entered the Paris office of satirical magazine *Charlie Hebdo* and assassinated eleven members of staff.

2. I borrow Giovanna Borradori's term for describing 'the way in which we believe rather than what we believe in'. Giovanna Borradori, 'Introduction: Terrorism and the Legacy of the Enlightenment – Habermas and Derrida', in *Philosophy in a Time of Terror: Dialogues with Jürgen Habermas and Jacques Derrida*, ed. by Giovanna Borradori (Chicago: Chicago University Press, 2003), pp. 1–22 (p. 18).

3. Peter Morey and Amina Yaqin, *Framing Muslims: Stereotyping and Representation after 9/11* (Cambridge, MA: Harvard University Press, 2011), p. 3.

4. Morey and Yaqin, *Framing Muslims*, p. 21.

5. Amin Malak, *Muslim Narratives and the Discourse of English* (Albany: State University of New York Press, 2005), p. 17.

6. See, for example, Franco Moretti, *The Way of the World: The Bildungsroman in European Culture*, new edition, trans. by Albert Sbragia (London: Verso, 2000), p. 3.

7. Moretti, *The Way of the World*, p. 10.

8. Moretti, *The Way of the World*, p. 11.

9. Morey and Yaqin, *Framing Muslims*, p. 36.

10. Mark Stein, *Black British Literature: Novels of Transformation* (Columbus: Ohio State University Press, 2004), p. xv.

11. Stein, *Black British Literature*, p. 43.

12. Feroza Jussawalla, 'Kim, Huck and Naipaul: Using the Postcolonial Bildungsroman to (Re)define Postcoloniality', *Links and Letters*, 4 (1997), 25–38 (p. 35).

13. Esra Mirze Santesso, *Disorientation: Muslim Identity in Contemporary Anglophone Literature* (Basingstoke: Palgrave Macmillan, 2013), p. 18.

14. Santesso, *Disorientation*, p. 19.

15. Arthur Bradley and Andrew Tate, *The New Atheist Novel: Fiction, Philosophy and Polemic after 9/11* (London: Continuum, 2010), p. 106.

16. Robin Yassin-Kassab, *The Road from Damascus* (London: Penguin, 2009), p. 334. All further references shall be given parenthetically in the text.

17. Sigmund Freud, *Penguin Freud Library*, ed. by Angela Richards, trans. by James Strachey, 15 vols (London: Penguin, 1958), *IV: The Interpretation of Dreams*, p. 364.

18. Peter Brooks, *Reading for the Plot: Design and Intention in Narrative* (London: Harvard University Press, 1992), p. 36.

19. Hanif Kureishi, *The Black Album* (London: Faber and Faber, 2003), p. 165. All further references shall be given parenthetically in the text.

20. Robin Yassin-Kassab, 'Islam in the Writing Process', *Religion and Literature*, 43.1 (2011), 139–44 (p. 140).

21. Salman Rushdie, *The Satanic Verses* (London: Vintage, 2006), p. 295.

22. C. E. Rashid, 'British Islam and the Novel of Transformation: Robin Yassin-Kassab's *The Road from Damascus*', *Journal of Postcolonial Writing*, 48.1 (2012), 92–103 (p. 93).

23. Yassin-Kassab, 'Islam in the Writing Process', p. 139.

24. Frederic M. Holmes, 'The Postcolonial Subject Divided between East and West: Kureishi's *The Black Album* as an Intertext of Rushdie's *The Satanic*

Verses', *Papers on Language and Literature: A Journal for Scholars and Critics of Language and Literature*, 37.3 (2001), 296–313 (p. 310).

25. Hans Robert Jauss, 'Theory of Genres and Medieval Literature', in *Modern Genre Theory*, ed. by David Duff (London: Longman, 1999), pp. 127–47 (p. 131).

26. Maria Degabriele, 'Prince of Darkness Meets Priestess of Porn: Sexual and Political Identities in Hanif Kureishi's *The Black Album*', *Intersections: Gender and Sexuality in Asia and the Pacific*, 2 (May 1999), http://www.inter sections.anu.edu.au/issue2/Kureishi.html (accessed 3 August 2010) (para. 8 of 29).

27. Brian McHale, *Postmodernist Fiction* (London: Methuen, 1994), p. 10.

28. Holmes, 'The Postcolonial Subject', p. 306.

29. McHale, p. 4.

30. Degabriele, para. 25 of 29.

31. Degabriele, para. 29 of 29.

32. Holmes, *Postmodernist Fiction*, p. 308.

33. Conversely, in other works Kureishi often figures love as the great uniter against selfish individualism or in the face of struggle. An example of this can be found in the film *My Beautiful Laundrette*, dir. by Stephen Frears (Film4, 1985).

34. Moretti, *The Way of the World*, p. 8.

35. Yassin-Kassab, *The Road from Damascus*, p. 6.

36. Renaldo J. Maduro and Joseph B. Wheelright, 'Archetype and Archetypal Image', in *Jungian Literary Criticism*, ed. by Richard P. Sugg (Evanston: Northwestern University Press, 1992), pp. 181–6 (p. 184).

37. Elleke Boehmer, *Stories of Women: Gender and Narrative in the Postcolonial Nation* (Manchester: Manchester University Press, 2005), p. 3.

38. Boehmer, *Stories of Women*, p. 27.

39. Leila Aboulela, *The Translator* (Edinburgh: Polygon, 2008), p. 12. All further references shall be given parenthetically in the text.

40. William Wordsworth, 'Ode: Intimations of Immortality from Recollections of Early Childhood', in *The Norton Anthology of Poetry*, ed. by Margaret Ferguson, Mary Jo Salter and Jon Stallworthy, 5th edition (New York: Norton, 2005), pp. 796–801.

41. Boehmer, *Stories of* Women, p. 29.

42. Waïl S. Hassan, 'Leila Aboulela and the Ideology of Muslim Immigrant Fiction', *Novel: A Forum on Fiction*, 41.2 (Spring–Summer 2008), 298–319 (pp. 304–5).

43. Amartya Sen, *Identity and Violence: The Illusion of Destiny* (London: Penguin, 2006), p. xv.

44. Leila Aboulela, *Minaret* (London: Bloomsbury, 2006), p. 110. All further references shall be given parenthetically in the text.

45. Sen, *Identity and Violence*, p. 99.

46. Hassan, 'Leila Aboulela', p. 299.

47. Anna Ball, '"Here is where I am": Rerouting Diasporic Experience in Leila Aboulela's Recent Novels', in *Rerouting the Postcolonial: New Directions for the New Millennium*, ed. by Janet Wilson, Cristina Şandru and Sarah Lawson Welsh (London: Routledge, 2010), pp. 118–27 (p. 125).

48. Simon Gikandi, 'Between Roots and Routes: Cosmopolitanism and the Claims of Locality', in *Rerouting the Postcolonial: New Directions for the New Millennium*, ed. by Janet Wilson, Cristina Şandru and Sarah Lawson Welsh (London: Routledge, 2010), pp. 22–35 (p. 29).

49. Anna Ball, '"Here is where I am"', p. 118.

50. Aboulela, *The Translator*, p. 22.
51. Hassan, 'Leila Aboulela', p. 314.
52. Hassan, 'Leila Aboulela', p. 316.
53. Morey and Yaqin, *Framing Muslims*, p. 36.
54. Morey and Yaqin, *Framing Muslims*, p. 36.
55. Geoffrey Nash, *The Anglo-Arab Encounter: Fiction and Autobiography by Arab Writers in English* (Bern: Peter Lang, 2007), p. 150.
56. Edward Said, *Orientalism* (London: Penguin, 2003), p. 1.
57. Said, *Orientalism*, p. 5.
58. Said, *Orientalism*, p. 45.
59. Ian Buruma and Avishai Margalit, *Occidentalism: The West in the Eyes of its Enemies* (New York: Penguin, 2004), p. 10.
60. Anna Ball, '"Here is where I am"', p. 125.
61. Tina Steiner, 'Strategic Nostalgia, Islam and Cultural Translation in Leila Aboulela's *The Translator* and *Coloured Lights*', *Current Writing: Text and Reception in Southern Africa*, 20.2 (2008), 7–25 (p. 22).
62. *Qur'an* 30.21.
63. Shelina Zahra Janmohamed, *Love in a Headscarf: Muslim Woman Seeks the One* (London: Aurum Press, 2009).
64. Olivier Roy, *Globalised Islam: The Search for a New Ummah* (London: C. Hurst, 2004), p. 3.
65. Bradley and Tate, *The New Atheist Novel*, p. 109.
66. Bradley and Tate, *The New Atheist Novel*, p. 105.
67. Bradley and Tate, *The New Atheist Novel*, p. 109.
68. Claire Chambers, 'Religion and the Lions of Literature', *Times Higher Education* (8 November 2012), http://www.timeshighereducation.co.uk/story.asp?story Code=410565&sectioncode=26 (accessed 10 June 2010) (para. 4 of 8).
69. Chambers, 'Religion', para. 5 of 8.
70. Claire Chambers, 'An Interview with Leila Aboulela', *Contemporary Women's Writing*, 3.1 (2009), http://cww.oxfordjournals.org/content/3/1/86.extract (accessed 21 February 2011), 86–102 (p. 100).
71. Roy, *Globalised Islam*, p. 3.
72. Sadia Abbas, 'Leila Aboulela, Religion and the Challenge of the Novel', *Contemporary Literature*, 52.3 (2011), 430–61 (pp. 436, 437).
73. Abbas, 'Leila Aboulela', p. 445.
74. Abbas, 'Leila Aboulela', p. 455.
75. Christina Phillips, 'Leila Aboulela's *The Translator*: Reading Islam in the West', *Wasafiri*, 27.1 (2012), 66–72 (p. 68).
76. Yassin-Kassab, *The Road from Damascus*, p. 60.
77. Rushdie, *The Satanic Verses*, p. 8.

2   Gothic Tales of Postcolonial England

1. James Procter and Angela Smith, 'Gothic and Empire', in *The Routledge Companion to Gothic*, ed. by Catherine Spooner and Emma McEvoy (Abingdon: Routledge, 2007), pp. 95–104 (p. 96).
2. Alexandra Warwick, 'Feeling Gothicky?', *Gothic Studies*, 9 (2007), 5–19 (p. 11).
3. Chris Baldick, 'Introduction', in *The Oxford Book of Gothic Tales*, ed. by Chris Baldick (Oxford: Oxford University Press, 1992), pp. xi–xxiii (p. xix).

4. For more on links between gothic, colonialism and postcolonialism see Andrew Smith and William Hughes (eds), *Empire and the Gothic: The Politics of Genre* (Basingstoke: Palgrave Macmillan, 2003); Tabish Khair, *The Gothic, Postcolonialism and Otherness: Ghosts from Elsewhere* (Basingstoke: Palgrave Macmillan, 2009); Alison Rudd, *Postcolonial Gothic Fictions from the Caribbean, Canada, Australia and New Zealand* (Cardiff: University of Wales Press, 2010).

5. David Punter, *Postcolonial Imaginings: Fictions of a New World Order* (Edinburgh: Edinburgh University Press, 2000), pp. 5–6.

6. CFMEB (Commission on the Future of Multi-Ethnic Britain), *The Future of Multiethnic Britain: The Parekh Report* (London: Profile Books, 2000), pp. 36, 25.

7. Anne-Marie Fortier, *Multicultural Horizons: Diversity and the Limits of the Civil Nation* (London: Routledge, 2008), p. 25.

8. Robert Miles, *Gothic Writing 1750–1820: A Genealogy* (London: Routledge, 2003), p. 31.

9. Paul Gilroy, *After Empire: Melancholia or Convivial Culture?* (Abingdon: Routledge, 2004), p. 95.

10. Iain Banks, *The Wasp Factory* (London: Abacus, 2004).

11. Meera Syal, *Anita and Me* (London: Flamingo, 1997), pp. 149–50. All further references shall be given parenthetically in the text.

12. Kelly Hurley, 'Abject and Grotesque', in *The Routledge Companion to Gothic*, ed. by Catherine Spooner and Emma McEvoy (Abingdon: Routledge, 2007), pp. 137–46 (p. 144).

13. Julia Kristeva, *Powers of Horror: An Essay on Abjection* (New York: Columbia University Press, 1982), p. 1.

14. Kristeva, *Powers of Horror*, p. 4.

15. Helen Oyeyemi, *The Icarus Girl* (London: Bloomsbury, 2006), p. 257. All further references shall be given parenthetically in the text.

16. Sarah Ilott and Chloe Buckley, '"Fragmenting and Becoming Double": Supplementary Twins and Abject Bodies in Helen Oyeyemi's *The Icarus Girl*', *Journal of Commonwealth Literature* (2015) [published online first at http://www.jcl.sagepub.com/content/early/2015/01/28/0021989414563999.full.pdf+html], 1–14 (p. 1). I make brief reference to this article in the course of the current chapter, but to see the expanded argument on processes of abjection within *The Icarus Girl*, please see the full article.

17. Nadeem Aslam, *Maps for Lost Lovers* (London: Faber and Faber, 2005), p. 304. All further references shall be given parenthetically in the text.

18. Lindsey Moore, 'British Muslim Identities and Spectres of Terror in Nadeem Aslam's Maps for Lost Lovers', *Postcolonial Text*, 5.2 (2009), http://www.postcolonial.org/index.php/pct/article/view/1017/946 (accessed 24 August 2012), 1–19, p. 10.

19. For Kristeva, abjection is associated with primal repression and enables the constitution of subject/object boundaries. Kristeva, *Powers of Horror*, p. 12.

20. Judith Butler, *Precarious Life: The Powers of Mourning and Violence* (London: Verso, 2004), p. 26.

21. Helen Oyeyemi, *White is for Witching* (London: Picador, 2009). All further references shall be given parenthetically in the text.

22. This synopsis is paraphrased from a longer article that I wrote as an entry on the novel for the *Literary Encyclopedia*. See Sarah Ilott, 'White Is for

Witching', *The Literary Encyclopedia*, (1 August 2013), http://www.litencyc. com/php/sworks.php?rec=true&UID=35030 (accessed 8 January 2015).

23. Ngũgĩ wa Thiong'o, *Decolonising the Mind: The Politics of Language in African Literature* (Martlesham: James Currey, 2011).

24. Patrick Colm Hogan, *Colonialism and Cultural Identity: Crises of Tradition in the Anglophone Literatures of India, Africa and the Caribbean* (Albany: State University of New York Press, 2000), p. 10.

25. Ilott and Buckley, "Fragmenting and Becoming Double", p. 7.

26. Vron Ware, 'The White Fear Factor', in *Terror and the Postcolonial*, ed. by Elleke Boehmer and Stephen Morton (Chichester: Wiley-Blackwell, 2009), pp. 99–112 (p. 106).

27. William Wordsworth, 'At Dover', in *The Sonnets of William Wordsworth: Collected In One Volume With A Few Additional Ones Now First Published* (1838) (Whitefish, MT: Kessinger Publishing, 2008), p. 212; Lord Byron, *Don Juan* (Kindle Edition), p. 246; Vera Lynn, 'The White Cliffs of Dover', 1942.

28. Maud Ellmann, *The Hunger Artists: Starving, Writing and Imprisonment* (London: Virago, 1993), pp. 30–1.

29. Syal, *Anita and Me*, p. 314.

30. See further Jacques Lacan, 'The Mirror Stage as Formative of the Function of the I as Revealed in Psychoanalytic Experience', in *Ecrits: A Selection*, trans. by Alan Sheridan (London: Tavistock, 1985), pp. 1–8.

31. Homi Bhabha, *The Location of Culture* (London: Routledge, 2000), p. 77.

32. Bhabha, *The Location of Culture*, p. 77.

33. Diana Adesola Mafe, 'Ghostly Girls in the "Eerie Bush": Helen Oyeyemi's *The Icarus Girl* as Postcolonial Female Gothic Fiction', *Research in African Literatures*, 42.3 (2012), 21–35 (p. 28).

34. Mafe, 'Ghostly Girls', p. 29.

35. Frantz Fanon, *Black Skin, White Masks*, trans. by Charles Lam Markmann (London: Paladin, 1972), p. 82.

36. Khair, *The Gothic, Postcolonialism and Otherness* p. 4.

37. See further Edward W. Said, *Orientalism* (London: Penguin, 2003).

38. Bhabha, *The Location of Culture*, p. 75.

39. Khair, *The Gothic, Postcolonialism and Otherness*, p. 4.

40. Sigmund Freud, 'The Uncanny', in *Collected Papers*, ed. by Ernest Jones, trans. by Joan Riviere, 4 vols (London: Hogarth,1934) IV, pp. 368–407 (p. 387).

41. Christine Vogt-William, 'Rescue Me? No thanks!: *A Wicked Old Woman* and *Anita and Me*', in *Towards a Transcultural Future: Literature and Society in a 'Post'-Colonial World*, ASNEL Papers 9.2, ed. by Geoffrey V. Davis, Peter H. Marsden, Bénédicte Ledent and Marc Delrez (Amsterdam: Rodopi, 2005), pp. 387–97 (p. 391).

42. Patricia Bastida-Rodriguez, 'Evil Friends: Childhood Friendship and Diasporic Identities in Meera Syal's *Anita and Me* and Helen Oyeyemi's *The Icarus Girl*', *Philologia*, 6 (2008), 163–71, p. 169.

43. Ilott and Buckley, "Fragmenting and Becoming Double", p. 12.

44. Giselle Anatol, 'Transforming the Skin-Shedding Soucouyant: Using Folklore to Reclaim Female Agency in Caribbean Literature', *Small Axe*, 7 (2000), 44–59 (p. 52).

45. For more on the figure of the 'abiku', see Timothy Mobolade, 'The Concept of Abiku', *African Arts*, 7.1 (1973), 62–4.

46. For more on the versatility of the gothic monster, see Judith Halberstam, *Skin Shows: Gothic Horror and the Technology of Monsters* (Durham, NC: Duke University Press, 1995).
47. Kristen Guest, 'Introduction: Cannibalism and the Boundaries of Identity', in *Eating Their Words: Cannibalism and the Boundaries of Cultural Identity*, ed. by Kristen Guest (Albany: State University of New York Press, 2001), pp. 1–10 (p. 3).
48. Hélène Cixous, *The Book of Promethea*, trans. by Betsy Wing (Lincoln, NE: University of Nebraska Press, 1991), p. 59.
49. Chris Foss, '"There Is No God Who Can Keep Us From Tasting": Good Cannibalism in Hélène Cixous's *The Book of Promethea*', in *Scenes of the Apple: Food and the Female Body in Nineteenth- and Twentieth-Century Women's Writing*, ed. by Tamar Heller and Patricia Moran (Albany: State University of New York Press, 2003), pp. 149–66 (p.150).
50. See further Kate Ferguson Ellis, *The Contested Castle: Gothic Novels and the Subversion of Domestic Ideology* (Champaign, IL: University of Illinois, 1989).
51. Maggie Kilgour, *From Communion to Cannibalism: An Anatomy of Metaphors of Incorporation* (Princeton, NY: Princeton University Press, 1990), pp. 5–6.
52. Ilott and Buckley, "Fragmenting and Becoming Double", p. 1.
53. Freud, 'The Uncanny', p. 375.
54. Freud, 'The Uncanny', p. 399.
55. Bhabha, *The Location of Culture*, p. 9.
56. Ian Baucom, *Out of Place: Englishness, Empire and the Locations of Identity* (Princeton: Princeton University Press, 1999), pp. 38–9.
57. Rupert Brooke, 'The Soldier', in *1914 and Other Poems*, by Rupert Brooke (West Norwood: Complete Press, 1915), p. 15.
58. Bhabha, *The Location of Culture*, p. 39.
59. Mafe, 'Ghostly Girls', pp. 31, 33.
60. Thomas Macaulay, 'Minute on Indian Education', in *The Post-Colonial Studies Reader*, ed. by Bill Ashcroft, Gareth Griffiths and Helen Tiffin (London: Routledge, 1995), pp. 428–30 (p. 430).
61. Khair, *The Gothic, Postcolonialism and Otherness*, p. 173.
62. Punter, *Postcolonial Imaginings*, pp. 140–1.
63. Moore argues that moths are also 'associated with the dangers of sexual transgression' in the novel. See further 'British Muslim Identities', p. 8.
64. Gayatri Spivak, 'Can the Subaltern Speak?' in *Marxism and the Interpretation of Culture*, ed. by Cary Nelson and Lawrence Grossberg (Urbana: University of Illinois Press, 1988), pp. 271–313 (pp. 308, 279).
65. Gayatri Spivak, 'Negotiating the Structures of Violence', in *The Post-Colonial Critic: Interviews, Strategies, Dialogues*, ed. by Sarah Harasym (New York: Routledge, 1990), pp. 138–51 (p. 144).
66. Spivak, 'Can the Subaltern Speak?', p. 295.
67. Moore, 'British Muslim Identities', p. 11.
68. Spivak, 'Can the Subaltern Speak?', p. 285.
69. Frantz Fanon and Edward Said are among the earliest and most prominent of these voices. See further Fanon, *Black Skin, White Masks* and Said, *Orientalism*.
70. See *Qur'an* 2.230. The novel's interpretation of this piece of Qur'anic scripture is controversial, however. The practice of taking a second husband in order to return to the first is widely condemned within Islam. Suraya could only

conceivably return to the first husband if the second divorce had happened for genuine reasons. I thank Aroosa Kanwal for this observation.

71. Patricia Meyer Spacks, *Gossip* (London: University of Chicago, 1986), pp. 6–7.

72. Tamar Heller and Patricia Moran, 'Introduction: Scenes of the Apple: Appetite, Desire, Writing', in *Scenes of the Apple: Food and the Female Body in Nineteenth- and Twentieth-Century Women's Writing*, ed. by Tamar Heller and Patricia Moran (Albany: State University of New York Press, 2003), pp. 1–44 (p. 26).

73. Heller and Moran, 'Introduction', p. 3.

74. Ben Machell, 'Helen Oyeyemi: The Times Interview', *The Times* (23 May 2009), http://www.thetimes.co.uk/tto/arts/books/article2454862.ece (accessed 12 June 2013).

75. Heller and Moran, 'Introduction', p. 1.

76. Heller and Moran, 'Introduction', p. 4.

77. Sandra M. Gilbert and Susan Gubar, *The Madwoman in the Attic: The Woman Writer and the Nineteenth-Century Literary Imagination* (New Haven: Yale University Press, 1979), p. 58.

78. Cathy Caruth, *Unclaimed Experience: Trauma, Narrative and History* (Baltimore: John Hopkins University Press, 1996), p. 4.

79. Caruth, *Unclaimed Experience*, pp. 9, 8.

80. Cathy Caruth, 'Introduction to Psychoanalysis, Trauma and Culture I', *American Imago*, 48.1 (1991), pp. 1–12 (p. 7).

81. Susan Brison, 'Trauma Narratives and the Remaking of the Self', in *Acts of Memory: Cultural Recall in the Present*, ed. by M. Bla, J. Crewe, and L. Spitzer (Hanover, NH: University of New England Press, 1999), pp. 39–54 (p. 40).

82. Stef Craps and Gert Buelens, 'Introduction: Postcolonial Trauma Novels', *Studies in the Novel*, 40.1 (2008), 1–12 (pp. 3–4).

83. Warwick, 'Feeling Gothicky?', p. 10.

84. Hanif Kureishi, *Something to Tell You* (London: Faber & Faber, 2008), p. 62. All further references shall be given parenthetically in the text.

85. Warwick, 'Feeling Gothicky?', p. 11.

86. Ranjana Khanna, 'Post-Palliative: Coloniality's Affective Dissonance', *Postcolonial Text*, 2.1 (2006), http://journals.sfu.ca/pocol/index.php/pct/article/view/385/815 (accessed 26 March 2010), (para. 2 of 37).

87. Warwick, 'Feeling Gothicky?', p. 11.

88. Khanna, 'Post-Palliative', para. 6–8 of 37.

89. Kai Erikson, 'Notes on Trauma and Community' in *Trauma: Explorations of Memory*, ed. by Cathy Caruth (Baltimore: John Hopkins University Press, 1995), pp. 183–99 (pp. 185, 186).

90. Erikson, 'Notes on Trauma and Community', p. 190.

91. Roger Luckhurst, *The Trauma Question* (London: Routledge, 2008), p. 93.

92. Victor Sage and Allan Lloyd Smith, 'Introduction', in *Modern Gothic: A Reader*, ed. by Victor Sage and Allan Lloyd Smith (Manchester: Manchester University Press, 1996), pp. 1–5 (p. 5).

3   The Subcultural Urban Novel

1. This paradigm was put forward in Bill Ashcroft, Gareth Griffiths and Helen Tiffin's seminal work *The Empire Writes Back* (London: Routledge, 1989).

2. Graham Huggan discusses the techniques of staged marginality and strategic exoticism at length in *The Postcolonial: Exotic Marketing the Margins* (London: Routledge, 2001).

3. Laura Mulvey, *Fetishism and Curiosity* (London: British Film Institute, 1996), p. 2.

4. Sigmund Freud, 'Three Essays on the Theory of Sexuality', in *The Freud Reader*, ed. by Peter Gay (London: Vintage, 1995), pp. 239–92 (p. 249).

5. Karl Marx, *Capital: A Critique of Political Economy*, trans. by Ben Fowkes (Harmondsworth: Penguin, 1976), pp. 164–5.

6. Marx, *Capital*, p. 165.

7. Mulvey, *Fetishism and Curiosity*, p. 2.

8. Huggan, *The Postcolonial Exotic*, p. 19.

9. Pierre Bourdieu, *The Field of Cultural Production: Essays on Art and Literature* (Cambridge: Polity Press, 1993), p. 30.

10. Michel Foucault, 'What is an Author?', in *Language, Counter-Memory, Practice: Selected Essays and Interviews by Michel Foucault*, ed. by Donald F. Bouchard, trans. by Donald F. Bouchard and Sherry Simon (Ithaca: Cornell University Press, 1977), pp. 113–38 (p. 124).

11. Foucault, 'What is an Author?', p. 117.

12. Huggan, *The Postcolonial Exotic*, pp. 5, 6.

13. Huggan, *The Postcolonial Exotic*, p. vii.

14. Huggan, *The Postcolonial Exotic*, p. 25.

15. Sarah Brouillette, *Postcolonial Writers in the Global Literary Marketplace* (Basingstoke: Palgrave Macmillan, 2007), pp. 5–6.

16. Brouillette, *Postcolonial Writers*, p. 7.

17. Brouillette, *Postcolonial Writers*, p. 19.

18. Brouillette, *Postcolonial Writers*, p. 3.

19. Neil Lazarus, *The Postcolonial Unconscious* (Cambridge: Cambridge University Press, 2011), p. 36.

20. Lazarus, *The Postcolonial Unconscious*, pp. 47–8.

21. Gérard Genette, *Paratexts: Thresholds of Interpretation*, trans. by Jane E. Lewin (Cambridge: Cambridge University Press, 1997), p. 1.

22. Richard Watts, *Packaging Post/Coloniality: The Manufacture of Literary Identity in the Francophone World* (Lanham: Lexington, 2005), p. 4.

23. Corinne Fowler, 'A Tale of Two Novels: Developing a Devolved Approach to Black British Writing', *Journal of Commonwealth Literature*, 43 (2008), 75–94 (p. 76).

24. Fowler, 'A Tale of Two Novels', p. 81.

25. Fowler,'A Tale of Two Novels', p. 89.

26. Lee Horsley, *Twentieth-Century Crime Fiction* (Oxford: Oxford University Press, 2005), pp. 229, 230.

27. Hanif Kureishi, 'Interview with Susan Fischer', Hanif Kureishi: In Analysis Conference, Roehampton University (25 February 2012).

28. Hanif Kureishi, *The Buddha of Suburbia* (London: Faber and Faber, 1990), p. 3. All further references shall be given parenthetically in the text.

29. Roger Bromley, *Narratives for a New Belonging: Diasporic Cultural Fictions* (Edinburgh: Edinburgh University Press, 2000), p. 152.

30. James Procter, *Dwelling Places: Postwar Black British Writing* (Manchester: Manchester University Press, 2003), p. 146.

31. Huggan, *The Postcolonial Exotic*, p· 94.
32. Doris Sommer, *Foundational Fictions: The National Romances of Latin America* (Berkeley: University of California Press, 1991), p. 32.
33. Sommer, *Foundational Fictions*, p. 29.
34. Mary Louise Pratt, *Imperial Eyes: Travel Writing and Transculturation* (New York: Routledge, 1992), p. 97.
35. *My Beautiful Laundrette*, dir. by Stephen Frears (Film4, 1985).
36. Stephanie Merritt, 'She's young, black, British - and the first publishing sensation of the millennium', *The Observer*, 16 January 2000, http://www.guard ian.co.uk/books/2000/jan/16/fiction.zadiesmith (accessed 12 March 2012).
37. Zadie Smith, *White Teeth* (London: Penguin, 2001), p. 269. All further references shall be given parenthetically in the text.
38. René Girard, *Deceit, Desire and the Novel: Self and Other in Literary Structure*, trans. by Yvonne Freccero (Baltimore: John Hopkins University Press, 1976), pp. 14, 7.
39. Philip Tew, *Zadie Smith* (Basingstoke: Palgrave Macmillan, 2010), p. 57.
40. Eve Kosofsky Sedgwick, *Between Men: English Literature and Male Homosocial Desire* (New York: Columbia University Press, 1985), pp. 1, 2.
41. *Make Bradford British*, dir. by Martin Fuller (Love West Productions, 2012).
42. Lanre Bakare, 'Make Bradford British failed to go beyond the racial stereotypes', *The Guardian*, 2 March 2012, http://www.guardian.co.uk/commentisfree/2012/ mar/02/make-bradford-british-channel-4-race (accessed 18 March 2012).
43. Kathryn Perry, 'The Heart of Whiteness: White Subjectivity and Interracial Relationships', in *Romance Revisited*, ed. by Lynne Pearce and Jackie Stacey (New York: New York University Press, 1995), pp. 171–84 (p. 176).
44. Elleke Boehmer, *Stories of Women: Gender and Narrative in the Postcolonial Nation* (Manchester: Manchester University Press, 2005), p. 28.
45. Maurice Godelier, 'The Origins of Male Domination', *New Left Review*, 127 (1981), 3–17 (p. 17).
46. Ken Gelder, *Subcultures: Cultural Histories and Social Practice* (London: Routledge, 2007), p. 90.
47. John Clarke, Stuart Hall, Tony Jefferson and Brian Roberts, 'Subculture, Cultures and Class [1975]', in *The Subcultures Reader*, ed. by Ken Gelder and Sarah Thornton (London: Routledge, 1997), pp. 100–11 (p. 101).
48. Clarke et al., 'Subculture', p. 101.
49. Sarah Thornton, 'General Introduction', in *The Subcultures Reader*, ed. by Ken Gelder and Sarah Thornton (London: Routledge, 1997), pp. 1–7 (p. 5).
50. Dick Hebdige, *Subculture: The Meaning of Style* (London: Routledge, 1979), p. 103.
51. Dick Hebdige, 'Posing... Threats, Striking... Poses: Youth, Surveillance and Display [1983]', in *The Subcultures Reader*, ed. by Ken Gelder and Sarah Thornton (London: Routledge, 1997), pp. 393–405 (p. 401).
52. Sarah Thornton, 'The Social Logic of Subcultural Capital', in *The Subcultures Reader*, ed. by Ken Gelder and Sarah Thornton (London: Routledge, 1997), pp. 200–9 (pp. 207–8).
53. Angela McRobbie and Jenny Garber, 'Girls and Subcultures [1975]', in *The Subcultures Reader*, ed. by Ken Gelder and Sarah Thornton (London: Routledge, 1997), pp. 112–20 (p. 114).
54. Karline Smith, *Full Crew* (London: The X Press, 2002), p. 68. All further references shall be given parenthetically in the text.

55. Karline Smith, *Moss Side Massive* (London: The X Press, 1994), p. 252. All further references shall be given parenthetically in the text.
56. Lynne Pearce, 'Manchester's Crime Fiction: The Mystery of the City's Smoking Gun', in *Postcolonial Manchester: Diaspora Space and the Devolution of Literary Culture*, by Lynne Pearce, Corinne Fowler and Robert Crawshaw (Manchester: Manchester University Press, 2013), pp. 110–53 (p. 113).
57. Pearce, 'Manchester's Crime Fiction', p. 124.
58. Horsley, *Twentieth-Century Crime Fiction*, p. 202.
59. Horsley, *Twentieth-Century Crime Fiction*, p. 230.
60. Gelder, *Subcultures*, p. 3.
61. Gelder, *Subcultures*, p. 119.
62. Sommer, *Foundational Fictions*, p. 38.
63. Gautam Malkani, *Londonstani* (London: Harper Perennial, 2007), p. 6. All further references shall be given parenthetically in the text.
64. James Graham, 'An Interview with Gautam Malkani: Ealing, Broadway, 6 November 2007', *Literary London*, 6.1 (2008), http://www.literarylondon.org/london-journal/march2008/graham.html (accessed 21 July 2012) (para. 3 of 37).
65. Hebdige, *Subculture*, p. 96.
66. Robert McCrum, 'Has the novel lost its way?', *The Observer*, 28 May 2006, http://www.guardian.co.uk/books/2006/may/28/fiction.features (accessed 23 July 2012) (para. 26 of 29).
67. McCrum, 'Has the novel lost its way?', para. 27 of 29.
68. James Graham, '"This in't Good Will Hunting": Londonstani and the Market for London's Multicultural Fictions', *Literary London*, 6.2 (2008), http://www.literarylondon.org/london-journal/september2008/graham.html (accessed 22 May 2012) (para. 13 of 23).
69. Graham, 'This in't Good Will Hunting', para. 18 of 23.
70. Huggan, *The Postcolonial Exotic*, p. 87.
71. Graham, 'Interview', paras 7 of 37, 10 of 37.
72 Nirpal Singh Dhaliwal, *Tourism* (London: Vintage, 2006), p. 85. All further references shall be given parenthetically in the text.
73. Gelder, *Subcultures*, p. 105.
74. Felly Nkweto Simmonds, 'Love in Black and White', in *Romance Revisited*, ed. by Lynne Pearce and Jackie Stacey (New York: New York University Press, 1995), pp. 210–22 (p. 217).
75. Simmonds, 'Love in Black and White', pp. 220–21.
76. Gelder, *Subcultures*, p. 106.

4   Multicultural British Comedy/The Comedy of Multicultural Britain

1. Thomas Hobbes, *The English Works of Thomas Hobbes*, ed. by W. Molesworth, 11 vols (London: John Bohn, 1840), IV: Human Nature, pp. 1–77 (p. 46).
2. Northrop Frye, 'Norms, Moral or Other, in Satire: A Symposium', *Satire Newsletter*, ed. by George A. Test, 2.1 (1964), 2–25 (p. 9).
3. Susan Purdie, *Comedy: The Mastery of Discourse* (Hemel Hempstead: Harvester Wheatsheaf, 1993), p. 66.

4. Purdie, *Comedy*, p. 14.
5. Purdie, *Comedy*, p. 58.
6. Purdie, *Comedy*, p. 5.
7. Marie Gillespie, 'From Comic Asians to Asian Comics: *Goodness Gracious Me*, British Television Comedy and Representations of Ethnicity', in *Group Identities on French and British Television*, ed. by Michael Scriven and Emily Roberts (New York: Berghahn, 2003), pp. 93–107 (p. 93).
8. John Morreall, *Taking Laughter Seriously* (Albany: State University of New York Press, 1983), p. 16.
9. Mikhail Bakhtin, 'Rabelais and his World', excerpt in *The Bakhtin Reader*, ed. by Pam Morris (Edward Arnold: London, 1994), pp. 194–244 (p. 198).
10. Bakhtin, 'Rabelais and his World', p. 199.
11. In Aldous Huxley's novel *Brave New World* (1932), the socially condoned and rationed drug 'soma' is used to give citizens temporary relief from the monotony of their work, ultimately reconciling them to it and making them better, more placid workers, who in their chemically numbed state are less prone to any revolutionary action.
12. Bakhtin, 'Rabelais and his World', p. 201.
13. Andrew Stott, *Comedy* (Oxon: Routledge, 2005), p. 12.
14. Susanne Reichl and Mark Stein, 'Introduction', in *Cheeky Fictions: Laughter and the Postcolonial*, ed. by Susanne Reichl and Mark Stein (Amsterdam: Rodopi, 2005), pp. 1–23 (p. 9).
15. Sigmund Freud, *Jokes and their Relation to the Unconscious*, trans. and ed. by James Strachey (London: Routledge & Kegan Paul, 1960), p. 151.
16. Freud, *Jokes*, *p.* 174.
17. As well as Damien O'Donnell's *East is East*, Andy de Emmony's *West is West* and Chris Morris's *Four Lions*, which are discussed later in the chapter, Josh Apignanesi's film *The Infidel* (2010) and Adil Ray's television sitcom *Citizen Khan* (2012–) also centre on British Muslims.
18. Alana Lentin and Gavan Titley, *The Crises of Mulitculturalism: Racism in a Neoliberal Age* (London: Zed Books, 2011), p. 3.
19. Virginia Richter, 'Laughter and Aggression: Desire and Derision in a Postcolonial Context', in *Cheeky Fictions: Laughter and the Postcolonial*, ed. by Susanne Reichl and Mark Stein (Amsterdam: Rodopi, 2005), pp. 61–72 (p. 71).
20. Homi Bhabha, *The Location of Culture* (London: Routledge, 2000), p. 85.
21. Bhabha, *The Location of Culture*, p. 67.
22. Bhabha notes that stereotypes are 'always already known' yet have to be 'anxiously repeated', p. 66.
23. Bhabha, *The Location of Culture*, p. 86.
24. Bhabha, *The Location of Culture*, p. 88.
25. Bhabha, *The Location of Culture*, p. 89.
26. Frantz Fanon, *Black Skin, White Masks*, trans. by Charles Lam Markmann (London: Paladin, 1972), p. 82.
27. Gurinder Chadha in interview with Claudia Sternberg, in Barbara Korte and Claudia Sternberg, *Bidding for the Mainstream? Black and Asian British Film since the 1990s* (Amsterdam: Rodopi, 2004), p. 246.
28. *Bend It Like Beckham*, dir. by Gurinder Chadha (Kintop Films, 2002); *Bhaji on the Beach*, dir. by Gurinder Chadha (Film4, 1993); *East is East*, dir. by Damien O'Donnell (Film4, 1999).

29. Anne-Marie Fortier, *Multicultural Horizons: Diversity and the Limits of the Civil Nation* (London: Routledge, 2008), p. 3.
30. Ali Nobil, 'Is East ... East?', *Third Text*, 49 (1999/2000), 105–7 (p. 105).
31. Korte and Sternberg, *Bidding for the Mainstream?*, p. 11.
32. It is interesting to note that scenes of white-on-white domestic violence were cut when adapting Ayub Khan-Din's play, meaning that George's violence stands in isolation. Thanks to Claire Chambers for this observation.
33. *West is West*, dir. by Andy De Emmony (Assassin Films, 2010).
34. Rainer Emig, 'The Empire Tickles Back: Hybrid Humour (and its Problems) in Contemporary Asian-British Comedy', in *Hybrid Humour: Comedy in Transcultural Perspectives*, ed. by Graeme Dunphy and Rainer Emig (Amsterdam: Rodopi, 2010), pp. 169–90 (p. 181).
35. Chadha in interview, Korte and Sternberg, *Bidding for the Mainstream?*, p. 250.
36. Jean Marsden, 'Performing the West Indies: Comedy, Feeling, and British Identity', *Comparative Drama*, 42 (2008), 73–88 (p. 75).
37. Chadha in interview, Korte and Sternberg, *Bidding for the Mainstream?*, p. 249.
38. Justine Ashby, 'Postfeminism in the British Frame', *Cinema Journal*, 44 (2005), 127–33 (p. 130).
39. John Clement Ball, *Satire and the Postcolonial Novel: V. S. Naipaul, Chinua Achebe, Salman Rushdie* (London: Routledge, 2003), p. 21.
40. Ashby, 'Postfeminism in the British Frame', p. 131.
41. This is similarly evident in Monica Ali's *Brick Lane* (London: Black Swan, 2004).
42. Sandra Heinen, 'Multi-Ethnic Britain on Screen: South Asian Diasporic Experience in Recent Feature Films', in *Multi-Ethnic Britain 2000+: New Perspectives in Literature, Film and the Arts*, ed. by Lars Eckstein, Barbara Korte, Eva Ulrike Pirker and Christoph Reinfandt (Amsterdam: Rodopi, 2008), pp. 65–78 (p. 77).
43. Chadha in interview, Korte and Sternberg, *Bidding for the Mainstream?*, p. 251.
44. Korte and Sternberg, *Bidding for the Mainstream?*, p. 8.
45. CCRT (Community Cohesion Review Team), 'Community Cohesion: A Report of the Independent Review Team, chaired by Ted Cantle', Cohesion Institute (2001), http://www.resources.cohesioninstitute.org.uk/Publications/Documents/Document/DownloadDocumentsFile.aspx?recordId=96%26file=PDFversion (accessed 16 December 2014), pp. 2, 10.
46. David Blunkett, 'The full text of David Blunkett's speech, made in the West Midlands to highlight the publication of reports into inner-city violence this summer', *The Guardian*, 11 December 2001, http://www.theguardian.com/politics/2001/dec/11/immigrationpolicy.race (accessed 17 December 2014) (para. 11 of 15).
47. Lentin and Titley, *The Crises of Mulitculturalism*, p. 43.
48. Lentin and Titley, *The Crises of Mulitculturalism*, p. 24.
49. In her review of the film, Claire Chambers suggests that the topic of terrorism lends itself to comedy as 'the ineptitude of plans to bomb Glasgow airport and Tiger Tiger nightclub in London and the dark slapstick easily discernible

in the Detroit pants-bomber debacle, demonstrate that not only is the subject ripe for satire, but it also abounds with physical humour, screwball and character comedy'. 'Four Lions', *Critical Muslim*, 3 (2012), 185–201 (p. 186).

50. Fatimah Tobing Rony, *The Third Eye: Race, Cinema and Ethnographic Spectacle* (Durham: Duke University Press, 1996), p. 207.
51. Tobing Rony, *The Third Eye*, pp. 196–7.
52. Emig, 'The Empire Tickles Back', p. 176.
53. Tobing Rony, *The Third Eye*, p. 4.
54. Peter Morey and Amina Yaqin, *Framing Muslims: Stereotyping and Representation after 9/11* (Cambridge, MA: Harvard University Press, 2011), p. 3.
55. Morey and Yaqin, *Framing Muslims*, p. 21.
56. Ella Shohat and Robert Stam, *Unthinking Eurocentrism: Multiculturalism and the Media* (London: Routledge, 2004), p. 183.
57. Giovanna Borradori, 'Introduction: Terrorism and the Legacy of the Enlightenment – Habermas and Derrida', in *Philosophy in a Time of Terror: Dialogues with Jürgen Habermas and Jacques Derrida*, ed. by Giovanna Borradori (Chicago: Chicago University Press, 2003), pp. 1–22 (p. 18).
58. Carl Boggs and Tom Pollard, 'Hollywood and the Spectacle of Terrorism', *New Political Science*, 28.3 (2006), 335–51 (p. 347).
59. For a detailed discussion of the concept of *jihad* according to both scriptural interpretation and popular understanding in Muslim communities, see Humayan Ansari, 'Attitudes to Jihad, Martyrdom and Terrorism among British Muslims', in *Muslim Britain: Communities Under Pressure*, ed. by Tahir Abbas (London: Zed Books, 2005), pp. 144–63 (pp. 145-50).
60. Ansari, 'Attitudes to Jihad', p. 147.
61. Ansari, 'Attitudes to Jihad', p. 147.
62. 'Film4', Channel 4 Sales, http://www.channel4sales.com/platforms/Film4 (accessed 12 January 2012).
63. Jean Baudrillard, *The Transformation of Evil* (London: Verso: 1993), pp. 75–6.
64. Boggs and Pollard, 'Hollywood and the Spectacle of Terrorism', p. 351.
65. John McLeod, *Postcolonial London: Rewriting the Metropolis* (London: Routledge, 2004), pp. 15, 16.
66. McLeod, *Postcolonial London*, p. 16.
67. McLeod, *Postcolonial London*, p. 16.
68. Within the film there are also nods to dystopian and science fiction authors: the tower block is called Wyndham Tower, connoting the science fiction author John Wyndham, and an arrest is made in Ballard Street, referencing the dystopian author J. G. Ballard, who wrote the novel *High Rise* (1975), a social satire on Thatcherite greed that led to social degeneration according to wealth and status in a high rise block.
69. Lentin and Titley, *The Crises of Mulitculturalism*, p. 8.
70. Simon Dentith, *Parody* (London: Routledge, 2000), pp. 15–16.
71. KRS-One, 'Sound of da Police' (1993).
72. Bhabha, *The Location of Culture*, p. 38.
73. Stephen Hessel, 'Horrifying Quixote: The Thin Line between Fear and Laughter', in *Fear Itself: Reasoning the Unreasonable*, ed. by Stephen Hessel and Michele Huppert (Amsterdam: Rodopi, 2010), pp. 23–41 (p. 28).
74. Purdie, *Comedy*, p. 58.

75. Ziauddin Sardar, *Balti Britain: A Provocative Journey through Asian Britain* (London: Granta, 2008), p. 295.
76. Sardar, *Balti Britain*, pp. 316-17, 325.
77. Avril Horner and Sue Zlosnik, *Gothic and the Comic Turn* (Basingstoke: Palgrave Macmillan, 2005), p. 3.
78. Horner and Zlosnik, *Gothic and the Comic Turn*, p. 15.
79. Umberto Eco, 'The Frames of Comic "Freedom"', *in Carnival!*, ed. by Thomas A. Sebeok (Berlin: Monton Publishers, 1984), pp. 1–9 (p. 6).

Bibliography

Primary sources

Books

Aboulela, Leila, *Minaret* (London: Bloomsbury, 2006).

——— *The Translator* (Edinburgh: Polygon, 2008).

Ali, Monica, *Brick Lane* (London: Black Swan, 2004).

Aslam, Nadeem, *Maps for Lost Lovers* (London: Faber and Faber, 2005).

Ballard, J. G., *High Rise* (London: Harper Perennial, 2006).

Banks, Iain, *The Wasp Factory* (London: Abacus, 2004).

Brooke, Rupert, 'The Soldier', in *1914 and Other Poems*, by Rupert Brooke (West Norwood: Complete Press, 1915), 15.

Byron, Lord, *Don Juan* (Kindle edition).

Dhaliwal, Nirpal Singh, *Tourism* (London: Vintage, 2006).

Huxley, Aldous, *Brave New World* (London: Vintage, 2004).

Janmohamed, Shelina Zahra, *Love in a Headscarf: Muslim Woman Seeks the One* (London: Aurum Press, 2009).

Kay, Jackie, 'So You Think I'm a Mule', in *Writing Black Britain 1948–1998*, ed. by James Procter (Manchester: Manchester University Press, 2000), 202–04.

Kureishi, Hanif, *The Black Album* (London: Faber and Faber, 2003).

——— *The Buddha of Suburbia* (London: Faber and Faber, 1990).

——— *Something to Tell You* (London: Faber & Faber, 2008).

Lynn, Vera, 'The White Cliffs of Dover' (1942).

Malkani, Gautam, *Londonstani* (London: Harper Perennial, 2007).

Naipaul, V. S., *The Mimic Men* (London: Vintage, 2001).

Oyeyemi, Helen, *The Icarus Girl* (London: Bloomsbury, 2006).

——— *White is for Witching* (London: Picador, 2009).

Rushdie, Salman, *The Satanic Verses* (London: Vintage, 2006).

Smith, Karline, *Full Crew* (London: The X Press, 2002).

——— *Moss Side Massive* (London: The X Press, 1994).

Smith, Zadie, *White Teeth* (London: Penguin, 2001).

Syal, Meera, *Anita and Me* (London: Flamingo, 1997).

Williams, Charlotte, *Sugar and Slate* (Aberystwyth: Planet, 2002).

William Wordsworth, 'At Dover', in *The Sonnets of William Wordsworth: Collected In One Volume With A Few Additional Ones Now First Published* (1838) (Whitefish, MT: Kessinger Publishing, 2008), 212.

——— 'Ode: Intimations of Immortality from Recollections of Early Childhood', in *The Norton Anthology of Poetry*, ed. by Margaret Ferguson, Mary Jo Salter and Jon Stallworthy, 5th edition (New York: Norton, 2005), 796–801.

Yassin-Kassab, Robin, *The Road from Damascus* (London: Penguin, 2009).

Films

Attack The Block, dir. by Joe Cornish (Studio Canal Features Film4, 2011).

Bend It Like Beckham, dir. by Gurinder Chadha (Kintop Films, 2002).
Bhaji on the Beach, dir. by Gurinder Chadha (Film4, 1993).
East is East, dir. by Damien O'Donnell (Film4, 1999).
Four Lions, dir. by Chris Morris (Film4, 2010).
The Infidel, dir. Josh Apignanesi (Slingshot Productions, 2010).
My Beautiful Laundrette, dir. by Stephen Frears (Film4, 1985).
West is West, dir. by Andy De Emmony (Assassin Films, 2010).

Television

Citizen Khan, dir. by Adil Ray (BBC, 2012–).
Make Bradford British, dir. by Martin Fuller (Love West Productions, 2012).

Secondary sources

Abbas, Sadia, 'Leila Aboulela, Religion and the Challenge of the Novel', *Contemporary Literature*, 52.3 (2011), 430–61.
Allen, Chris, 'From Race to Religion: The New Face of Discrimination', in *Muslim Britain Communities Under Pressure*, ed. by Tahir Abbas (London: Zed Books, 2005), pp. 49–65.
Altman, Rick, *Film/Genre* (London: BFI Publishing, 1999).
Anatol, Giselle, 'Transforming the Skin-Shedding Soucouyant: Using Folklore to Reclaim Female Agency in Caribbean Literature', *Small Axe*, 7 (2000), 44–59.
Anderson, Benedict, *Imagined Communities* (London: Verso, 1991).
Ansari, Humayan, 'Attitudes to Jihad, Martyrdom and Terrorism among British Muslims', in *Muslim Britain: Communities under Pressure*, ed. by Tahir Abbas (London: Zed Books, 2005), pp. 144–63.
Ashby, Justine, 'Postfeminism in the British Frame', *Cinema Journal*, 44 (2005), 127–33.
Ashcroft, Bill, Gareth Griffiths and Helen Tiffin, *The Empire Writes Back*, 2nd edition (London: Routledge, 2003).
—— *Key Concepts in Post-Colonial Studies* (London: Routledge, 1998).
Bakare, Lanre, '*Make Bradford British* failed to go beyond the racial stereotypes', *The Guardian*, 2 March 2012, http://www.guardian.co.uk/commentis-free/2012/mar/02/make-bradford- british-channel-4-race (accessed 18 March 2012).
Bakhtin, Mikhail, 'Rabelais and his World', excerpt in *The Bakhtin Reader*, ed. by Pam Morris (Edward Arnold: London, 1994), pp. 194–244.
Baldick, Chris, 'Introduction', in *The Oxford Book of Gothic Tales*, ed. by Chris Baldick (Oxford: Oxford University Press, 1992), pp. xi–xxiii.
Ball, Anna, '"Here is where I am": Rerouting Diasporic Experience in Leila Aboulela's Recent Novels', in *Rerouting the Postcolonial: New Directions for the New Millennium*, ed. by Janet Wilson, Cristina Şandru and Sarah Lawson Welsh (London: Routledge, 2010), pp. 118–27.
Ball, John Clement, *Satire and the Postcolonial Novel: V. S. Naipaul, Chinua Achebe, Salman Rushdie* (London: Routledge, 2003).
Bastida-Rodriguez, Patricia, 'Evil Friends: Childhood Friendship and Diasporic Identities in Meera Syal's *Anita and Me* and Helen Oyeyemi's *The Icarus Girl*', *Philologia*, 6 (2008), 163–71.

Baucom, Ian, *Out of Place: Englishness, Empire and the Locations of Identity* (Princeton: Princeton University Press, 1999).

Baudrillard, Jean, *The Transformation of Evil* (London: Verso: 1993).

Bhabha, Homi K., 'DissemiNation: Time, Narrative, and the Margins of the Modern Nation', in *Nation and Narration*, ed. by Homi K. Bhabha (London: Routledge, 1990), pp. 291–322.

_____ 'Introduction: Narrating the Nation', in *Nation and Narration*, ed. by Homi K. Bhabha (London: Routledge, 1990), pp. 1–7.

_____ *The Location of Culture* (London: Routledge, 2000).

Blunkett, David, 'The full text of David Blunkett's speech, made in the West Midlands to highlight the publication of reports into inner-city violence this summer', *The Guardian*, 11 December 2001, http://www.theguardian.com/politics/2001/dec/11/immigrationpolicy.race (accessed 17 December 2014).

Boehmer, Elleke, *Stories of Women: Gender and Narrative in the Postcolonial Nation* (Manchester: Manchester University Press, 2005).

Boggs, Carl, and Tom Pollard, 'Hollywood and the Spectacle of Terrorism', *New Political Science*, 28.3 (2006), 335–51.

Borradori, Giovanna, 'Introduction: Terrorism and the Legacy of the Enlightenment – Habermas and Derrida', in *Philosophy in a Time of Terror: Dialogues with Jürgen Habermas and Jacques Derrida*, ed. by Giovanna Borradori (Chicago: Chicago University Press, 2003), pp. 1–22.

Bourdieu, Pierre, *The Field of Cultural Production: Essays on Art and Literature* (Cambridge: Polity Press, 1993).

Bradley, Arthur, and Andrew Tate, *The New Atheist Novel: Fiction, Philosophy and Polemic after 9/11* (London: Continuum, 2010).

Brison, Susan, 'Trauma Narratives and the Remaking of the Self', in *Acts of Memory: Cultural Recall in the Present*, ed. by M. Bla, J. Crewe and L. Spitzer (Hanover, NH: University of New England Press, 1999), pp. 39–54.

Bromley, Roger, *Narratives for a New Belonging: Diasporic Cultural Fictions* (Edinburgh: Edinburgh University Press, 2000).

Brooks, Peter, *Reading for the Plot: Design and Intention in Narrative* (London: Harvard University Press, 1992).

Brouillette, Sarah, *Postcolonial Writers in the Global Literary Marketplace* (Basingstoke: Palgrave Macmillan, 2007).

Buruma, Ian, and Avishai Margalit, *Occidentalism: The West in the Eyes of its Enemies* (New York: Penguin, 2004).

Butler, Judith, *Precarious Life: The Powers of Mourning and Violence* (London: Verso, 2004).

Caruth, Cathy, 'Introduction to Psychoanalysis, Trauma and Culture I', *American Imago*, 48.1 (1991), 1–12.

_____ *Unclaimed Experience: Trauma, Narrative and History* (Baltimore: John Hopkins University Press, 1996).

CCRT (Community Cohesion Review Team), 'Community Cohesion: A Report of the Independent Review Team, chaired by Ted Cantle', *Cohesion Institute* (2001), http://www.resources.cohesioninstitute.org.uk/Publications/Documents/Document/DownloadDocumentsFile.aspx?recordId=96%26file=PDFversion (accessed 16 December 2014).

CFMEB (Commission on the Future of Multi-Ethnic Britain), *The Future of Multiethnic Britain: The Parekh Report* (London: Profile Books, 2000).

Chadha, Gurinder, and Sonia Friedman, 'Exclusive: A New British Musical About Where We Are Now: Gurinder Chadha and Sonia Friedman on what inspired them to tackle *Bend It Like Beckham* the musical', *Bend it Like Beckham: The Musical*, http://benditlikebeckhamthemusical.co.uk/?gclid=Cj0KEQiAiamlBRCgj 83PiYm6--gBEiQArnojD8OY81uGgNtQDEKMgO7m0SJ1xzV4U4wR0S-J-Tpx7AYaAqiL8P8HAQ#content (accessed 5 January 2015).

Chambers, Claire, 'Four Lions', *Critical Muslim*, 3 (2012), 185–201.

—— 'An Interview with Leila Aboulela', *Contemporary Women's Writing*, 3.1 (2009), http://www.cww.oxfordjournals.org/content/3/1/86.extract (accessed 21 February 2011), 86–102.

—— 'Religion and the Lions of Literature', *Times Higher Education* (8 November 2012), http://www.timeshighereducation.co.uk/story.asp?storyCode=410565& sectioncode=26 (accessed 10 June 2010).

Cixous, Hélène, *The Book of Promethea*, trans. by Betsy Wing (Lincoln, NE: University of Nebraska Press, 1991).

Clarke, John, Stuart Hall, Tony Jefferson and Brian Roberts, 'Subculture, Cultures and Class [1975]', in *The Subcultures Reader*, ed. by Ken Gelder and Sarah Thornton (London: Routledge, 1997), pp. 100–11.

Craps, Stef, and Gert Buelens, 'Introduction: Postcolonial Trauma Novels', *Studies in the Novel*, 40.1 (2008), 1–12.

Currie, Mark, *About Time: Narrative, Fiction and the Philosophy of Time* (Edinburgh: Edinburgh University Press, 2007).

Degabriele, Maria, 'Prince of Darkness Meets Priestess of Porn: Sexual and Political Identities in Hanif Kureishi's *The Black Album*', *Intersections: Gender and Sexuality in Asia and the Pacific*, 2 (May 1999) http://intersections.anu.edu. au/issue2/Kureishi.html (accessed 3 August 2010).

Dentith, Simon, *Parody* (London: Routledge, 2000).

Duff, David, 'Introduction', in *Modern Genre Theory*, ed. by David Duff (Harlow: Longman, 2000), pp. 1–24.

Eco, Umberto, 'The Frames of Comic "Freedom"', in *Carnival!*, ed. by Thomas A. Sebeok (Berlin: Monton Publishers, 1984), pp. 1–9.

Ellmann, Maud, *The Hunger Artists: Starving, Writing and Imprisonment* (London: Virago, 1993).

Emig, Rainer, 'The Empire Tickles Back: Hybrid Humour (and its Problems) in Contemporary Asian-British Comedy', in *Hybrid Humour: Comedy in Transcultural Perspectives*, ed. by Graeme Dunphy and Rainer Emig (Amsterdam: Rodopi, 2010), pp. 169–90.

Erickson, John, *Islam and Postcolonial Narrative* (Cambridge: Cambridge University Press, 1998).

Erikson, Kai, 'Notes on Trauma and Community' in *Trauma: Explorations of Memory*, ed. by Cathy Caruth (Baltimore: John Hopkins University Press, 1995), pp. 183–99.

Fanon, Frantz, *Black Skin, White Masks*, trans. by Charles Lam Markmann (London: Paladin, 1972).

Ferguson Ellis, Kate, *The Contested Castle: Gothic Novels and the Subversion of Domestic Ideology* (Champaign: University of Illinois, 1989).

Fortier, Anne-Marie, *Multicultural Horizons: Diversity and the Limits of the Civil Nation* (London: Routledge, 2008).

Foss, Chris, '"There Is No God Who Can Keep Us From Tasting": Good Cannibalism in Hélène Cixous's *The Book of Promethea*', in *Scenes of the Apple:*

Food and the Female Body in Nineteenth- and Twentieth-Century Women's Writing, ed. by Tamar Heller and Patricia Moran (Albany: State University of New York Press, 2003), pp. 149–66.

Foucault, Michel, 'What is an Author?', in *Language, Counter-Memory, Practice: Selected Essays and Interviews by Michel Foucault*, ed. by Donald F. Bouchard, trans. by Donald F. Bouchard and Sherry Simon (Ithaca: Cornell University Press, 1977), pp. 113–38.

Fowler, Corinne, 'A Tale of Two Novels: Developing a Devolved Approach to Black British Writing', *Journal of Commonwealth Literature*, 43 (2008), 75–94.

Freud, Sigmund, *Penguin Freud Library*, ed. by Angela Richards, trans. by James Strachey, 15 vols (London: Penguin, 1958), IV: *The Interpretation of Dreams*.

—— *Jokes and their Relation to the Unconscious*, trans. and ed. by James Strachey (London: Routledge & Kegan Paul, 1960).

—— 'Three Essays on the Theory of Sexuality', in *The Freud Reader*, ed. by Peter Gay (London: Vintage, 1995), pp. 239–92.

—— 'The Uncanny', in *Collected Papers*, ed. by Ernest Jones, trans. by Joan Riviere, 4 vols (London: Hogarth, 1934) IV, pp. 368–407.

Frye, Northrop, 'Norms, Moral or Other, in Satire: A Symposium', *Satire Newsletter*, ed. by George A. Test, 2.1 (1964), 2–25.

Gelder, Ken, *Subcultures: Cultural Histories and Social Practice* (London: Routledge, 2007).

Genette, Gérard, *Paratexts: Thresholds of Interpretation*, trans. by Jane E. Lewin (Cambridge: Cambridge University Press, 1997).

Gikandi, Simon, 'Between Roots and Routes: Cosmopolitanism and the Claims of Locality', in *Rerouting the Postcolonial: New Directions for the New Millennium*, ed. by Janet Wilson, Cristina Şandru and Sarah Lawson Welsh (London: Routledge, 2010), pp. 22–35.

Gilbert, Sandra M., and Susan Gubar, *The Madwoman in the Attic: The Woman Writer and the Nineteenth-Century Literary Imagination* (New Haven: Yale University Press, 1979).

Gillespie, Marie, 'From Comic Asians to Asian Comics: *Goodness Gracious Me*, British Television Comedy and Representations of Ethnicity', in *Group Identities on French and British Television*, ed. by Michael Scriven and Emily Roberts (New York: Berghahn, 2003), pp. 93–107.

Gilroy, Paul, *After Empire: Melancholia or Convivial Culture?* (Abingdon: Routledge, 2004).

Girard, René, *Deceit, Desire and the Novel: Self and Other in Literary Structure*, trans. by Yvonne Freccero (Baltimore: John Hopkins University Press, 1976).

Godelier, Maurice, 'The Origins of Male Domination', *New Left Review*, 127 (1981), 3–17.

Graham, James, 'An Interview with Gautam Malkani: Ealing, Broadway, 6 November 2007', *Literary London*, 6.1 (2008), http://www.literarylondon.org/london- journal/march2008/graham.html (accessed 21 July 2012).

—— '"This in't Good Will Hunting": *Londonstani* and the Market for London's Multicultural Fictions', *Literary London*, 6.2 (2008), http://www.literarylondon.org/london-journal/september2008/graham.html (accessed 22 May 2012).

Guest, Kristen, 'Introduction: Cannibalism and the Boundaries of Identity', in *Eating Their Words: Cannibalism and the Boundaries of Cultural Identity*, ed. by Kristen Guest (Albany: State University of New York Press, 2001), pp. 1–10.

Halberstam, Judith, *Skin Shows: Gothic Horror and the Technology of Monsters* (Durham, NC: Duke University Press, 1995).

Hassan, Waïl S., 'Leila Aboulela and the Ideology of Muslim Immigrant Fiction', *Novel: A Forum on Fiction*, 41.2 (Spring–Summer 2008), 298–319.

Hebdige, Dick, 'Posing ... Threats, Striking ... Poses: Youth, Surveillance and Display [1983]', in *The Subcultures Reader*, ed. by Ken Gelder and Sarah Thornton (London: Routledge, 1997), pp. 393–405.

_____ *Subculture: The Meaning of Style* (London: Routledge, 1979).

Hegerfeldt, Anne, 'The Stars that Spring from Bastardising: Wise Children Go For Shakespeare', *Zeitschrift Für Englische Philologie*, 121 (2003), 351–72.

Heinen, Sandra, 'Multi-Ethnic Britain on Screen: South Asian Diasporic Experience in Recent Feature Films', in *Multi-Ethnic Britain 2000+: New Perspectives in Literature, Film and the Arts*, ed. by Lars Eckstein, Barbara Korte, Eva Ulrike Pirker and Christoph Reinfandt (Amsterdam: Rodopi, 2008), pp. 65–78.

Heller, Tamar, and Patricia Moran, 'Introduction: Scenes of the Apple: Appetite, Desire, Writing', in *Scenes of the Apple: Food and the Female Body in Nineteenth- and Twentieth-Century Women's Writing*, ed. by Tamar Heller and Patricia Moran (Albany: State University of New York Press, 2003), pp. 1–44.

Hessel, Stephen, 'Horrifying Quixote: The Thin Line between Fear and Laughter', in *Fear Itself: Reasoning the Unreasonable*, ed. by Stephen Hessel and Michele Huppert (Amsterdam: Rodopi, 2010), pp. 23–41.

Hobbes, Thomas, *The English Works of Thomas Hobbes*, ed. by W. Molesworth, 11 vols (London: John Bohn, 1840), IV: *Human Nature*, pp. 1–77.

Hogan, Patrick Colm, *Colonialism and Cultural Identity: Crises of Tradition in the Anglophone Literatures of India, Africa and the Caribbean* (Albany: State University of New York Press, 2000).

Holmes, Frederic M., 'The Postcolonial Subject Divided between East and West: Kureishi's *The Black Album* as an Intertext of Rushdie's *The Satanic Verses*', *Papers on Language and Literature: A Journal for Scholars and Critics of Language and Literature*, 37.3 (Summer 2001), 296–313.

Horner, Avril, and Sue Zlosnik, *Gothic and the Comic Turn* (Basingstoke: Palgrave Macmillan, 2005).

Horsley, Lee, *Twentieth-Century Crime Fiction* (Oxford: Oxford University Press, 2005).

Huggan, Graham, *The Postcolonial Exotic: Marketing the Margins* (London: Routledge, 2001).

Hurley, Kelly, 'Abject and Grotesque', in *The Routledge Companion to Gothic*, ed. by Catherine Spooner and Emma McEvoy (Abingdon: Routledge, 2007), pp. 137–46.

Ilott, Sarah, 'White Is for Witching', *The Literary Encyclopedia* (1 August 2013), http://www.litencyc.com/php/sworks.php?rec=true&UID=35030 (accessed 8 January 2015).

_____, and Chloe Buckley, '"Fragmenting and Becoming Double": Supplementary Twins and Abject Bodies in Helen Oyeyemi's *The Icarus Girl*', *Journal of Commonwealth Literature* (2015), published online first at http://www.jcl.sage-pub.com/content/early/2015/01/28/0021989414563999.full.pdf+html, 1–14.

Jameson, Fredric, 'Magical Narratives: On the Dialectical Use of Genre Criticism', in *Modern Genre Theory*, ed. by David Duff (Harlow: Longman, 2000), pp. 167–92.

Jauss, Hans Robert, 'Theory of Genres and Medieval Literature', in *Modern Genre Theory*, ed. by David Duff (London: Longman, 1999), pp. 127–47.

Jussawalla, Feroza, 'Kim, Huck and Naipaul: Using the Postcolonial Bildungsroman to (Re)define Postcoloniality', *Links and Letters*, 4 (1997), 25–38.

Khair, Tabish, *The Gothic, Postcolonialism and Otherness: Ghosts from Elsewhere* (Basingstoke: Palgrave Macmillan, 2009).

Khanna, Ranjana, 'Post-Palliative: Coloniality's Affective Dissonance', *Postcolonial Text*, 2.1 (2006), http://www.journals.sfu.ca/pocol/index.php/pct/article/view/385/815 (accessed 26 March 2010).

Kilgour, Maggie, *From Communion to Cannibalism: An Anatomy of Metaphors of Incorporation* (Princeton, NY: Princeton University Press, 1990).

Korte, Barbara, and Claudia Sternberg, *Bidding for the Mainstream: Black and Asian British Film since the 1990s* (Amsterdam: Rodopi, 2004).

Kristeva, Julia, *Powers of Horror: An Essay on Abjection* (New York: Columbia University Press, 1982).

Kureishi, Hanif, 'Interview with Susan Fischer', *Hanif Kureishi: In Analysis Conference*, Roehampton University (25 February 2012).

Lacan, Jacques, 'The Mirror Stage as Formative of the Function of the I as Revealed in Psychoanalytic Experience', in *Ecrits: A Selection*, trans. by Alan Sheridan (London: Tavistock, 1985), pp. 1–8.

Lazarus, Neil, *The Postcolonial Unconscious* (Cambridge: Cambridge University Press, 2011).

Lentin, Alana, and Gavan Titley, *The Crises of Mulitculturalism: Racism in a Neoliberal Age* (London: Zed Books, 2011).

Luckhurst, Roger, *The Trauma Question* (London: Routledge, 2008).

Macaulay, Thomas, 'Minute on Indian Education', in *The Post-Colonial Studies Reader*, ed. by Bill Ashcroft, Gareth Griffiths and Helen Tiffin (London: Routledge, 1995), pp. 428–30.

Machell, Ben, 'Helen Oyeyemi: The Times interview', *The Times* (23 May 2009), http://www.thetimes.co.uk/tto/arts/books/article2454862.ece (accessed 12 June 2013).

Maduro, Renaldo J. and Joseph B. Wheelright, 'Archetype and Archetypal Image', in *Jungian Literary Criticism*, ed. by Richard P. Sugg (Evanston: Northwestern University Press, 1992), pp. 181–6.

Mafe, Diana Adesola, 'Ghostly Girls in the "Eerie Bush": Helen Oyeyemi's *The Icarus Girl* as Postcolonial Female Gothic Fiction', *Research in African Literatures* 42.3 (2012), 21–35.

Malak, Amin, *Muslim Narratives and the Discourse of English* (Albany: State University of New York Press, 2005).

Marsden, Jean, 'Performing the West Indies: Comedy, Feeling, and British Identity', *Comparative Drama*, 42 (2008), 73–88.

Marx, Karl, *Capital: A Critique of Political Economy*, trans. by Ben Fowkes (Harmondsworth: Penguin, 1976), pp. 164–5.

McCrum, Robert, 'Has the novel lost its way?', *The Observer*, 28 May 2006, http://www.guardian.co.uk/books/2006/may/28/fiction.features (accessed 23 July 2012).

McHale, Brian, *Postmodernist Fiction* (London: Methuen, 1994).

McLeod, John, *Postcolonial London: Rewriting the Metropolis* (London: Routledge, 2004).

McRobbie, Angela, and Jenny Garber, 'Girls and Subcultures [1975]', in The Subcultures Reader, ed. by Ken Gelder and Sarah Thornton (London: Routledge, 1997), pp. 112–20.

Mercer, Kobena, 'Back to My Routes: A Postscript to the 1980s (1990)', in Writing Black Britain 1948–1998, ed. by James Procter (Manchester: Manchester University Press, 2000), pp. 285–93.

Merritt, Stephanie, 'She's young, black, British – and the first publishing sensation of the millennium', The Observer, 16 January 2000, http://www.guardian.co.uk/books/2000/jan/16/fiction.zadiesmith (accessed 12 March 2012).

Meyer Spacks, Patricia, Gossip (London: University of Chicago, 1986).

Miles, Robert, Gothic Writing 1750–1820: A Genealogy (London: Routledge, 2003).

Mobolade, Timothy, 'The Concept of Abiku', African Arts, 7.1 (1973), 62–4.

Modood, Tariq, 'British Asian Muslims and the Rushdie Affair', Political Quarterly, 61.2 (1990), 143–60.

_____ Multicultural Politics: Racism, Ethnicity and Muslims in Britain (Edinburgh: Edinburgh University Press, 2005).

Moore, Lindsey, 'British Muslim Identities and Spectres of Terror in Nadeem Aslam's Maps for Lost Lovers', Postcolonial Text, 5.2 (2009), http://www.postcolonial.org/index.php/pct/article/view/1017/946 (accessed 24 August 2012), 1–19.

_____ 'Special Issue: Glocal Imaginaries: Preface', Postcolonial Text, 6.2 (2011), http://www.postcolonial.org/index.php/pct/article/download/1323/1169 (accessed 18 November 2012), 1–7.

Moretti, Franco, The Way of the World: The Bildungsroman in European Culture, new edition, trans. by Albert Sbragia (London: Verso, 2000).

Morey, Peter, and Amina Yaqin, Framing Muslims: Stereotyping and Representation after 9/11 (Cambridge, MA: Harvard University Press, 2011).

Morreall, John, Taking Laughter Seriously (Albany: State University of New York Press, 1983).

Mulvey, Laura, Fetishism and Curiosity (London: British Film Institute, 1996).

Nash, Geoffrey, The Anglo-Arab Encounter: Fiction and Autobiography by Arab Writers in English (Bern: Peter Lang, 2007).

Ngũgĩ wa Thiong'o, Decolonising the Mind: The Politics of Language in African Literature (Martlesham: James Currey, 2011).

Nobil, Ali, 'Is East ... East?', Third Text, 49 (1999/2000), 105–7.

Pearce, Lynne, 'Manchester's Crime Fiction: The Mystery of the City's Smoking Gun', in Postcolonial Manchester: Diaspora Space and the Devolution of Literary Culture, ed. by Lynne Pearce, Corinne Fowler and Robert Crawshaw (Manchester: Manchester University Press, 2013), pp. 110–53.

_____, Corinne Fowler and Robert Crawshaw, Postcolonial Manchester: Diaspora Space and the Devolution of Literary Culture (Manchester: Manchester University Press, 2013).

Perry, Kathryn, 'The Heart of Whiteness: White Subjectivity and Interracial Relationships', in Romance Revisited, ed. by Lynne Pearce and Jackie Stacey (New York: New York University Press, 1995), pp. 171–84.

Phillips, Christina, 'Leila Aboulela's The Translator: Reading Islam in the West', Wasafiri, 27.1 (2012), 66–72.

Pickles, Eric, 'Letter to Muslim leaders: The text in full', The Independent, 19 January 2015, http://www.independent.co.uk/news/uk/eric-pickles-letter-to-muslim-leaders-the-text-in-full-9987249.html (accessed 15 February 2015).

Pratt, Mary Louise, *Imperial Eyes: Travel Writing and Transculturation* (New York: Routledge, 1992).

Procter, James, *Dwelling Places: Postwar Black British Writing* (Manchester: Manchester University Press, 2003).

＿＿ 'General Introduction', in *Writing Black Britain 1948–1998*, ed. by James Procter (Manchester and New York: Manchester University Press, 2000), pp. 1–12.

＿＿, and Angela Smith, 'Gothic and Empire', in *The Routledge Companion to Gothic*, ed. by Catherine Spooner and Emma McEvoy (Abingdon: Routledge, 2007), pp. 95–104.

Propp, Vladimir, 'Fairy Tale Transformations', in *Modern Genre Theory*, ed. by David Duff (Harlow: Longman, 2000), pp. 50–67.

Punter, David, *Postcolonial Imaginings: Fictions of a New World Order* (Edinburgh: Edinburgh University Press, 2000).

Purdie, Susan, *Comedy: The Mastery of Discourse* (Hemel Hempstead: Harvester Wheatsheaf, 1993).

Quinn, Ben, '*Bend It Like Beckham* to be made into musical', *Guardian*, 31 October 2014, http://www.theguardian.com/stage/2014/oct/31/bend-it-like-beckham-musical (accessed 5 January 2015).

Rashid, C. E., 'British Islam and the Novel of Transformation: Robin Yassin-Kassab's *The Road from Damascus*', *Journal of Postcolonial Writing*, 48.1 (2012), 92–103.

Reichl, Susanne, and Mark Stein, 'Introduction', in *Cheeky Fictions: Laughter and the Postcolonial*, ed. by Susanne Reichl and Mark Stein (Amsterdam: Rodopi, 2005), pp. 1–23.

Richter, Virginia, 'Laughter and Aggression: Desire and Derision in a Postcolonial Context', in *Cheeky Fictions: Laughter and the Postcolonial*, ed. by Susanne Reichl and Mark Stein (Amsterdam: Rodopi, 2005), pp. 61–72.

Roy, Olivier, *Globalised Islam: The Search for a New Ummah* (London: C. Hurst, 2004).

Rudd, Alison, *Postcolonial Gothic Fictions from the Caribbean, Canada, Australia and New Zealand* (Cardiff: University of Wales Press, 2010).

Rushdie, Salman, *Imaginary Homelands* (London: Vintage, 2010).

＿＿ *Joseph Anton: A Memoir* (London: Jonathan Cape, 2012).

Sage, Victor, and Allan Lloyd Smith, 'Introduction', in *Modern Gothic: A Reader*, ed. by Victor Sage and Allan Lloyd Smith (Manchester: Manchester University Press, 1996), pp. 1–5.

Said, Edward, *Orientalism* (London: Penguin, 2003).

Santesso, Esra Mirze, *Disorientation: Muslim Identity in Contemporary Anglophone Literature* (Basingstoke: Palgrave Macmillan, 2013).

Sardar, Ziauddin, *Balti Britain: A Provocative Journey through Asian Britain* (London: Granta, 2008).

Sedgwick, Eve Kosofsky, *Between Men: English Literature and Male Homosocial Desire* (New York: Columbia University Press, 1985).

Sen, Amartya, *Identity and Violence: The Illusion of Destiny* (London: Penguin, 2006).

Shohat, Ella, and Robert Stam, *Unthinking Eurocentrism: Multiculturalism and the Media* (London: Routledge, 2004).

Simmonds, Felly Nkweto, 'Love in Black and White', in *Romance Revisited*, ed. by Lynne Pearce and Jackie Stacey (New York: New York University Press, 1995), pp. 210–22.

Smith, Andrew, and William Hughes (eds), *Empire and the Gothic: The Politics of Genre* (Basingstoke: Palgrave Macmillan, 2003).

Sommer, Doris, *Foundational Fictions: The National Romances of Latin America* (Berkeley: University of California Press, 1991).

Spivak, Gayatri, 'Can the Subaltern Speak?' in *Marxism and the Interpretation of Culture*, ed. by Cary Nelson and Lawrence Grossberg (Urbana: University of Illinois Press, 1988), pp. 271–313.

—— 'Negotiating the Structures of Violence', in *The Post-Colonial Critic: Interviews, Strategies, Dialogues*, ed. by Sarah Harasym (New York: Routledge, 1990), pp. 138–51.

—— 'Reading *The Satanic Verses*', in *What is an Author?*, ed. by Maurice Biriotti and Nicola Miller (Manchester: Manchester University Press, 1993), pp. 104–34.

Stein, Mark, *Black British Literature: Novels of Transformation* (Columbus: Ohio State University Press, 2004).

Steiner, Tina, 'Strategic Nostalgia, Islam and Cultural Translation in Leila Aboulela's *The Translator* and *Coloured Lights*', *Current Writing: Text and Reception in Southern Africa*, 20.2 (2008), 7–25.

Stott, Andrew, *Comedy* (Oxon: Routledge, 2005).

Tew, Philip, *Zadie Smith* (Basingstoke: Palgrave Macmillan, 2010).

Thornton, Sarah, 'General Introduction', in *The Subcultures Reader*, ed. by Ken Gelder and Sarah Thornton (London: Routledge, 1997), pp. 1–7.

—— 'The Social Logic of Subcultural Capital', in *The Subcultures Reader*, ed. by Ken Gelder and Sarah Thornton (London: Routledge, 1997), pp. 200–9.

Tobing Rony, Fatimah, *The Third Eye: Race, Cinema and Ethnographic Spectacle* (Durham: Duke University Press, 1996).

Vogt-William, Christine, 'Rescue Me? No thanks!: *A Wicked Old Woman* and *Anita and Me*', in *Towards a Transcultural Future: Literature and Society in a 'Post'-Colonial World*, ASNEL Papers 9.2, ed. by Geoffrey V. Davis, Peter H. Marsden, Bénédicte Ledent and Marc Delrez (Amsterdam: Rodopi, 2005), pp. 387–97.

Ware, Vron, 'The White Fear Factor', in *Terror and the Postcolonial*, ed. by Elleke Boehmer and Stephen Morton (Chichester: Wiley-Blackwell, 2009), pp. 99–112.

Warwick, Alexandra, 'Feeling Gothicky?', *Gothic Studies*, 9 (2007), 5–19.

Watts, Richard, *Packaging Post/Coloniality: The Manufacture of Literary Identity in the Francophone World* (Lanham: Lexington, 2005).

Weller, Paul, *A Mirror For Our Times: 'The Rushdie Affair' and the Future of Multiculturalism* (London: Continuum, 2009).

Wexler, Joyce, 'What is a Nation? Magic Realism and National Identity in *Midnight's Children* and *Clear Light of Day*', *Journal of Commonwealth Literature*, 37 (2002), 137–55.

Yassin-Kassab, Robin, 'Islam in the Writing Process', *Religion and Literature*, 43.1 (2011), 139–44.

Index

Printed and bound by CPI Group (UK) Ltd, Croydon, CR0 4YY